The Evolution of the Russian Communist Party

The Regional Focus

BY
Julia Wishnevsky

EDITED BY
Elizabeth Teague

The Jamestown Foundation

THE EVOLUTION OF THE RUSSIAN COMMUNIST PARTY

ISBN 0-9675009-0-7

Published by the Jamestown Foundation
1528 18th Street NW, Washington DC 20036 USA
Printed in the USA

Acknowledgements

The author is grateful to many people who kindly helped her in the preparation of this study, and especially to Dmitrii Furman, Gabriel Superfin, Vera Tolz, Joan Barth Urban, Mikhail Sokolov, Pavel Korenbaum and Keith Bush. She made four trips to Russia to research the study, visiting Moscow, St Petersburg, Pskov, Novgorod, Tula, Bryansk and Blagoveshchensk. She is deeply grateful to Gennadii Zyuganov, Valentin Kuptsov, Yurii Lodkin, Nataliya Morozova, Aleksei Zotikov, Nataliya Akimova, Vladimir Nikitin, Vladimir Gudim, Mikhail Filshin, Vladimir Semago, Gennadii Gamza and other members and associates of the CPRF who graciously agreed to be interviewed. She would also like to thank her friends Ada and Oleg Gorbachev for their hospitality. She is indebted to Erin Long of the Jamestown Foundation for her unfailing patience and cheerful encouragement, and to Eugene Levitsky, Paul Tann and Glenn Court for expert editing, proofreading and design assistance.

JuliaWishnevsky
July 1999

The Jamestown Foundation

The Jamestown Foundation is a non-profit, non-partisan research and publication organization providing information and analysis of trends in the former Soviet Union that affect vital Western interests. The Foundation through its programs encourages the development of democracy, civil liberty, and free enterprise in Russia and the former Soviet states.

Contents

1: The Roots of Russia's Communist Party

Boasting some half a million members, the Communist Party of the Russian Federation (CPRF) is post-Soviet Russia's only political party with a strong regional and social base. The CPRF was indeed described, throughout the 1990s, as Russia's only political party worthy of the name, since it was the only political organization possessing a relatively well-organized regional network and a loyal base of support across a clearly defined swath of Russian provinces.

The CP RSFSR

The CPRF was often described as the largest of the successor organizations of the Communist Party of the Soviet Union (CPSU). In fact, it was the direct descendant not of the CPSU but of the Communist Party of the Russian Soviet Federative Socialist Republic (RSFSR). The distinction is important since the CP RSFSR was effectively created in opposition to the CPSU. Specifically, it was set up by hard-line communists as a form of protest against the attempts of Soviet Party leader and President Mikhail Gorbachev to reform the CPSU and turn it into a "democratic" party. This was something the CPSU was not, did not want to be, and could not become.

The RSFSR occupied 76 percent of the territory of the USSR. Until 1990, however, the Russian Republic was the only one of the USSR's fifteen constituent Union republics forbidden to have its own communist party. This had been the case since 1925, three years after the Soviet Union was established, when the Russian Communist Party of Bolsheviks was absorbed into the CPSU. Soviet leaders feared—justifiably, as it turned out—that a Russian communist party would be so large and powerful that it would rival the CPSU, and that Russian particularism might turn to separatism and undermine the "indestructible union of free republics" otherwise known as the USSR.

Soviet leaders accordingly met the establishment of the CP RSFSR in June 1990 with considerable apprehension. In the event, the CP RSFSR survived for little more than a year. It vanished from the political scene in the general upheaval that followed the failed coup d'etat of August 1991 and the December 1991 dissolution of the USSR. Russian separatism did indeed play a major role in the destruction of the USSR. With hindsight, the creation of the CP RSFSR may accordingly be seen as the penultimate act in the death agony of the USSR and the CPSU. But while the USSR broke up like a piece of glass or a thing of clay—along the geographical borders between the USSR's Union republics—the CPSU disintegrated, as often happens with political parties, in accordance with its members' personal beliefs, career aspirations and institutional loyalties.

Background

This chapter outlines the birth and brief life of the CP RSFSR. Before we delve further, a few points are in order:

On the eve of Mikhail Gorbachev's rise to power in 1985, the CPSU claimed 19.5 million members—about 10 percent of the adult population of the USSR and some 50 percent of males with higher education. Although the overwhelming majority of the Soviet population did not belong to the Communist Party, the CPSU penetrated not only all Soviet government institutions but also all those non-government organizations whose existence was officially sanctioned. This enabled the CPSU and its youth wing, the Komsomol, to monitor activities both official and unofficial at all levels throughout the country. A Soviet citizen who was not a Party member could not expect to make a career in any prestigious sphere of activity. The only exception was religion, but even that was not really an exception, since religion was barely tolerated in the Soviet Union and churches were permitted to operate only under the supervision of the secret police (KGB) and Communist-dominated bodies such as the Council on Religious Affairs or the Council on Affairs of the Russian Orthodox Church.

The only alternative spot on the Soviet political map was the dissident community which, somewhat to its own surprise, succeeded in inculcating Soviet society, including some top CPSU officials, with ideals such as the desirability of glasnost (openness), human rights and the rule of law. But the dissident movement was never strong enough to influence more than a handful of professional managers or politicians. By the time Mikhail Gorbachev became Soviet leader (his official title being General Secretary of the CPSU Central Committee), the dissident movement had been bled white by arrests and forced emigration.

Contrasts with Political Elites in Europe

Post-Soviet Russia differs in one particularly important respect from most of the post-communist countries of Central and Eastern Europe. The political elite in Russia today—be it ruling or in opposition, liberal or conservative, pro- or anti- Western, pro- or anticommunist—consists very largely of members of the former communist nomenklatura who have adjusted to Russia's new capitalist conditions. (The nomenklatura was the vast patronage network which, under the control of the CPSU, controlled appointments to responsible posts at every level of Soviet society.)

This was not the case in countries such as Hungary, Poland, the Czech Republic and Lithuania, where the collapse of communism brought to power a new generation of democratic leaders with non-communist, often dissident backgrounds. They included people such as Jozsef Antall in Hungary, Lech Walesa in Poland, Vaclav Havel in the Czech Republic and Vytautas Landsbergis in Lithuania. Many of these leaders later lost power in democratic elections to former Communists, most of whom proved neither less friendly toward the West nor significantly less democratic than their non-communist predecessors.

Yeltsin Appears on the Scene

In Russia, by contrast, reform-minded communists from Gorbachev's generation were replaced in 1991 by a maverick, Boris Yeltsin, who had served almost all his life in leading positions in the CPSU. Yeltsin joined the Party in 1961. Following a career in the Sverdlovsk Regional Committee of the CPSU he moved to Moscow where, in 1986, he was appointed First Secretary of the Moscow City Committee of the CPSU, a post that gave him candidate membership in the party's ruling Politburo. There, his rebellious behavior provoked his ouster from power and a period in the wilderness. Yeltsin fought back, winning a seat in 1989 in the first multi-candidate elections in Soviet history. In May 1990, Yeltsin was elected Speaker of the Russian parliament. He ostentatiously quit the Communist Party in July 1990, during its Twenty-seventh Congress and, in June 1991, he became Russia's first democratically elected president. He was re-elected in 1996. Russia has not yet, therefore, gone through the process whereby one democratically elected president hands power peacefully over to another.

Yeltsin was supported in his new position by thousands of officials with similar nomenklatura backgrounds. It is these people who now make up the elite in post-Soviet Russia. The presence of former dissidents in today's Russian elite is barely noticeable: only a couple of such individuals presently occupy seats in the lower house of the Russian parliament, the State Duma, while a handful have second- or third ranking positions in small reform-oriented parties and movements, such as Russia's Democratic Choice and Yabloko. Even the masterminds of Yeltsin's market reforms—liberal academics noted for the militancy of their anticommunist views—had as a rule served until 1991 as research analysts in the CPSU

Central Committee or occupied other positions in the CPSU hierarchy. The man often described as the father of Russia's market reforms, former acting prime minister Yegor Gaidar, worked during the Soviet period for the CPSU daily newspaper, *Pravda*, and the Party's theoretical monthly, *Kommunist*. Yeltsin's second prime minister, Viktor Chernomyrdin, had been USSR Minister of the Gas Industry and oversaw its transformation into Gazprom, the world's largest gas producer. Even Yeltsin's third prime minister, Sergei Kirienko, who was only twenty-six when the USSR collapsed, made his early career in the Komsomol which, in the late Gorbachev period, provided many young Communists with an entry to the world of business (see Chapter 3). Yevgenii Primakov, the man who in 1998 stepped into Kirienko's shoes as prime minister, was a veteran communist widely believed to have worked as a KGB agent in the late 1960s, when he was *Pravda* correspondent in the Middle East. Primakov appointed Yurii Maslyukov, a leading communist parliamentarian and one-time chairman of USSR Gosplan, as his first deputy prime minister.

Composition of the CPRF

While the new Russian elite contains few former dissidents, the CPRF, by the same token, does not consist of "former communists" of the Central and Eastern European type. Instead, the CPRF is largely made up of non-enterprising and unimaginative people who remained in the Communist Party after their more daring and pragmatic comrades had gone. Unlike its Central and Eastern European cousins, the CPRF has not thought of removing the word "Communist" from its name. Official CPRF documents and the writings and speeches of party leaders demonstrate that in many respects the CPRF has evolved in the opposite direction to that taken by most former Central and Eastern European communist parties and even, in its final years, by the late and unlamented CPSU. While paying lip service to democratic principles and the mixed economy, many CPRF leaders express in their published materials their nostalgia for Joseph Stalin and their disdain for his successor, Nikita Khrushchev, who denounced Stalin's terror and had the tyrant's mummified body removed from public display. Their contempt for Gorbachev and his liberal colleague Aleksandr Yakovlev — the "grandfather of glasnost"—knows no bounds.

To all intents and purposes, today's CPRF is a party not of revolutionaries but of unemployed has-been apparatchiks. The CPRF remains, nonetheless, Russia's only nationally organized political party. It has survived several attempts to ban its activities and close its newspapers. This apparent anomaly requires an explanation. The answer seems to be that the harsh anticommunist rhetoric employed by Yeltsin and his entourage has allowed the communists to capitalize on the errors of the "party of power" and the hardships suffered by the population as a result of Yeltsin's economic reforms. The lower Yeltsin's popularity in the opinion polls, the more the older and more vulnerable members of the population long for the "good old days." As a result, the CPRF retains its influence in the country and in the corridors of power.

This is a paradoxical situation. As will be seen from the discussion that follows, the ideology of today's CPRF is in almost all respects the complete opposite of everything that was stood for not only by Karl Marx but also by Bolshevik leader Vladimir Lenin. The difference may be summarized in the following terms. Whereas Lenin and his comrades were driven by their vision of some bright, yet unknown, future when they would realize "the age-old dream of all mankind," today's Russian communists seek inspiration in their country's glorious past as one of the world's two superpowers. They draw their strength from that common human sentiment, nostalgia.

Gorbachev Launches His Reforms

The process of democratization launched by the CPSU's last General Secretary Mikhail Gorbachev (1985-1991) brought about the collapse of communist rule in Central and Eastern Europe and part of Asia. Gorbachev's reforms, called perestroika (restructuring), ended the Cold War between East and West and gave the citizens of the Communist bloc many of the democratic rights and freedoms they had been denied, including the right to elect their own governments. According to Gorbachev, perestroika was supposed to fulfill the following tasks:

- Persuade the Communist Party to relinquish its monopoly on power and its undivided sway over social and spiritual life;
- Free the economy from state control; recognize the right to private property; and redirect economic activity to serve the interests of the people;
- Introduce real political freedoms, the fundamentals of parliamentary rule, pluralism of opinions and parties, freedom of speech and conscience, and the right freely to leave and return to the country;
- Foster public discussion and democratic choice of the best possible projects of social development;
- Pursue a foreign policy based on common sense rather than ideological confrontation fraught with the danger of universal catastrophe.

It does not belittle Gorbachev's real achievements to deny that many errors were made during the six years that he was in power, or that some of the ideas of the Gorbachev era were ill thought-through. Beset by economic crisis and murderous ethnic conflicts, perestroika was bound to provoke resistance from all points of the Soviet political compass. Many of those who opposed Gorbachev's reforms a decade ago make up the nucleus of the CPRF and its Russian nationalist allies today. They were as keen then as now to preserve as much as possible of the Russian Empire that was built by the czars and consolidated by Stalin and his heirs. Back in the 1980s, however, it took them some time to form themselves into a conservative opposition to the ruling elite.

Two factors slowed them down. First was the long shadow of the totalitarian state and the single party that ruled it. Terror and a relentless propaganda machine had enforced the habit of rigid discipline on all Party members and ensured that dissidents and "splitters" were punished with the utmost severity. Gorbachev's opponents needed the freedom of expression that Gorbachev gave them before they could muster the courage to voice their opposition. Secondly, almost everyone involved in politics in those days, including Gorbachev himself, changed their minds and, consequently, their loyalties as events progressed. A large part of the opposition to Gorbachev—and, later, to Yeltsin—were initially supporters of perestroika. Some of today's opposition leaders were originally Gorbachev's closest allies. They include Gorbachev's one-time Party deputy, Yegor Ligachev; two Soviet prime ministers, Nikolai Ryzhkov and Valentin Pavlov; and Gorbachev's friend from his student years, Anatolii Lukyanov, now a prominent CPRF leader.

GORBACHEV'S GLASNOST

Gorbachev came to power in March 1985, replacing as Kremlin leader a colorless bureaucrat, Konstantin Chernenko, who had spent most of his thirteen months in office on his deathbed. Chernenko was the third General Secretary to die in office within two and half years, following Yurii Andropov (1982-84) and Leonid Brezhnev (1964-82). All in all, the world's second superpower had been ruled from an intensive care ward for almost a decade prior to Gorbachev's accession.

The 54-year-old Gorbachev was, by contrast, the youngest member of the Politburo (the executive body that ruled the CPSU and, to all intents and purposes, the country). As the first Soviet leader to appreciate the power of television, Gorbachev delivered his message to the people in a series of informal walkabouts that ranged from the Baltic states in the west to Vladivostok in the east, and from Stavropol in the south to Leningrad in the north. He captured the imagination of the population with an openness of manner that no former Soviet leader had possessed. One of Gorbachev's characteristics commanded special attention. This was the new leader's ability to speak spontaneously, not just to read aloud from a piece of paper, as had all previous Soviet leaders since Lenin and Trotsky. All in all, Gorbachev's appearance was welcomed as a breath of fresh air in the stagnant atmosphere of the Communist Party Central Committee headquarters in Moscow.

"Everything is rotten in our country." "We cannot live like this any more." These were Gorbachev's slogans when he came to power. Though it is often forgotten today, at that time the sentiment that things needed to be changed was shared by many people, including a large proportion of those belonging to what George Orwell would have called the "Inner Party." As later became clear, however, people's ideas of the particular kinds of changes needed varied and often contradicted each other.

There were, for all that, few if any dissenting voices when Gorbachev issued his first call for a thorough restructuring of the system. At that time, Gorbachev and his allies did not themselves appreciate just how rotten the system was. They believed it could be modernized and reformed. To this end, the new leaders employed the traditional Soviet method of personnel changes, removing the Old Guard and replacing them with new and energetic Party officials from the provinces. Such a policy was not, of course, enough to solve the problems nationwide even though the wave of personnel changes was accompanied, not unusual for the Soviet Union, by a massive campaign of criticism of the Brezhnevite "era of stagnation." The Twenty-seventh Congress of the CPSU, held in February 1986, did not differ greatly from Communist Party Congresses of earlier periods. The monolithic regime appeared intact, and surely no one at that moment imagined that this was to be the last such gathering in Russian history.

Reaction to Reform

As Gorbachev proceeded with his plans to democratize the social, political and economic spheres of Soviet life, the Communist Party apparatus responded with quiet sabotage. Gorbachev recalled in his memoirs that, although many ordinary people appeared to support his policies, the Party itself dug in its heels and adopted a policy of passive resistance. "No one seemed to oppose us, everyone seemed to support [perestroika]," Gorbachev wrote, "and yet nothing changed." Heads of government departments and local officials either ignored the decisions and instructions of the central leadership or amended them with comments and instructions of their own, altering the meaning of the new policies in precisely the opposite direction. Gorbachev later confessed that he invented his trademark policy of glasnost as a means of overcoming "outright sabotage" of his reforms by Party bureaucrats. Usually translated as "openness," the policy was based on the assumption that the public was entitled to be informed about developments in the public domain and to play a role in the decision-making process.

Soon, Party bureaucrats found themselves unable to maintain their policy of "agree, but do the opposite." Instead, they were forced to voice their disagreements openly, if such a word can be used to describe criticism voiced behind the closed doors of the CPSU Central Committee's plenary sessions. In January 1987, the Party leader in Krasnodar Krai, Ivan Polozkov, addressed a Central Committee plenum with a speech attacking Gorbachev's policy of glasnost in the media, literature and arts. "Look what our young people are engrossed in reading!" Small-minded people, Polozkov complained, were lapping up novels, plays and media articles that exposed the ills of Soviet life, while the Party struggled to maintain its ideals. Other speakers at the plenum supported Polozkov, saying the media should not be allowed to criticize the Party's shortcomings but should be encouraged to draw public attention to its positive achievements. After January 1987, no CPSU Central Committee plenum passed without an attack on glasnost. The ensuing polarization of opinion in the Party and the country assumed the following broad outlines: the intelligentsia of Moscow and Leningrad on one side, and provincial Party bureaucrats on the other.

Of course, as always happens at a time of great and historic changes, there were exceptions to this generalization. As a rule, Party officials attacked the media whenever they found it uncomfortable to reveal the real reason for their displeasure with the Gorbachev leadership, which was that Gorbachev's policies directly threatened the vested interests of the Soviet ruling class. The draft resolution of the January 1987 Central Committee plenum, for example, included a proposal that the heads of Party committees at all levels should be directly elected by all the members of the given Party organization. This change was supposed to end the nomenklatura method of selection of Party cadres, under which leaders were appointed from above. Had the plan been approved, it might have made the democratization process in the USSR smoother. Had the elections been conducted fairly, they might have fostered the emergence of different factions within the Party and even, in time, the creation of a multiparty system on the ruins of the CPSU. Such a democratization would still, however, have deprived the overwhelming majority of Soviet citizens—those who were not members of the CPSU and who had, for whatever reason, no intention of joining it—of a say in the government of their country. In any case, the proposal was vetoed by the Central Committee's Party Organs Department, which, to all intents and purposes, controlled the Party. It was the failure of this attempt to democratize the Party that prompted Gorbachev to change tack and to try instead to transfer the Party's responsibility for administrative functions to the Soviets—the USSR's network of local legislative councils, which were elected by universal suffrage.

The CPSU Splits Along Ideological Lines

Certain groups of Soviet society proved particularly active in opposing Gorbachev's reforms. The conservative opposition found a rostrum in the pages of Russian nationalist literary publications such as the monthly journals *Nash sovremennik* and *Molodaya gvardiya* or the weekly newspaper *Literaturnaya Rossiya*. Literary feuds were nothing new in Russia: they were always simmering below the surface and would explode from time to time into open hostilities. With the advent of perestroika, liberal authors were allowed to voice their views freely, and some were even promoted to positions of responsibility. This aroused the wrath of their illiberal opponents, eager to return to the status quo ante. All in all, as Peter Reddaway has pointed out, the leadership of the RSFSR Writers' Union became the first body publicly to oppose the liberalization of public and cultural life. In retrospect, it is clear that the body served as a laboratory for Russia's future Communist Party.

In March 1987, the secretariat of the RSFSR Writers' Union held a meeting at which reactionary writers, including board chairman Sergei Mikhalkov and his deputy, Yurii Bondarev, threatened to unleash "a new Battle of Stalingrad" against editors who dared to publish the works of previously banned writers or who printed articles criticizing works by them. The meeting and the threats uttered at it forced Gorbachev to take an unusual step—he intervened personally in the literary dispute with a comment to the effect that the outburst aroused the grave displeasure of the

CPSU leadership. Nonetheless, the leadership of the RSFSR Writers' Union continued to foment what Bondarev termed "a civil war in Soviet literature." In the ensuing years, the Secretariat of the Writers' Union arranged a series of meetings in various Russian cities at which speakers lambasted the newly acquired cultural freedoms as a manifestation of a worldwide Judeo-Masonic conspiracy directed against all things Russian.

In July 1991, a number of ultra-orthodox Communist newspapers published a collective appeal to the nation (*Slovo k narodu*). In it, the letter-writers sounded an alarm over the consequences of perestroika, which, they claimed, had driven Russia to "darkness and extinction." Generally believed to have served as a propaganda overture to the August 1991 putsch against Gorbachev, the manifesto bore the signature of Gennadii Zyuganov—a founder-member of the CP RSFSR and chairman of its Commission on Humanitarian and Ideological Problems, now leader of the CPRF—along with those of soon-to-be putschists Valentin Varennikov, Vasilii Starodubtsev and Aleksandr Tizyakov, and prominent nationalists Yurii Blokhin, Yurii Bondarev, General Boris Gromov, Lyudmila Zykina, General Albert Makashov, Aleksandr Prokhanov, Valentin Rasputin and Eduard Volodin.

The disputes in the Writers' Union and, to a lesser extent, in some other artistic bodies, revealed the existence of a situation that was particularly astonishing for the CPSU. Until that stage in its history, the CPSU had preserved a monolithic unity of opinion and punished any deviation from the "Party line" with a zeal comparable only to that of Tomas de Torquemada. And yet the Party had found itself, for a critical period in 1987-88, with two "chief ideologists." Although the position of "second" secretary was not at that time officially recognized, such a rank existed de facto if only because someone had to stand in for the General Secretary whenever the latter was absent. This role was customarily entrusted to the Politburo member in charge of ideology, who also chaired the meetings of the Party Secretariat—the body responsible for the day-to-day running of the Party. Gorbachev himself had served as such a deputy to Chernenko and he in turn elevated his ally, Yegor Ligachev, to this position as a reward for his assistance in engineering Gorbachev's election as Party leader in March 1985.

The Ligachev-Yakovlev Controversy & Nina Andreeva's Letter

In 1987 Gorbachev appointed the most daring of his associates, Alexander Yakovlev, to membership of both the Politburo and the Secretariat. In promoting Yakovlev to full Politburo membership, Gorbachev recalls, he was deliberately seeking to ensure that Ligachev would not be left alone to supervise the sphere of ideology. The reason for such a decision, Gorbachev went on, was the growing conservatism of Ligachev's mindset. Thanks to this division of authority, all the interested parties—cultural figures, academics, editors and even the employees of the Central Committee apparatus—found themselves faced with a choice of mentor. Many preferred the academic Yakovlev, a wise man with charming manners but a sharp tongue, to the dogmatic Ligachev, who gradually evolved into a bogeyman for the entire country.

Though Gorbachev and Ligachev repeatedly denied the existence of disagreements in the Politburo, the discord became public knowledge following the publication on March 15, 1988, of a full-page article, entitled "I cannot betray my principles" in the daily *Sovetskaya Rossiya*. Purporting to be a letter to the editor from a Leningrad chemistry teacher, Nina Andreeva, the letter defended Stalin's achievements against his detractors. Andreeva's letter became the political event of the season, not so much for what it said, since it was only one of a number of such articles published at around that time, as for the fact that Ligachev praised it at a meeting of newspaper editors and recommended that it be reprinted in as many regional newspapers as possible. Liberal intellectuals felt that glasnost was at an end.

Within days, however, Gorbachev and Yakovlev, who had been abroad when the article appeared, had returned to Moscow and opened a series of debates with Party officials. Everyone had to be either for or against Nina Andreeva. The Politburo devoted two full days to discussing her letter. Three years later, in an interview with an obscure journal for young peasants, former Politburo member Viktor Nikonov recalled his own position in the discussion, which illustrates the mood that prevailed among CPSU officials at the time. "You have ruined the media, which are now obsessed with blackening our history," Nikonov remembered telling Yakovlev. "You're to blame for the attacks being made on us from the social democratic standpoint. You are yourself a Social Democrat!"

Gorbachev carried the day, a fact that underlines the authority that the post of General Secretary still carried in the CPSU at that time. On April 5, *Pravda* printed a hard-hitting piece attacking Andreeva's piece as the "manifesto of anti-perestroika forces." Although penned by Yakovlev, the rebuff was unsigned in order to underline its authority. While few Party officials really shared Andreeva's extreme Stalinist and anti-Semitic convictions, many backed her as a covert way of demonstrating their dislike of Gorbachev's policies. At least one of them lost his job and suffered the punishment usually meted out to members of the nomenklatura who managed to offend the leadership. This was none other than Yurii Petrov, Yeltsin's crony from his hometown of Sverdlovsk who would serve as the first head of the Russian President's Administration after Yeltsin was elected President of the RSFSR in 1991. At one of Gorbachev's meetings with Party "generals," held in the middle of April 1988, Petrov told Gorbachev to his face that he agreed with Nina Andreeva. Gorbachev was furious. He dismissed Petrov from the position of First Secretary of the Sverdlovsk Regional Party Committee, which Petrov—Yeltsin's handpicked replacement—had held since Yeltsin moved to Moscow in 1985. As punishment, Gorbachev exiled Petrov to Cuba as Soviet ambassador.

Once again, the secrecy in which Party affairs were conducted enabled Yeltsin to attract support from both poles of the growing opposition to Gorbachev and his policies—from those who thought the General Secretary was going too far too fast, and from those who thought he was not going far or fast enough. It seems unlikely that many of Yeltsin's future associates among the liberal intelligentsia would have joined his camp had they known that sympathizers of Nina Andreeva were present in the headquarters.

As it happened, the Nina Andreeva affair played a key role in ensuing developments. On the one hand, it contributed to the birth of a free press in Russia. Never again would the situation be repeated in which all the media kept silent for three weeks for fear of repercussions. On the other hand, it turned the editorial board of *Sovetskaya Rossiya* into an incubator for hard-line opposition to reform; chief editor Valentin Chikin was elevated to the Politburo of the CP RSFSR in 1990 and elected to the State Duma, on the CPRF ticket, in 1993 and 1996. The newspaper played a central role in a party whose leaders never tired of recalling Lenin's description of its first newspaper, *Iskra*: that it served not merely as a propaganda tool but as the Party's collective organizer.

Had it been deliberately orchestrated, the diarchy in the domain of CPSU ideology might have served a useful purpose. It could have made it possible for different currents to coexist within the Party, and prepared their proponents for a civilized divorce. Certainly it was not long before it became clear that the views of the CPSU's two ideologists—Yegor Ligachev and Aleksandr Yakovlev—could not be reconciled within a single party. They were too far apart for that. Although by no means a Stalinist himself, Ligachev felt more comfortable with Stalinists and anti-Semites than he did with most of his comrades on the Gorbachev team. Yakovlev, for his part, held beliefs that could only be termed anticommunist. In 1988, he went so far as to commission one of his subordinates, the philosopher Aleksandr Tsipko, to write a critique of Marxist doctrine. The result was that a staffer in the Propaganda Department of the CPSU Central Committee penned the first article denouncing Karl Marx's teachings from positions reflecting those of the anticommunist exile, Alexander Solzhenitsyn, printed in an official Soviet journal.

Such a divergence of views would be divisive for any political party. For the CPSU—a party that had put ideology above politics ever since Lenin split from the dissident Mensheviks in 1903—it was fatal. In the words of Gorbachev's aide Georgii Shakhnazarov, those who stood behind Nina Andreeva knew that the gravest danger for the Party was to allow it to doubt the infallibility of its doctrines.

In an attempt to justify his involvement in the August 1991 putsch, former KGB Chairman Vladimir Kryuchkov claimed that, by mid-1991, Gorbachev and Yakovlev were intent on splitting the CPSU and setting up in its place at least two parties—one dogmatic and the other social-democratic—capable of competing for power with other parties at the ballot box. There seems to be a good deal of truth to this. As early as December 1995, Yakovlev, in a memorandum to Gorbachev, had proposed splitting the CPSU into two in order to create an organized way out of the differences in opinions of the party members. At the time, Gorbachev dismissed Yakovlev's idea as "premature." According to Gorbachev's biographer Archie Brown, this was an impractical suggestion for Gorbachev's first year in power; had Gorbachev attempted to implement the plan at that time, Brown argues, it would almost certainly have resulted in the ouster of both men. In the years that followed, however, the political situation in the USSR and Russia changed dramatically. During the Twenty-eighth Congress of the CPSU, held in June 1990, reform-minded delegates urged Yakovlev and fellow Politburo progressive Eduard Shevardnadze to engineer a split in precisely the way depicted by Kryuchkov. These two leaders favored splitting with Party conservatives and creating a social democratic party, but were reportedly stopped by Gorbachev at the last moment.

Gorbachev Scrambles for Reform Amidst Growing Public Discontent and Violence

Back in 1988, Gorbachev certainly had no intention of using the Ligachev-Yakovlev controversy to split the CPSU, even if this could have been achieved in a more or less civilized way. Instead, in September of that year, Gorbachev reorganized the CPSU leadership. He removed Ligachev as his deputy and put him in charge of agriculture—traditionally the "graveyard" post of the CPSU. At the same time, Gorbachev put Yakovlev in charge of foreign policy and entrusted the ideology portfolio to a colorless nonentity, Vadim Medvedev, who was equally unpopular with the Ligachevites as with Yakovlev's sympathizers. Finally, he suspended meetings of the Central Committee Secretariat, traditionally the nerve center for the Party's intervention in the economy, and replaced its specific economic departments by commissions with sketchily drawn responsibilities. In the end, this reshuffle wrought the opposite to that which Gorbachev apparently desired: instead of making the Party more open and democratic, it precipitated the collapse of the CPSU and the emergence from its ruins of the CPRF.

Gorbachev made full use of his victory over Ligachev in the Nina Andreeva controversy, since at that time the CPSU was preparing to elect delegates to the Nineteenth Party Conference. Gorbachev needed a pro-reform momentum throughout the Party to ensure that reform-oriented delegates were chosen. He wanted to persuade the conference to approve the revolutionary (in the Soviet context) principle of contested elections to a new Soviet parliament, the USSR Congress of People's Deputies. Gorbachev also wanted the conference to relinquish the Communist Party's traditional role of managing the Soviet command economy in favor of governmental bodies which would, in turn, be accountable to elected Soviets (local legislative councils). Because of the rather undemocratic way in which delegates were selected (after being nominated by their primary Party organizations the candidates were filtered through a number of committees at district and regional levels), Gorbachev failed in his attempt to secure the election of large numbers of reform-minded intellectuals as conference delegates. There nonetheless seems little doubt that Gorbachev's victory over Ligachev strengthened the General Secretary's authority even among conservative delegates, who voted unanimously for everything that was put before them, including Gorbachev's sweeping changes to the Soviet system of government that gave the USSR its first standing parliament.

By the time the conference opened at the end of June 1988, public discontent with the CPSU was growing. The primary reason was the poor performance of the economy. Gorbachev came to power in 1985 promising the population higher living standards in return for harder work. However, living standards deteriorated during Gorbachev's first years in power. Meat continued to be rationed in many Soviet cities, just as it had been under Brezhnev, while the 1985 campaign against alcohol rendered vodka almost unobtainable also. To make matters worse, sugar had to be rationed because bootleggers snapped up stocks. The long list of "deficit" goods grew rapidly until it included soap, toothpaste, washing powder and other staples.

In addition to economic hardship, the country experienced the first ethnic conflict of the kind that would eventually provoke the collapse of the USSR. The first such incident occurred in December 1986, when troops attacked an ethnically inspired rally in Almaty, capital of the Central Asian Republic of Kazakhstan. Local youths rioted because Moscow had replaced the ethnic Kazakh leader of the republic, Dinmukhamed Kunaev, with Gennadii Kolbin, a Russian newcomer from the Volga city Ulyanovsk. Many people were wounded and some were killed. Then, in early 1988, fighting broke out between the inhabitants of two Soviet republics—Azerbaijan and Armenia—over the status of the predominantly Armenian enclave of Nagorno-Karabakh within Azerbaijan. While the significance of the riots in Almaty remained limited to the republic, the bloodshed in Nagorno-Karabakh commanded attention in Moscow and in Leningrad and even outside the USSR because of the presence of large and influential Armenian diaspora communities.

First Shoots Of Civil Society

Yet another reason for the CPSU's growing unpopularity was the appearance on the scene of alternative political organizations in the guise of so-called "informal" groups. Initially, such groups attracted ecologists, rock-music fans or people eager to preserve historical monuments. Before long, however, these apolitical groups were joined by groups of religious believers, clubs in support of perestroika, or groups professing more precise aims, such as the anti-Stalinist "Memorial" society, which was dedicated to preserving the memory of the victims of the Soviet-era terror. In August 1987, forty-seven unofficial groups held a conference in Moscow on the theme of "Public Initiatives under Perestroika." That conference adopted a common manifesto and founded the Federation of Social Clubs. Although one of the conference working groups came up with a proposal for abolishing the USSR's single-party system and replacing it with political pluralism, that almost unthinkable suggestion was rejected by the majority of the conference. The conference saw, nonetheless, the appearance in the USSR of the first shoots of a civil society.

One of the activities undertaken on the streets of Moscow by activists of the new informal groups was campaigning for the election as delegates to the Nineteenth Party Conference of such reformers as the editor of the outspoken magazine *Ogonek*, Vitalii Korotich; the philosopher Yurii Karyakin; and the co-chairman of "Memorial," Yurii Afanasyev. Some of them were elected, thanks to Gorbachev's personal intervention on their behalf. But at least one—Boris Yeltsin—was elected in spite of Gorbachev. Yeltsin became the star of the conference both because of his address attacking the perks of the Party privilegentsia and because of his very public argument with Ligachev, who made a fool of himself by taking issue with Yeltsin in front of television cameras. Sad to say, the conference demonstrated the immaturity of Soviet society, since scenes such as Yeltsin's argument with Ligachev, or Korotich's defense of *Ogonek's* decision to publish an article on corruption in the Party, distracted public attention from the deeper historic significance of the conference's decisions.

Nineteenth Party Conference

The Nineteenth Party Conference was the beginning of the end for the CPSU. It left many professional Party bureaucrats bewildered and wondering what they were supposed to do, now that the Party had resolved to stop ordering the Soviets around and to stop monitoring the economic activities of factories and farms. At the same time, the bodies that were supposed to replace the Party proved unsuitable either for governing the country or for managing the economy. As a result, Moscow started to lose control over affairs of state.

The most decisive break with the past was represented by the decision of the Nineteenth Party Conference to introduce contested elections for a new legislature that would replace the existing Supreme Soviet, a body which had traditionally rubber-stamped legislation at the behest of the CPSU apparatus. As the Conference drew to a close, Gorbachev persuaded it to approve the idea of a constitutional amendment providing for elections to a new Soviet "superparliament," the Congress of People's Deputies (CPD). The CPD would be elected by the population in April 1989 and would, in turn, elect from among its own members a smaller, bicameral Supreme Soviet. The Supreme Soviet would serve as a standing legislature.

The setting up of the new Soviet legislature played a vital role in the process of democratization in the USSR. In the two years and seven months that it existed, the Congress of People's Deputies succeeded in abolishing media censorship and removing from the Soviet Constitution the CPSU's right to control all areas of the country's activity. These were only some of the progressive measures approved by the Congress, which also fostered a flock of new, democratic politicians. It made hitherto omnipotent government ministers, Politburo members and even the General Secretary himself accountable to the people's representatives, while allowing the electorate to watch the powers-that-be report back to parliament in live television broadcasts. And yet, the structure of the new parliament, the way deputies were elected, and the organization of its sessions proved a bitter disappointment to the very same democratic deputies who owed their fame to the innovation. In addition, the April 1989 elections to seats in the Congress of People's Deputies struck a fatal blow to Gorbachev's relations with Party officials.

During discussions over which form of democracy to adopt, Gorbachev had set his heart on a peculiar system of semi-corporatist government suggested by his old friend from university, Anatolii Lukyanov. Lukyanov, for his part, had concocted the scheme on the basis of archive materials dealing with the way the Soviets conferred in Lenin's day. The difference, of course, lay in the fact that back then the Soviets did not govern the country for a single day: Lenin saw to it that they were swiftly co-opted by the Bolshevik Party. The parliament elected under Lukyanov's system also bore a vague resemblance to another historic gathering: the Estates-General convened by France's Louis XVI in May 1789. In both cases, the deputies were elected on an unequal basis, depending on their social class. Under Lukyanov's plan, Soviet citizens elected deputies to a 2,250-seat "superparliament" on the following basis: (a) 750 deputies were elected in constituencies across the USSR, on the basis of an equal number of electors per constituency; (b) 750 deputies were elected to represent national-territorial formations, including the USSR's constituent Union-republics and its major cities, Moscow and Leningrad; (c) the remaining 750 deputies were selected by "public organizations" such as the CPSU, Komsomol, Trade Union Federation, USSR Academy of Sciences, and so on. The problem with this scheme was that it undermined the basic principle of "one citizen, one vote." Most citizens had only one vote, but other, more privileged people had two or more.

The CPSU had the right to elect one hundred deputies. These were chosen by members of the Central Committee from a list of precisely one hundred candidates. Gorbachev was taking no chances. He arranged an old-style, uncontested election for himself and his Politburo cronies (except for those who, like Foreign Minister Eduard Shevardnadze, held ministerial posts) while lower-ranking Party officials were forced, kicking and screaming, to stand in contested elections. This put Gorbachev in a vulnerable position with Party bureaucrats, particularly when it became known that thirty-two of 160 regional Party bosses had failed to win election, as did all those in top Party or government posts in Leningrad. Little wonder that, at a Central Committee plenum one month before the Congress was due to hold its first session, Party hierarchs turned on Gorbachev for the first time and attacked his policies in rude terms. One speaker, Aleksandr Melnikov, accused the leadership of driving the Party to ruin because it was unaware of what was going on in the provinces.

The Congress opened on May 25 and lasted until June 9, 1989. For sixteen days, the USSR's 300 million-strong population sat glued to their television sets, unsure of whether or not to believe their ears. They had never before heard such heresies. On July 8, Gorbachev read the riot act to a meeting of first secretaries of regional Party committees. The speakers at the meeting sounded the alarm over attacks on the higher-ups, particularly on Ligachev, that had been voiced at the Congress. Gorbachev responded with a threat to fire the conservative officials.

CPD Takes on Conservative Hue

In all fairness to the Party secretaries, it should be admitted that the institutions Gorbachev created were quite unsuited to carry out the functions from which he was determined to detach the CPSU. "We have destroyed the old mechanism, but we have not created a new one in its stead," was the consensus of those days. Prime Minister Nikolai Ryzhkov, who headed the first Soviet government to have been approved by the parliament, complained that his orders and those of his economic ministers were ignored by the officials who were supposed to implement them. The disappearance of basic goods from the shelves eventually provoked unrest on the part even of the long-suffering Soviet workforce. The summer of 1989 saw huge strikes by coal miners in various parts of the Soviet Union, while bloody conflicts between different nationalities also intensified. Meanwhile, Popular Fronts in the Baltic states started their peaceful march toward independence, and their example was soon copied in other republics. The collapse of Communism in Central and Eastern Europe and the end of its military arm, the Warsaw Pact, encouraged secessionists in the Union republics as well as their liberal Russian allies to anticipate a similar fate for their respective countries.

The fate of the CPD bore some resemblance to that of its French predecessor on the eve of the 1789 Revolution. In France, members of the Third Estate abandoned the Estates-General to form the National Assembly. In the Soviet Union, reform-minded deputies found both the CPD and the Supreme Soviet to have been too easily manipulated by Gorbachev and his deputy, Lukyanov. One by one, they lost interest in the all-Union bodies and abandoned them to make politics in their own republics. As a result of this process, the CPD evolved in the opposite direction to that taken by the electorate at large. While the Soviet population was gradually becoming more radical, the Congress became more and more conservative, adding fuel to the radicals' belief that the parliament could not represent the will of the country.

The elections to the CPD exposed the myth of Party unity. While Communist Party members constituted 87.6 percent of the deputies to the CPD (as opposed to a mere 71.5 percent in the old, unreformed Supreme Soviet, whose numbers were padded out by token workers and peasants), about a quarter of the deputies were elected in the face of active opposition from the Party apparatus. The first Soviet parliamentary opposition, the radical Interregional Group of Deputies, which emerged in 1989, was made up mostly of Communist Party members, as was its conservative counterpart, the opposition "Soyuz" (Union) group. Nonetheless, the CPSU turned out, more often than not, to be the only political party capable of persuading the CPD to vote for its proposals. This trend persisted even after the CPSU was gone. At the last session of the CPD, held at the end of August 1991, after the CPSU had been banned and Gorbachev had handed in his Party card, the Congress meekly approved the proposal put forward by Gorbachev and endorsed by the leaders of the Soviet republics, and voted itself out of existence.

The CPSU Relinquishes Its Leading Role

In the meantime, the Party apparatus tried to make a comeback by setting up informal groups of its own. In May 1989, the notorious Nina Andreeva set up an organization called "Unity for a Return to Leninist Principles and Communist Ideals." Her movement attracted only about a hundred neo-Stalinists, but it inspired those Party officials in Leningrad who had, a few months earlier, failed to win election to the CPD. In mid-June 1989, the United Workers' Front held its constituent congress in Leningrad with Nina Andreeva as guest of honor. Two days later, members of the new movement rallied in downtown Leningrad to declare their determination to fight against liberal intellectuals and members of cooperatives (the USSR's first officially tolerated private enterprises). Their ire was aroused by their antipathy to the idea of a market-oriented economy and, in particular, to the possibility of land reform. They also demanded changes in the rules for the elections to local Soviets due to be held in March the following year. The Front wanted two-thirds of the seats in the city Soviet to be reserved for deputies elected by industrial workers and for all election campaigning to take place at factories. The Front's activists declared that such rules would prevent members of the democratic intelligentsia from being elected. Despite the support the Front enjoyed from the Leningrad city and regional Party committees, the city Soviet rejected the Front's openly undemocratic proposals by a vote of 385 to 16.

In the following months, conservatives in other towns and cities followed Leningrad's example and established their own branches of the United Workers' Front. Before long, they decided to join ranks and set up an umbrella organization at republic level. The founding congress of the United Front of Workers of Russia met in Sverdlovsk on September 8 and 9, 1989. It was attended by 110 delegates from twenty-nine cities of the RSFSR, as well as by groups of ethnic Russians from Moldova, Tajikistan and the Baltic republics. The delegates reiterated the goals earlier proclaimed by local branches—opposition to market reform and amendment to the electoral law to increase the representation of workers in the USSR CPD. However, the Front attracted very little grassroots support. Before long, it merged itself into the so-called Leningrad Initiative Congress of Communists of Russia. This would pave the way for the June 1990 establishment of the Communist Party of the RSFSR.

Before that, however, two developments took place that were to play a key role in the fate of the CPSU. The first was the removal of Article 6 from the Soviet Constitution. The second was the decision of the Lithuanian Communist Party to leave the CPSU.

Article 6 Under Attack

Article 6 described the CPSU as "the leading and guiding force in Soviet society" and "the nucleus of its political system." The provision was seen as blocking the emergence of a multi-party system or a civil society in the USSR because it subordinated every public and state institution to the Communist Party rather than to the people and their elected representatives. As early as July 24, 1989, a deputy representing striking coal miners in Pechora in the Far North had addressed the Supreme Soviet with a list of the strikers' political demands, among which was the removal of Article 6 from the Constitution. The demand was picked up and adopted as a campaign goal by the Interregional Group of deputies and their leader, Andrei Sakharov.

The measure did not, in fact, contradict the policies of Gorbachev and the reform wing of the Party leadership. Addressing a group of students at the Moscow Higher Komsomol School in November 1989,

Aleksandr Yakovlev endorsed the idea of removing Article 6; however, Yakovlev recommended waiting until the following year when, he predicted, a new Soviet constitution would be adopted. At a plenum of the CPSU Central Committee in December 1989, Gorbachev's progressive Minister of Internal Affairs, Vadim Bakatin, tried to persuade his audience to jettison the offending article. Bakatin claimed that a multi-party system was, in any case, emerging in various parts of the Soviet Union. Gorbachev favored a gradual, step-by-step transfer of power from the CPSU to the Soviets. In his view, however, the time was not ripe to finalize the process because the Soviets were as yet institutionally too weak, and lacking in the necessary personnel and experience, to take power into their own hands.

When the second session of the USSR CPD opened on December 12, 1989, Andrei Sakharov tried to read a petition calling for the abolition of Article 6. Gorbachev brusquely cut him off. Two days later, the Nobel laureate was dead, having made an emotional address at a meeting of the Moscow democratic intelligentsia in which he criticized the slow pace of reform. Death transformed Sakharov into a cult figure. Three months later, in March 1990, a plenum of the CPSU Central Committee prepared to consider constitutional amendments abolishing Article 6 and the introduction of the post of executive president of the USSR. On the eve of the plenum, the Interregional Group organized the greatest rally ever held on the streets of Moscow. Half a million people demonstrated in support of Gorbachev's reforms and against Party conservatives. At the next session of the CPD that same month, Gorbachev committed probably the gravest error in his political career when he had himself elected as the first Soviet president in an uncontested vote by members of the Congress rather than by universal suffrage.

Lithuanian Communists Break Away From CPSU

At the end of 1989, the Lithuanian Communist Party held a Congress at which 82 percent of the delegates, led by First Secretary Algirdas Brazauskas, voted to break ties with the CPSU and set up an independent party with their own program and rules. The Party split, and the remaining 18 percent formed the "Temporary Central Committee of the Lithuanian Communist Party on the Platform of the CPSU." The impact of the split on the rest of the CPSU was complex. It enraged the conservatives and undermined the authority of the Soviet state and Party leadership; at the same time, it encouraged various currents within the Party to act as their wisdom dictated.

The Yeltsin Factor

The final blow to Gorbachev's authority in the CPSU was the election, on May 28, 1990, of Boris Yeltsin as chairman (speaker) of Russia's new parliament, the RSFSR Supreme Soviet. Yeltsin was nominated for the post by the Democratic Russia Movement, an umbrella organization embracing pro-reform activists from various electoral clubs, newly formed political parties and one relatively strong movement identifying itself as "Communists for Perestroika." In the elections to local Soviets held on March 4 and 18, 1990, Democratic Russia's candidates won landslide victories in Moscow, Leningrad and several other smaller cities. However, the system for electing deputies at republic level was such that, while Democratic Russia swept the board in elections to the city Soviets, the movement and its allies won only 40 percent of the seats in the RSFSR CPD. It therefore seems safe to assert that Yeltsin owed his rise to power as much to the carelessness of Gorbachev's leadership as to his success at the ballot box.

Although Yeltsin had announced his intention of running as chairman of the Supreme Soviet early on, the Soviet leadership failed either to put up an attractive alternative candidate or to accept Yeltsin's victory with good grace. Instead, Gorbachev chose the risky path of intervening personally in the electoral process. The first session of the RSFSR CPD opened on May 16, 1990. Eight days later, the Soviet President addressed the Russian deputies and enjoined them not to endorse Yeltsin's candidacy. Gorbachev accused Yeltsin of "betraying the cause of socialism." Gorbachev went on to warn the deputies—correctly, as it turned out, though there is some cause to doubt whether he believed his own words at the time—that the Soviet Union would collapse if Yeltsin was elected. The USSR could survive the loss of any of the other fifteen republics, Gorbachev declared, but without Russia there could be no Union. The warning went unheeded; it may even have been counterproductive, since being bullied by the CPSU General Secretary had by that time gone quite out of fashion.

Hardliners Put Up Polozkov Against Yeltsin

The CPSU Politburo did not help matters. It resolved to support the candidacy of none other than Ivan Polozkov, the Party leader from Krasnodar Krai whose reactionary views made him completely unacceptable to almost everybody. The bloc of hard-line Communists and ultranationalists who shared Polozkov's views had failed to win a single seat in the March 1990 elections to the Moscow and Leningrad Soviets. Gorbachev's aide and confidant, Georgii Shakhnazarov, told his boss that, forced to choose between Yeltsin and Polozkov, he too would have voted for Yeltsin. At the Congress, Polozkov's supporters campaigned by supplying the deputies with anti-Semitic leaflets accusing various Russian celebrities of concealing their Jewish origins.

Polozkov's controversial personality notwithstanding, Yeltsin's victory was by no means easy. Two rounds of voting failed to produce a winner. But, after offering concessions to the more conservative deputies, Yeltsin won by a narrow margin in the third round.

Decree on Power and Parliament Weaken CPSU

Following Yeltsin's victory, representatives of Democratic Russia worked at getting legislation adopted by Russia's new parliament that would undermine the power of the CPSU and assert Russia's autonomy vis-a-vis the center. Aimed at the CPSU and adopted during the Russian parliament's first session was the landmark Decree on Power. Among other provisions, this piece of legislation outlawed party organizations in the police, army and secret police, as well as in state-owned industrial enterprises. This was a major blow to the Communist Party, whose power was rooted in its presence in every workplace the length and breadth of the USSR.

On June 12, 1990, parliament adopted a declaration of state sovereignty and asserted that RSFSR laws took precedence over Soviet federal laws. Also introduced was a ban on combining positions in the Soviets or governmental bodies with leading positions in any political parties. As these laws were disadvantageous for middle-ranking CPSU officials, eager to hedge their bets and chair their respective regional or local Soviets, a backlash to reverse them became virtually inevitable.

Time and again, twentieth century Russia has repeated one and the same pattern. Those who have failed to dominate a particular body have not been content to bide their time and try again. Instead they have set up alternative bodies and attempted to oust their rivals from power. When Lenin's Bolsheviks lost the elections to the State Duma in 1917, they established the Soviets and set about dominating them instead. Finding themselves a minority within the CPSU, Gorbachev and his colleagues invented the Congress of People's Deputies. Unable to dominate the USSR Supreme Soviet, Yeltsin and his supporters turned to its hitherto insignificant Russian equivalent. Yeltsin's hard-line opponents proved no exception to this rule. Within days of his election as chairman of the RSFSR Supreme Soviet, the Secretariat of the RSFSR Writers' Union issued an appeal for the creation of a Russian Communist Party.

Birth of the Russian Communist Party

Pressure for a Russian Party organization was first expressed at the end of 1989. Gorbachev was always strongly opposed to the creation of a Russian Communist Party and, for that matter, to the idea that Russia should have equal status with the other Soviet republics. Such a move would mean the end of the empire, Chernyaev remembers Gorbachev warning—correctly, as it turned out.

In December 1989, Gorbachev managed to fight off demands for a Russian Communist Party. Instead, he revived the Russian Bureau—a department of the CPSU Central Committee that had been closed down in the 1960s—and had himself appointed as its head. But this was only a temporary measure. By April 1990, hard-line intellectuals set up the Leningrad Initiative Congress of Communists of Russia with the aim of paving the way for the establishment of a full-fledged Russian Communist Party. Support for the idea came from a wide range of leading communists, of whom Boris Yeltsin was one. On June 20, 1990, conservative delegates to the CPSU's Twenty-eighth Congress convened what they proceeded to declare the First Founding Congress of the Communist Party of the RSFSR. The hall rang with strident attacks on Gorbachev and his allies for betraying the Socialist camp (the USSR and its Central and Eastern European allies) into the hands of foreign powers. The Decree on Power came in for special criticism. Polozkov was elected first secretary of the new party, defeating Yeltsin's ally, Oleg Lobov, by 1,396 votes to 1,066. The Russian Communist Party (CP RSFSR) had been born.

2: From the CP RSFSR to the CPRF

The CPRF, as explained in Chapter 1, is the successor to a party that was set up within the CPSU but in virtual opposition to it—the CP RSFSR. The CP RSFSR never achieved the status of ruling party to which it aspired. Boris Yeltsin's election in May 1990 as chairman of the RSFSR Supreme Soviet, and in June 1991 as Russia's first democratically elected president, put paid to the party's hopes of leading the country. And, two months after Yeltsin was elected president, the failure of the August 1991 coup set in motion the processes that led to the collapse of the USSR and the temporary outlawing of the Communist Party on Russian territory.

Today's CPRF is therefore a very different party animal than its parent. Established in February 1993 with Gennadii Zyuganov as its leader, the CPRF is an opposition party that professes its determination to win a leading role exclusively through the ballot box. This transformation was accompanied by changes in political base, party structure, philosophy and ideology that reflected the change from a ruling to an opposition party.

The CPRF's gravest problem is perhaps the absence of industrial or "blue-collar" workers in its ranks. This explains why the 1997 election to the State Duma of Nikolai Kolometsev, a worker at the agricultural machinery factory Rostselmash, inspired a half-page article in a CPRF newspaper. It is cold comfort for the CPRF leadership that workers are in no rush to join other Russian parties, either.

The CPRF has nonetheless played a crucial role in the colossal changes that have taken place in the Russian political system during the country's brief post-Soviet history. The CPRF has emerged from this chaotic process as the most (if not the only) viable party in Russia today. This is true despite the fact that the CPRF has been unable to maintain the iron discipline that prevailed in the CPSU in the days of its power and glory. Like the CPSU, the CPRF does not recognize factions or allow them to organize platforms within the party. Unlike the CPSU, however, the CPRF has been forced to tolerate the existence within its ranks of groups expressing a wide range of different opinions, and its meetings are characterized by heated discussion rather than by the unanimous voting that typified the CPSU.

CPRF Idiosyncracies

The most profound way in which the CPRF differs from the CPSU is ideology. The evolution of the CPRF's ideology is discussed in detail in Chapter 4. Suffice it to say here that CPRF has made a radical departure from Communist orthodoxy. Abandoning the lip service that the CPSU used to pay to proletarian internationalism, the CPRF has opted instead for a Russian nationalism that often slides over into outright xenophobia. It has also jettisoned the orthodox Marxist preference for revolutionary and violent ways of coming to power. Instead, its leaders have concluded an unwritten alliance with the more conservative segments of the Russian Orthodox Church and have adopted their worldview.

Along with this shift toward Russian nationalist sentiment, the CPRF has adapted to the economic realities of today's post-Soviet Russia and jettisoned the idea of central planning and large-scale state-ownership. It has recognized the "plurality of forms of property," the right to private enterprise that is central to capitalism and the free market.

Although Gennadii Zyuganov and other leaders of today's CPRF have fought off attempts to rename their party a Social-Democratic instead of a Communist party, they have changed the date of the party's founding from 1902 to 1898. In so doing, they followed the example set by Mikhail Gorbachev. Until Gorbachev became General Secretary of the CPSU, leaders of the CPSU dated the birth of the party to 1902. That was the year in which the Russian Social Democratic Workers' Party (RSDWP) held its second congress. A group of delegates led by Lenin split off from the RSDWP to form a radical party "of a new type"—the Bolsheviks. Gorbachev set a precedent by declaring 1898—the year in which the RSDWP held its first congress—the founding date of the Soviet Communist Party. In so doing, he was trying deliberately to identify the CPSU with the more moderate Menshevik wing of the RSDWP, and not just with Lenin and the radical Bolsheviks. It is striking and significant that Zyuganov's CPRF has followed Gorbachev's precedent and claimed the same date for its own founding.

The CPRF and Yeltsin

Relations between the Yeltsin regime and Russia's Communists have passed through some very tense patches, including several attempts by Yeltsin to ban the party. Over the course of time, however, the leaders of the CPRF have gradually come to terms with the powers-that-be. This has laid them open to accusations of hypocrisy and fraternization with the enemy. In their book on the CPRF (*Russia's Communists at the Crossroads*), Joan Urban and Valerii Solovei stress the pervasiveness among Russia's neo-Communists of a worldview that divides the Russian political elite into patriots and traitors. "Regardless of specific group affiliation," the authors write, "they were all but unanimous in denouncing Gorbachev, Yeltsin, and their respective inner circles as self-serving opportunists who were, to boot, guilty of high treason."

This view certainly exists and is strongly held and expressed. At the same time, however, the CPRF's parliamentary leaders have over the years come to terms with the Yeltsin leadership and have even cooperated with it. In this respect, the policy of the CPRF is not that different from any parliamentary opposition in any "normal" country. Allegations that the CPRF cuts deals with Yeltsin's administration in private and lambastes the "anti-people regime" in public can be heard from most of Zyuganov's critics, both pro- and anticommunist.

At times, this has given the CPRF the aura of being a split personality, but it has enabled the party to escape from the total isolation that was the fate of Ivan Polozkov's CP RSFSR. Unlike that political outcast, today's CPRF has been party to all the political negotiations between the Yeltsin government and parliament since the general elections of December 1993. This change can only be partly explained by the policies of Zyuganov's leadership. Other factors include the departures of radical firebrands Viktor Tyulkin and Viktor Anpilov, who left the CP RSFSR to form the Working Russia movement, and of the leaders of other splinter parties such as the Russian Communist Workers' Party or the Union of Communist Parties-CPSU. Last but not least, growing popular disillusion with the Yeltsin leadership also helped to end the isolation of the CPRF.

Communist "Support" of Yeltsin

The willingness of Zyuganov's party to cooperate with the Yeltsin administration is often explained by reference to the supposed growth of Social-Democratic trends within the CPRF. This implies that the party has adopted a more moderate position toward the present regime. In fact, the change may just as well be explained by reference to fading anticommunist zeal on the part of Yeltsin's supporters. In May 1990, when Yeltsin was elected chairman of the Russian parliament, many of the present leaders of the CPRF belonged to the "Communists of Russia" parliamentary faction, which controlled between 40 and 60 percent of the votes in the Russian parliament and was ostensibly in opposition to Yeltsin. "Communists of Russia" nonetheless failed to head off any of Yeltsin's moves during his struggle for power against Gorbachev and the rest of the Soviet leadership. The ambiguous attitude of the faction during this period may be illustrated by the following examples:

(1)In June 1990, the Russian parliament gave almost unanimous endorsement to the declaration of state sovereignty and the assertion of the supremacy of Russian laws over those of the USSR. These measures, proposed by Yeltsin, marked a major step toward the breakup of the USSR.

(2)In February 1991, eight leaders of the Russian parliament called for Yeltsin's ouster from his position as chairman of the Supreme Soviet. The attempt failed as a result of Polozkov's personal intervention on Yeltsin's behalf.

As long as the USSR remained in existence, the "Communists of Russia" faction had at least two reasons to cooperate with Yeltsin. The first was that, whether openly or covertly, most of them opposed Gorbachev's perestroika policies and supported Yeltsin's campaign to elevate the status of the RSFSR at the expense of the all-Union center. The second reason was that it was hard for any Russian to resist the irrational but widespread hero-worship of Yeltsin that prevailed at that time.

It may be added that as many as 87 percent of the deputies elected to seats in the RSFSR CPD in March 1990 were—at least on paper—members of the CPSU. By no means all of them joined the "Communists of Russia" faction, however, and still fewer supported Polozkov personally. Rightly or wrongly, Polozkov held the reputation of an odious reactionary. Communist Party members made up the overwhelming majority even among Yeltsin's most radical supporters—the "Democratic Russia" faction—where they mixed happily with former political prisoners and other dissidents. Only a few dozen "Democratic Russia" activists followed Yeltsin's example and quit the CPSU after the June 1990 founding congress of the CP RSFSR. Between these two poles were many Communist Party members who were unwilling to join either the "Communists of Russia" or the "Democratic Russia" faction, but felt more inclined to opt for Yeltsin than for Polozkov and his associates. This group even included some members of the Central Committee of the CP RSFSR itself, such as the head of the Control Commission, Colonel Nikolai Stolyarov, who voiced strong reservations about Polozkov's leadership in a series of interviews published at the time in the Soviet media.

On April 9, 1991, another Army officer and member of the CP RSFSR Central Committee, Colonel Aleksandr Rutskoi, attracted attention by publicly attacking the leadership of the CP RSFSR and setting up a faction called "Communists for Democracy," which declared its support for Yeltsin. Later, some rank-and-file supporters of democratic reform who still retained their Communist Party membership, announced their intention of forming a faction inside the CP RSFSR, provisionally entitled "Democratic Party of Russia's Communists" (DPRC). Yeltsin rewarded Rutskoi for splitting the CP RSFSR by inviting him to run as his Vice-

President in the presidential election held on June 12, 1991. The resounding victory of the Yeltsin-Rutskoi team further accelerated the death throes of the CP RSFSR and of the Soviet Union.

Defining the CPSU and the CP RSFSR Down

Within weeks of the presidential election, Yeltsin struck his first blow against the CPSU and the CP RSFSR. On July 20, 1991, just a month before the abortive coup that was to bring down the USSR, Russia's new president issued his Decree No. 2. This banned the activities of political parties in all state agencies on the territory of the RSFSR. At that time, the CPSU maintained cells (known as "primary Party organizations") in every state-owned enterprise throughout the USSR. That ensured the Party's presence in factories, farms, schools, universities, courts, police stations and government ministries. The CPSU was, of course, the only political party with this privilege. Throughout the Soviet period, these cells had enabled the CPSU to control every sphere of life in the country, from the economy and the army to the personal lives of Soviet citizens. Indeed, the fact that it operated in this way prompted many analysts to claim that the Communist Party was not really a political party at all in the generally accepted sense of the term.

The CP RSFSR appealed against Yeltsin's decree to the USSR Constitutional Oversight Committee (the equivalent of a Constitutional Court, though with fewer powers), which displayed no enthusiasm to intervene. When the decree came into force on August 5, 1991, the CP RSFSR had little choice but to start to transfer its cells from workplaces to the premises of local Communist Party committees. The following day, the Central Committee of the CP RSFSR held what was to prove to be (though of course no one foresaw this at the time) its last plenary session. At that meeting, Vice-President-elect Rutskoi and his supporters were expelled from the Party. Included in the expulsion was Vasilii Lipitsky, ideologue of the DPRC. The plenum also dismissed Polozkov as first secretary, replacing him as party leader with the moderate head of the Vologda Oblast Party Committee, Valentin Kuptsov.

In sharp contrast to the expulsion of Rutskoi and his colleagues, the ouster of Polozkov passed almost unnoticed by the media. The Russian media at the time rarely commented on personnel developments within the CP RSFSR. But Polozkov's ouster was indeed an important event. Back in 1990, the CPSU Central Committee's Department on Organizational Party Work had recommended Kuptsov, not Polozkov, as a suitable candidate to lead the Russian Communist Party. In view of this decision,

Polozkov had promised Gorbachev that he would not stand for the post of Party First Secretary. When the conference took place, however, Polozkov failed to keep his word. He claimed that, between the time he gave Gorbachev his word and the time of the election, hundreds of conference delegates had approached him and urged him to stand for the post of first secretary. When it came to the vote, Kuptsov lost to Polozkov in the first round. Therefore, the changing of the guard on August 6, 1991 demonstrated two things. First, that up until the date of the impending coup, Gorbachev was capable of enforcing his will on the CP RSFSR, albeit with difficulty. Second, that the changing of the guard in the CP RSFSR was a symbolic event—that is, the last victory of the apparatus over elected Communist officials.

The August 1991 Coup

A few days later, with Gorbachev away on his annual summer vacation in Crimea, the Bureau of the Presidium of the CPSU Central Control Commission recommended that former Politburo member and Party Secretary Aleksandr Yakovlev be expelled from the CPSU for statements "intended to split the CPSU and remove it from the political scene." Yakovlev responded by submitting his resignation from the CPSU, following the example of another Gorbachev ally, Foreign Minister Eduard Shevardnadze, who had quit the CPSU a few weeks earlier. Yakovlev issued a statement alleging that "a Stalinist group has taken shape within the Party's leadership core" and that reactionaries were planning a coup d'etat against Gorbachev. Within days—on 19 August 1991—members of the top Soviet leadership did indeed attempt to replace Gorbachev with an unconstitutional body called the State Committee for the State of Emergency (GKChP). This was the short-lived coup of August 1991 that was to bring about the end of Communist rule in the Soviet Union. Much of the credit for the attempted coup's failure belongs to the brave resistance mounted by Yeltsin, his supporters in the Russian parliament and the thousands of Muscovites who rushed to defend Russia's fledgling democracy outside the Russian parliament (now government) building, commonly known as the "Russian White House."

CPSU and CP RSFSR Not Directly Involved in Coup

The expulsion from the Communist Party of Yeltsin's and Gorbachev's associates on the eve of the putsch created the erroneous impression that this ill-thought-out adventure had been inspired by reactionary forces within the Party apparatus. When the Russian Prosecutor-General's Office investigated the putsch, however, it found little evidence to indict either the CPSU or the CP RSFSR. True, all the members of the GKChP were Communist Party members, but so too was virtually every member of the Soviet hierarchy. No member of the GKChP served in his capacity as Party official. Six of them—USSR Vice-President Gennadii Yanaev, KGB chief Vladimir Kryuchkov, Prime Minister Valentin Pavlov, Minister of Internal Affairs Boris Pugo, Defense Minister Dmitrii Yazov and first deputy chairman of the Defense Council Oleg Baklanov—were more closely identified with the Soviet state and government than with the Party apparat, while the other two—Vasilii Starodubtsev and Aleksandr Tizyakov—represented the interests of Russia's state-owned agricultural and defense-industrial sectors, respectively. Only one member of the GKChP—CPSU Politburo member Oleg Shenin—was directly employed by the Party. Investigators unearthed no evidence to indicate that Shenin enjoyed any support from the rest of the Politburo. Similarly, the documents issued by the GKChP during the coup were marked by the absence of Marxist or Communist jargon, consisting rather of statements of concern about the integrity of the Soviet Union, problems of state security, law and order, and the economy.

The coup nonetheless exposed the CPSU as indecisive, cowardly and unfit to rule. For generations, the Party had claimed that it was the best and only champion of the people's interests, but, when crisis struck, it displayed a total lack of initiative. In the absence of General Secretary Gorbachev, under house arrest at his luxury summer residence, and of Gorbachev's deputy Volodymyr Ivashko, who was undergoing surgery, no Communist Party leader or leading institution dared to speak out. The only exception was the leadership of the Party's youth league, the Central Committee of the Komsomol, which immediately condemned the GKChP as unconstitutional. The Secretariat of the CPSU did not meet until the afternoon of August 21, by which time the failure of the coup was already obvious to everyone. By contrast with the Komsomol, the Secretariat did not condemn the coup outright, but merely called for a meeting with Gorbachev. As for the leaders of the CP RSFSR, they never commented at any time.

The KGB appears to have played a greater role in the coup than either the CPSU or the CP RSFSR. KGB chairman Kryuchkov was a member of the GKChP and seems to have been the brains behind it. Several other top KGB officials were involved in Gorbachev's arrest and isolation. It was nonetheless against the Communist Party, not the KGB, that the wrath of Yeltsin's propaganda machine and public opinion were directed.

As early as August 22, troops of the RSFSR and Moscow city authorities, accompanied by legislators and other supporters, seized all the Party buildings in the Russian capital. Party employees were searched before being thrown into the street. The crowd was not, by contrast, permitted to occupy KGB headquarters on Moscow's Lubyanka Square. The only exception made during that night of freedom was the removal from the square of the monument of KGB founder Feliks Dzerzhinsky. Of all the thousands of articles that have appeared since then in the Russian media, virtually all have asserted or implied that the KGB played a subordinate role in the crimes of the Communist era and that the handful of people who made up the CPSU Politburo and Secretariat bore responsibility for the seventy years of terror and oppression that overshadowed the lives of hundreds of millions of people.

The End of the CPSU

The power vacuum created by the coup was quickly filled. Yeltsin seized the opportunity to gather into his hands the reins of power hitherto controlled by the Soviet leadership—army, police, state security and so on. When the putsch was over and Gorbachev returned to Moscow, he found that all his earlier powers had evaporated.

On August 23, Gorbachev attended a meeting of the RSFSR Supreme Soviet, presided over by Yeltsin and acting speaker Ruslan Khasbulatov. Almost all observers of this meeting were shocked by the glee with which the Russian lawmakers humiliated the weakened Soviet President. Yeltsin announced, almost as an aside, that he had signed a decree suspending the activities of the CP RSFSR and sequestering its property, pending a court ruling on the Russian party's alleged involvement in the coup. Under Decree No. 79 of August 23, Russia's Interior Ministry was required to safeguard the Party's property, while the RSFSR Central Bank was ordered to cease all transactions on the accounts of the CP RSFSR, its branches and daughter organizations. This was the first of a series of documents that put an end to the old-style Communist Party and shaped the new one.

On August 24, Gorbachev announced his resignation as CPSU General Secretary and recommended that the CPSU Central Committee be disbanded. The CPSU Secretariat responded the following day with a statement defending its actions during the coup and disclaiming any prior knowledge of the coup. The statement called for the holding of a Central Committee plenum at which the question of disbanding the Central Committee would be examined. Within hours, Yeltsin signed Decree No. 90, expropriating the buildings and assets of the CPSU on the territory of the RSFSR and transferring them to the state. In a separate move, the Russian authorities halted publication of the Communist Party's newspapers, including *Pravda*, *Sovetskaya Rossiya* and *Leninskoe znamya*, as well as *Literaturnaya Rossiya* and *Den'*. The last two did not belong to the CPSU, though they were supportive of the views of the Polozkov leadership. The newspapers were permitted to resume publication within a few weeks, but the Central Committee was not allowed to call a last plenary session. On August 29, 1991, the USSR Supreme Soviet passed a law suspending the activities of the CPSU throughout the USSR.

CALLS FOR A NEW PARTY

The degree of anticommunist feeling that prevailed that autumn among the Russian political elite and the population at large was such that few observers imagined that Russia would ever see another Communist Party. Marxism, pundits declared, was dead, and nowhere more so than in Russia. The population would never stand for its revival. Few commentators therefore paid much attention when, in September 1991, a group of members of the "Communists of Russia" parliamentary faction—which had not been disbanded after the coup—issued an appeal calling for the establishment of a left-wing party to replace the CPSU. The appeal was drowned out by vociferous public demands for the CPSU to be put on trial by a court similar to that in Nuremberg in 1945-47. As the theme of their manifesto, the organizers of the appeal adopted the last draft Program of the CPSU, "Socialism, Democracy, Progress." This had been penned by Gorbachev's reform-minded associates in preparation for the split in the CPSU that they anticipated would take place at the Party's next congress, scheduled for later in 1991. The congress, of course, was never held.

The authors of the appeal acknowledged that the CPSU in its old form had lost the trust of the population and ceased, to all intents and purposes, to exist. They called on all politically active people to unite "in the name of civil concord" to find "a peaceful and constitutional way out for the country from chaos and collapse." To this end they proposed the creation of a "non-apparatus party of like-minded people, who share the ideals of freedom, truth, morality and justice." They appeared to have in mind the formation of a new party in which all former members of the CPSU could find a place, excluding extreme hard-liners, as had happened with many of the former ruling parties of Central and Eastern Europe.

The extent of the disenchantment with the past may be judged by the symbolic fact that the disgraced leaders of the CP RSFSR turned to

Roy Medvedev, a former dissident, to preside over this first attempt to revive their party. Former CP RSFSR leaders, such as Valentin Kuptsov, apparently deemed it safer to lie low and refrained from signing the appeal. Pride of place among the signatories went instead to Medvedev, one of the most prolific and famous Soviet samizdat authors of the 1970s. Medvedev, a Marxist historian, had been expelled from the CPSU in 1969 following the publication in the West of his book on Stalin's terror, *Let History Judge*. He escaped imprisonment but received several official warnings about his dissident activities from the KGB and the State Procuracy. In 1984-85, a police guard was placed outside Medvedev's front door in an attempt to prevent Western journalists and diplomats from entering his apartment. He had been reinstated in the CPSU only in the late 1980s, thanks to Gorbachev's liberalization.

The Socialist Workers' Party (SWP)

The founding conference of the new party opened on October 26, 1991. Medvedev was elected to the organizing committee and identified as the "spiritual leader" of the new party, which was called the Socialist Workers' Party (SWP). A moderate member of the "Communists of Russia" parliamentary faction, Ivan Rybkin (subsequently a member of Yeltsin's government) was elected chairman of the organizing committee. When the conference decided not to include the word "Communist" in the title, Viktor Tyulkin and Viktor Anpilov quit to set up their own party, the Russian Communist Workers' Party (RCWP). Shortly afterwards, activists of small groups who identified themselves as the "Russian Party of Communists" and the "Union of Communists" followed Tyulkin's and Anpilov's example.

The SWP held its first congress in Moscow on December 21-22, 1991. It was attended by 298 delegates from sixty-five of Russia's eighty-nine regions. Seven co-chairmen were elected: Anatolii Denisov, Mikhail Lapshin, Aleksandr Mal'tsev, Roy Medvedev, Ivan Rybkin, Gennadii Sklyar and Lyudmila Vartazarova. Although the policies of the SWP leadership were similar to those of former Communists in Central and Eastern Europe, their moderation was not shared by many of the rank-and-file members. During the first year of its existence, the SWP provided a shelter for former officials of the CP RSFSR, a number of whom had managed to preserve their influential positions in the provinces despite the banning of their party.

At its height in 1992, the SWP claimed 70,000 members. The party's efforts to establish a collective leadership, free of people with an apparatus background, lasted only about eighteen months, until the party's second congress in June 1993. That congress established the position of chairperson, which went to Vartazarova, a former district secretary of the CPSU. After the CPRF was set up, many SWP members joined, dropping SWP membership to a mere 7,000. Many former SWP members resigned from the CPRF following the victory at the CPRF founding congress in 1993 of Gennadii Zyuganov and his allies, but they did not return in large numbers to the SWP.

Today, the SWP is regarded as the most prominent party of the "democratic left." Its leaders avoid close contacts with the CPRF and seek alliances with other democratic left wing or centrist groups. It nonetheless remains a tiny party with few supporters. It failed to win a single seat in the parliamentary elections in either 1993 or 1995. Its fate supports the conclusion that the Central and Eastern European model of political development stood little chance of success in Russia.

Yeltsin Bans CPSU and CP RSFSR

On November 6, 1992, Yeltsin signed yet another decree banning the activities of the CPSU and the CP RSFSR on the territory of the Russian Federation. According to presidential Decree No. 169, the organizational structures of both parties were to be disbanded indefinitely. This was the straw that broke the camel's back.

Yeltsin's earlier decrees, Nos. 79 and 90, had merely "suspended" the activities of the CPSU and CP RSFSR pending an investigation of their involvement in the August 1991 coup. Communists had not dared to protest against the first two decrees, but they did muster the courage to challenge the third. Since Yeltsin's ban provoked this response, his Decree No. 169 can be said to have produced the opposite effect to that which he intended. Until then many Communists had seemingly resigned themselves to awaiting the outcome of the official investigation into the coup. Given that the investigation was to take three years, they might well have gone on waiting and not have bestirred themselves to revive their party. But the fact that Yeltsin was trying to outlaw the party even before the investigation had reported its findings provoked thirty-seven members of the "Communists of Russia" parliamentary faction to appeal to the Constitutional Court against all three of Yeltsin's decrees. In this sense, Yeltsin's third decree may be said to have provided the impulse that led to the creation of the CPRF in 1993.

It may be added that the "Communists of Russia" faction could hardly be accused of having provoked Yeltsin's ban by their opposition to his policies. Quite the contrary: Russia's "superparliament," the CPD, had a few days earlier granted Yeltsin's request for extraordinary powers for a period of one year to carry out economic reforms. Yeltsin acquired the power to act as both president and prime minister, to fill legislative gaps by means of presidential decrees, and to appoint government ministers without the consent of parliament.

Supreme Soviet Approves Dissolution of Soviet Union

Five weeks later, Russia's Supreme Soviet approved the Minsk agreement on the dissolution of the Soviet Union and the formation of the Commonwealth of Independent States (CIS). Addressing the session, Communist deputy Vitalii Sevastyanov urged the "Communists of Russia" faction to vote for the resolution because, he said, getting rid of the USSR had opened the way to getting rid of Gorbachev. In accordance with this reasoning, 188 deputies voted in favor of Yeltsin's proposal to annul the USSR, six voted against, while seven abstained. In a separate vote, the Russian parliament also denounced the Union treaty of 1922, which had created the USSR. Yeltsin described the vote as historic, saying that the republics that had made up the USSR had been driven to this action by Gorbachev's stubborn refusal to give up the idea of a strong center. A few years later, on March 15, 1996, the CPRF parliamentary faction led Russia's State Duma in adopting a resolution calling for the denunciation of the Minsk accords, and Sevastyanov would vote for this together with the rest of his faction. Needless to say, their belated condemnation yielded no practical results.

The CPSU on Trial

A watershed in Russia's post-Soviet history occurred when the Constitutional Court met to examine the legality of Yeltsin's decrees outlawing the CPSU and the CP RSFSR. The court sat from June to November 1992. The hearings were accompanied by a mass propaganda campaign in the Russian media, aimed at influencing the Court in favor of the President. It is true that the Communist side was free to argue its side of the case in the Communist media. In other respects, however, the way in which the Kremlin conducted its side of the argument reminded many people of the propaganda machine of the Soviet period.

In their deposition, the Communists argued that Yeltsin's Decree No. 79 violated the Law on Public Organizations which stated that the activities of public organizations such as political parties might be suspended in only two ways: by decision of the organization itself; or by a court decision in the event of a state of emergency. A state of emergency was not officially proclaimed in August 1991. Therefore, the Communists claimed Yeltsin exceeded his powers when he banned the activities of the CPSU and CP RSFSR. As for Yeltsin's Decree No. 90, which confiscated the property of the CPSU and the CP RSFSR, the petitioners argued that Russia's Law on Property did not list the President among the officials entitled by law to confiscate property.

Yeltsin's lawyers built their defense on the argument that the CPSU had never been a political party. Rather, they said, it was a "state structure" that directly controlled the activities of the Soviet armed forces, security police and industrial enterprises as well as exercising other functions of state power. Therefore, the Yeltsin side argued that the Law on Public Organizations was not applicable to either the CPSU or the CP RSFSR.

Both sides of the dispute apparently agreed on certain points that appeared less certain to the outside observer. Both claimed that the top leaders of the CPSU and they alone—that is, the members of the CPSU Politburo and Secretariat—were responsible for all the crimes and human rights violations committed in or by the USSR. According to this logic, rank-and-file Party members were guiltless. Similarly innocent were those employed by agencies such as the KGB, Glavlit, or the Army, which directly executed the orders of the Party leadership, including repression, censorship or armed invasion of foreign countries. Both sides were keen to shift at least some of the blame onto the last leaders of the CPSU, Gorbachev and his Politburo associates. When Gorbachev refused to testify at the hearings, his passport was withdrawn in punishment. The extent of complicity between the supposedly opposing sides comes as less of a surprise if one recalls that the overwhelming majority of Yeltsin's representatives at the Court and seven of the Constitutional Court's thirteen judges were former members of the CPSU.

The Constitutional Court's Verdict

At the end of November 1992, the Court delivered its ruling: none of Yeltsin's decrees was given a completely clean bill of constitutional health, but parts of all three were declared constitutional. In an interview with the Communist daily *Pravda*, Constitutional Court Chairman Valerii Zorkin called the ruling a "centrist" decision. Others termed it "Solomonic." The Court's circumspection permitted both sides to the dispute to claim victory.

For example, the Court dismissed Yeltsin's argument that he was justified in dissolving the CP RSFSR since the party was not registered. The Constitutional Court ruled that, as an integral part of the CPSU, the CP RSFSR had no need to register. On the other hand, the Court found that Yeltsin had been within his rights in suspending the activities of the CP RSFSR pending a trial, since Soviet law had empowered the authorities to halt the activities of parties posing a direct threat to the state or the citizenry.

As for Yeltsin's decree confiscating the property of the CPSU and the CP RSFSR, the Constitutional Court observed that property rights had been poorly defined in the USSR. The Court could not, therefore, rule which parts of the property of the CPSU and the CP RSFSR really belonged to the parties in the full legal sense—that is, had been purchased with membership dues or the profits from the publication of Party newspapers and journals—and which had been illegally expropriated. The Court suggested that disputes over property should be referred to a court of arbitration.

The Court ruled that Yeltsin had acted within his rights when he banned the Communist Party's organizational bodies—its district, city and oblast committees, up to and including the Central Committee, Politburo and Secretariat—but that he did not have the right to disband the locally-based primary Party organizations. Party committees might not be restored in their old forms, the Court ruled, but Communists were entitled to set up new organizational bodies "in accordance with the requirements of the Constitution and laws of the Russian Federation and on an equal footing with other parties."

The Constitutional Court declined to declare Yeltsin's decrees constitutional, arguing that every decision of the state power was assumed to be constitutional until ruled otherwise by the Court. But it also refused to rule the CPSU unconstitutional, arguing that there was no case to answer because both the CPSU and the CP RSFSR had by the time of the hearings been nonexistent for over a year. The way was, accordingly, cleared for the restoration of the Russian Communist Party.

Attempts to Restore the Communist Party

Although the leaders of the CP RSFSR who were to make up the leadership of the future CPRF had backed the creation of the SWP, the SWP was by no means the CPRF's only major component. Initiative groups dedicated to restoring the Communist Party sprang up in various parts of Russia in the early 1990s, including Moscow and St. Petersburg. Many of the members of such groups shared orthodox Marxist-Leninist, even Stalinist views, but others espoused Russian nationalist and anti-Semitic sentiments. It was in fact the latter group who were to play the main role at the founding congress of the CPRF held in February 1993 and in the Party's subsequent evolution. As the Party grew, it shed both the moderate supporters of "democratic Socialism" and the "internationalists."

Another trend characterizing the Russian political scene in the early 1990s was the defection from Yeltsin's camp of early supporters who disapproved of the Russian President's subsequent policies—particularly the December 1991 dissolution of the Soviet Union and the January 1992 "shock therapy" model of economic reform. While in the months that followed the failed August 1991 coup Yeltsin had enjoyed the support of the overwhelming majority of the population, that support began to wane following the dissolution of the USSR and the launch of market reform. Many of Yeltsin's former allies withdrew their support at this time. Some of them set up opposition liberal or centrist organizations, but others gravitated, along with Communists and other oppositionists, towards the various Russian nationalist associations. None of these joint enterprises participated directly in the restoration of the Russian Communist Party, yet the cumulative influence of their activities was quite significant. As well as widening the potential support-base of the CPRF, such associations influenced the ideology of the future party. And, at least for a while, they provided a haven for the party's future leader, Gennadii Zyuganov.

In January 1992, Viktor Anpilov and his militant Communist colleagues set up the "Working Russia" movement. Its declared aim was to organize street protests and rallies in Moscow and other big Russian cities. The following month, Communist and non-Communist Russian nationalist opponents of Yeltsin set up an organization called the Russian National Assembly (Sobor) (RNA). The second congress of the RNA was held in Moscow on June 12-13. It was attended by the Russian "village" writers Valentin Rasputin and Vasilii Belov, and by the veteran dissident, Academician Igor Shafarevich. The congress elected four co-chairmen: Valentin Rasputin, KGB General Aleksandr Sterligov, Gennadii Zyuganov and Petr Romanov, director of the Krasnoyarsk Aluminum Complex. The RNA proved short-lived. It was decimated by internecine squabbling soon after its second congress.

In March 1992, a group of Yeltsin's parliamentary opponents announced the creation of the "United Opposition." Leading this group were parliamentary deputies who had supported Yeltsin's election as Speaker of the Russian parliament in June 1990. "United Opposition" embraced a wide spectrum, from the Don Cossacks to Stalinists such as Richard Kosolapov, founding father of the RCWP and, in the early 1980s, chief editor of the CPSU's theoretical journal *Kommunist.* Despite its diversity, "United Opposition" proved more durable than the RNA. At a meeting in June 1992, its member-groups elected a Political Council, chiefly memorable from the point of view of this study because Zyuganov was a member. The following October, United Opposition activists set up the largest and strongest opposition organization of that time—the National Salvation Front (NSF). Neither the FNS nor any other umbrella opposition was ever as influential as today's CPRF, however.

The NSF held its founding congress on October 24, 1992, and elected nine co-chairmen, with a former activist of the Leningrad cultural underground, Ilya Konstantinov, heading the executive committee. Only three of the Front's nine leaders, of whom Zyuganov was one, belonged to the Communist wing of the opposition; the other six had non-communist or even anticommunist backgrounds. The non-Communists included Konstantinov himself, the monarchist Viktor Aksyuchits, and the leader of the Constitutional-Democratic Party, Mikhail Astafyev. They played a major role in the Front's subsequent activities. However, Zyuganov's presence in the leadership enabled the Yeltsin team to dismiss the Front's activities as a conspiracy of Communists and Fascists. Inaccurate as that description was, Zyuganov's early activity in various nationalist umbrella organizations does seem to have determined the future tendency of the CPRF to set up unions with various non-Communist opposition movements. Typical of this mode of operation was the creation in 1996 of the Popular Patriotic Union of Russia (PPUoR)—an alliance of Communist, Agrarian and nationalist parliamentarians that allowed the leaders of the CPRF in the State Duma to identify themselves as a "patriotic" rather than a "Communist" opposition.

Desperately Seeking to Become Heirs of the CPSU

As noted above, attempts to unite the various Communist movements and groups started long before the Constitutional Court pronounced judgment. As early as November 1991, Working Russia formed a series of ad hoc alliances in order to organize rallies in various Russian cities marking the anniversary of the 1917 Bolshevik Revolution. That same month, Anpilov, Tyul'kin and Kosolapov founded the hard-core Russian Communist Workers' Party (RCWP) in Ekaterinburg (Sverdlovsk during the Soviet era). To this day, the RCWP remains, after the CPRF, Russia's largest party of Communist orientation. Declaring itself the only true heir of the CPSU, the RCWP has repeatedly refused to join any other movement trying to restore either the CPSU or CP RSFSR. On the eve of the CPRF congress, however, a large number of RCWP founder members, including Kosolapov, General Makashov and Kuzbass miners' leader Teimuraz Avaliani, left the RCWP and joined the CPRF.

In the provinces, members of such seemingly incompatible organizations as the SWP and the RCWP formed joint committees, while Communists in a number of Russian regions attempted to restore the old-time district and city committees of the CP RSFSR. Regional Communist organizations were registered in North Ossetia, Bashkortostan and Stavropol Krai. In Moscow, splinter parties that emerged from the Marxist platform in the CPSU went so far as to attempt to restore the CPSU itself. In late 1991 two such groups—the Russian Party of Communists and the Union of Communists—formed an umbrella organization called the All-Union Committee of Communists (AUCC). The AUCC met in July 1992 in the town of Pushchino near Moscow and held what they billed as nothing less than the "Twenty-ninth Congress of the CPSU." At that meeting, a little-known economist, Sergei Skvortsov, was elected "first secretary of the CPSU Central Committee." Neither he nor his party has been heard of again.

A more serious attempt to restore the CPSU took place in the offices of the once powerful newspaper, *Pravda*, on June 13, 1992. The meeting was attended by sixty-two of the four hundred members of the CPSU Central Committee elected at the CPSU's last congress in 1990. Since all those elected in 1990 had been invited, those who did not put in an appearance were deemed to have resigned, while those present pressed ahead with what they declared to be a plenary session of the CPSU Central Committee. They expelled Gorbachev from the Communist Party for treason and resolved to convene the CPSU's Twentieth Conference.

In October 1992, two former members of the CPSU's Marxist platform, Aleksei Prigarin and Konstantin Nikolaev, presided over a conference at which they, too, decided to restore the CPSU. This organization held what it called the Twenty-ninth Congress of the CPSU on March 26-28, 1993. It was attended by four hundred delegates from all the former Union republics except Kyrgyzstan and Armenia. The participants set up an umbrella organization, the Union of Communist Parties-CPSU (UCP-CPSU) and elected as chairman Oleg Shenin, a former member of the CPSU Politburo who had been involved in the August 1991 coup.

The UCP-CPSU was organized for the purpose of uniting the communist parties of the former Soviet republics and restoring the USSR. The founders of the CPRF, by contrast, remained at that time determined to act strictly within the law and in accord with the Constitutional Court's ruling on the CPSU. Therefore, Zyuganov and his allies did not initially recognize the existence of the UCP-CPSU. Only in July 1994 did the CPRF ally itself with the UCP-CPSU, following many months of pressure on Zyuganov's leadership by Prigarin's allies in the Moscow Committee of the CPRF. Today, the UCP-CPSU numbers twenty-two member organizations and a total membership of 1.3 million. As a party that pays allegiance to a state that no longer exists, however, the UCP-CPSU participates in no elections. Notwithstanding its substantial membership, therefore, it is not an influential organization.

Russia's Communist Party Restored

While some Communists were seeking to restore the CPSU, others concentrated on restoring the Russian Communist Party. August 1992 saw the creation of a new organization formally known as the Political Consultative Coordinating Council of Russia's Communists—Roskomsovet for short—aimed at reestablishing a united Russian Communist Party. In November 1992, Roskomsovet convened a meeting of the leaders of the SWP, the Union of Communists and the Russian Party of Communists, along with representatives of regional Communist organizations, members of the Central Committees and Central Control Committees of both the CPSU and the CP RSFSR, and members of the "Communists of Russia" parliamentary faction. Valentin Kuptsov was elected Chairman of an Organizational Initiative Committee and charged with convening a unifying congress of Russian Communists. Kuptsov, a member of the "Gorbachevite" wing of the communist movement, attempted to steer the new organization in a moderate direction.

When, at the end of November 1992, the Constitutional Court ruled that Communists were entitled to set up a party, Gennadii Zyuganov joined the Organizational Initiative Committee and began to play an active role in it. At its meeting on December 27, 1992, the Committee resolved to conduct a "restoration," rather than a "unifying" congress, as initially promised. This decision reflected the decision to restore the old communist party—that is, the CP RSFSR—rather than just to unite the various communist and left wing groups and weld them into a new political party.

Meeting of the Second Congress

The Second Congress of the Communist Party of the Russian Federation was accordingly held on February 13 and 14, 1993, in the village of Voronovo in the suburbs of Moscow. The almost underground atmosphere of the event and the militantly anticommunist public mood that prevailed in Russia at that time were in striking contrast to subsequent CPRF gatherings in Moscow's prestigious House of Columns.

Originally, the congress organizers had intended the new party to be much broader and more pluralistic than turned out to be the case. It should, they thought, serve as an umbrella organization for all the different communist and left wing parties, in which the voices of all could be heard. To this end, the organizers suggested that the leaders of all parties should each address the congress. However, the congress delegates voted this proposal down, and only the last leader of the CP RSFSR, Kuptsov, was allowed to report to the congress. This decision was not taken because the delegates felt any particular sympathy for Kuptsov; rather, it reflected the delegates' deep-rooted conservatism and the difficulty they had in shaking off the ways in which the old Communist Party had been accustomed to hold such gatherings.

The intention of the organizers that the new party should be different from its "parent" parties—the CPSU and CP RSFSR—was evident in Kuptsov's report to the congress. In it, the outgoing leader attempted to analyze the errors of the CPSU and CP RSFSR, singling out their bureaucratic mentality and lack of political courage. Kuptsov stressed the determination of the communists to avoid violence or anything that could provoke another civil war in Russia. But Kuptsov did not stop there. He went on to say that anyone who suggested the restoration of either the USSR or the CPSU was "either a fool or an adventurer." Indeed, Kuptsov went so far as to urge that the rule of the majority in the new Russian communist movement be accompanied with respect for the views of the minority, adding that the existence of various factions and "platforms" in the new party was inevitable. This flew in the face of the fundamentals both of the party's Marxist-Leninist past and of its National-Stalinist future.

Another key address at the congress was delivered by yet another moderate, Viktor Zorkaltsev, former first secretary of the Tomsk Oblast Committee of the CP RSFSR (later to become chairman of the Duma's Committee on the Affairs of Public Associations and Religious Organizations). Zorkaltsev addressed the conference with a proposal for party statutes that would have provided for the possibility of dual membership in the CPRF along with that in one of the founding communist parties.

However, Stalinists such as Tyulkin, Kosolapov and Yurii Belov (later head of the Leningrad organization of the CPRF) seized the initiative at the congress and determined the future development of the CPRF. They were supported by delegates from the provinces and the moderate proposals of Kuptsov and Zorkaltsev were overruled. To all intents and purposes, the congress restored the CP RSFSR under the new name CPRF. It outlawed the establishment within the party of factions or platforms, and forbade members of the CPRF from simultaneously belonging to any other political party.

CEC Formed

The congress elected a Central Executive Committee (CEC) consisting of 148 members. Eighty-nine of them represented the various Russian regions; forty-four were prominent individuals elected on a central list; and ten were elected on a closed or secret list and their identities were not revealed. Five places were reserved for representatives of other Communist parties. The SWP was represented in the CEC by former CPSU and CP RSFSR officials, and other communist parties by activists of hard-core nationalist associations such as the National Salvation Front and Union of Officers. Only two former members of the top Soviet leadership were elected to the CEC: Shenin and Anatolii Lukyanov, former speaker of the USSR Supreme Soviet; both had been implicated in the August 1991 coup.

Initially, the congress organizers intended the CEC to be headed by a collective leadership, with Kuptsov as first among equals. But this idea came under attack at the congress from Makashov, who accused Kuptsov of "Gorbachevism" and demanded that Zyuganov be elected leader instead. Kuptsov backed off and Zyuganov was elected to chair the CEC, with Kuptsov as his first deputy. Thereafter, Kuptsov displayed conspicuous loyalty toward both the CPRF and Zyuganov. Other deputies were Zorkaltsev, SWP co-chair Ivan Rybkin, agrarian Mikhail Lapshin, the leader of the St. Petersburg Committee of the CP RSFSR Yurii Belov, and the former deputy speaker of the RSFSR Supreme Soviet Svetlana Goryacheva.

Results of the Second Congress

As a result of the outcome of the "founding-restoration" congress, hardliners such as Makashov and Kosolapov quit the RCWP for the CPRF, while SWP leaders such as Medvedev split away from the CPRF. Later, other founding fathers followed Medvedev's example. That devotee of "democratic socialism," Boris Slavin, quit the CPRF in November 1995, a few months prior to the June 1996 presidential election and joined the Party of Workers' Self-Government led by the famous eye-surgeon Svyatoslav Fedorov. Rybkin joined the governing camp and for some time served as a key member of Yeltsin's administration in the position of secretary of Russia's Security Council. Other leading communist personalities, who had been active on the Organizational Initiative Committee, also split away, albeit in a less demonstrative manner, and formed the Agrarian Party, led by Lapshin. (A junior partner of the CPRF, the Agrarian Party tends nonetheless to adopt a more moderate stance toward the Yeltsin administration and on political developments than the CPRF). All in all, the party established at the CPRF founding conference was very different from that planned by its organizers.

The CEC met for the first time on March 15, 1993, to elect a presidium and adopt a party program entitled "New Socialism for Russia." Also discussed was the policy of the CPRF toward the forthcoming April 25, 1993, referendum which was supposed to resolve (though of course it did not) the dispute between Yeltsin and the Russian parliament. It was decided that Communists should vote "No" to the question of whether or not they trusted the Russian president; "No" to the question of whether or not they had confidence in the economic and social policies of the Yeltsin administration; "Yes" to the proposal that there should be an early presidential election; and "No" to the idea of early parliamentary elections.

The Crisis of 1993

The early 1990s were dominated by fighting between Yeltsin and the Russian parliament (which still consisted, as it had in Soviet times, of the Supreme Soviet and the "superparliament," the Congress of People's Deputies). The Yeltsin team portrayed the conflict in black-and-white terms as a communist revolt against the democratically elected president and his team of liberal reformers. In reality, Yeltsin had appointed two key members of the parliamentary opposition himself. These two were Ruslan Khasbulatov, Yeltsin's choice to replace him as parliamentary speaker, and Vice-President Aleksandr Rutskoi, Yeltsin's handpicked running mate in the 1991 presidential election. Other opposition leaders who were active at that time, such as Konstantinov and Aksyuchits, came from dissident backgrounds. Unlike Yeltsin, who had served most of his life as a top CPSU official, they had never held Communist views. True, the Communists of Russia faction supported the parliamentary opposition, but so too did most of the other parliamentary factions.

Yeltsin Dissolves Parliament

On September 21, 1993, Yeltsin issued presidential Decree No. 1400, dissolving the Supreme Soviet and Congress of People's Deputies. The Russian Constitution and the Law on the Presidency both stated in no uncertain terms that the president was not entitled to dissolve parliament. In an address to the nation, Yeltsin himself conceded that he had violated the Constitution. In response, parliament blockaded itself inside the Russian White House and started the impeachment proceedings that were, in due course, approved by the Constitutional Court. The Moscow city authorities cut off electricity and water to the White House. People demonstrating in support of parliament were beaten up by the police and sometimes shot at. They responded by launching an armed assault on certain government buildings—the headquarters of the General Staff of the armed forces, the offices of the Moscow Mayor, and the Ostankino television tower. Dozens of people were killed or wounded during these clashes; to this day, there is no clear number. In all known cases except one, however, Yeltsin's supporters shot the victims.

The CPRF condemned Decree No. 1400, as did politicians across the political spectrum. Many members of the CPRF CEC—Rybkin, Makashov and Colonel Stanislav Terekhov, leader of the reactionary Union of Officers—played an active part in the opposition. As a party, however, the CPRF kept a low profile throughout the crisis. Zyuganov's restraint was rewarded when, on October 2, 1992, he became the only opposition leader permitted to address the nation on Russian television. He used the opportunity to call on the members of the CPRF to refrain from violence.

Following the dissolution of parliament, Yeltsin issued a decree banning the activities of the CPRF. Simultaneously, Press Minister Vladimir Shumeiko closed down *Pravda*, *Sovetskaya Rossiya* and other opposition newspapers and TV programs and imposed censorship on the rest of the media. Thanks to pressure from Western governments and human rights organizations, these restrictions were soon removed.

On October 4, 1993, Yeltsin dispatched tanks to storm the White House and the "communist revolt" was suppressed. Yeltsin then issued a string of new decrees, suspending the activities of the Constitutional Court and ordering a referendum on a new Constitution that would give the president vast powers while sharply curtailing those of parliament. A mixed electoral system was introduced by presidential decree which provided favorable conditions for the election of the pro-government party, Russia's Democratic Choice, to the new, emasculated parliament, the State Duma.

Parliamentary Elections of 1993

The First Conference of the CPRF, held in October 1993, drew up a list of candidates for the parliamentary elections slated for December of that year. First place in those elections went to the then "party of government,"

Yegor Gaidar's Russia's Democratic Choice, with 15.6 percent, while Vladimir Zhirinovsky's illiberal Liberal Democratic Party came in second with 14.2 percent. The CPRF came in third with 10.7 percent of the vote, winning 45 seats in the 450-member lower house of the new parliament, the State Duma. The CPRF was back in the mainstream of Russian politics.

3: Privatizing the State

The CPRF, set up in February 1993, consisted largely of those people who remained in the Communist Party after the more pragmatic members of the nomenklatura had gone. This chapter argues that these more adventurous comrades took advantage of the opportunities offered by Gorbachev's economic reforms to seize control of the new emerging economic system, and it traces the evolution of the more pragmatic members of the Soviet nomenklatura into today's entrepreneurial elite. Asserting control over key sectors of the state-owned Soviet economy, the "new Russians" converted formerly state-owned enterprises into their own private property. Boris Yeltsin was a case in point. Yeltsin, who joined the CPSU in 1961, served almost all his life in leading positions in the CPSU. Following a career in the Sverdlovsk Oblast in the Urals, where he rose to be Party First Secretary, he moved in 1986 to Moscow, where he was appointed First Secretary of the Moscow City Party Committee. That post gave him candidate membership in the Politburo. Before long, his rebellious behavior provoked his ouster from power and a period in the wilderness. Yeltsin fought back. In May 1990 he was elected Speaker of the Russian parliament and in June 1991 he became Russia's first democratically elected president.

As has already been stressed, Yeltsin was backed by thousands of officials with similar nomenklatura backgrounds who made up much of the elite in post-Soviet Russia. It was almost as if, wrote the newspaper *Nezavisimaya Gazeta*, the reformist wing of the Communist Party had come to power under Yeltsin's leadership.[1]

By contrast, the CPRF looked more like a right-wing party, highly suspicious of new ideas, than a left-wing party bent on revolutionary change. Zyuganov and his colleagues might perhaps be seen as the functional equivalents of former civil servants searching for a new role. Their colleagues, by contrast, seized hold of the opportunities offered by Gorbachev's economic reforms.

The Gorbachev Legacy

The USSR that Gorbachev inherited in spring 1985 was suffering from an alarming slowdown of economic growth. The new leader set out to try to

1. *Nezavisimaya Gazeta*, 3 December 1992, cited in Olga Kryshtanovskaya and Stephen White, "From Soviet Nomenklatura to Russian Elite," *Europe-Asia Studies*, No. 5, July 1996, pp. 711-733.

reverse this trend and to launch the USSR on the path of economic modernization. Gorbachev pledged early in his leadership to streamline the system of economic management, rationalize central planning and give enterprises greater independence. Gorbachev is often accused of having merely "tinkered" with economic reform. His initial economic reforms were indeed modest and assumed that public ownership would remain the foundation of the Soviet economy. In reality, he set the ball rolling and, whether he intended to or not, initiated changes that made the privatization of the Russian economy virtually inevitable.

Some would say that this had begun to happen even during the Soviet period. The economist Vitalii Naishul, for example, has argued that, as the post-Stalin leadership relaxed the iron grip on the country that Stalin had maintained, directors of Soviet plants and factories began to feel more and more in control of the assets they managed. That encouraged them, Naishul has argued, gradually to come to feel that they had de facto property rights to their formally state-owned enterprises. This process set the scene for the privatization that took place in the 1990s.[2]

Economic Reforms

Gorbachev's economic reforms began with the November 1986 "Law on Individual Labor Activity," which permitted Soviet citizens to engage in some limited private enterprise but did not envision the legalization of private property. The May 1988 "Law on Cooperatives" encouraged the development of cooperatives and small family businesses. Hundreds of cooperatives sprang up, even though Gorbachev was careful to maintain the Marxist taboo against "hired labor" and to restrict the newly legalized private businesses to single individuals or family members.

The "Law on the State Enterprise," which came into effect in January 1988, promised enterprises greater autonomy from central planners and freed them to decide what to produce and where to sell it. Firms were not immediately given the power to decide what price to charge for their products, but they were promised that some prices would gradually be freed from central control. Also in 1988, Gorbachev removed the CPSU from the day-to-day management of the economy, In November 1989 he authorized the leasing of state enterprises by workers and, the following year, the leasing of family farms.

2. V.A. Naishul', *The Supreme and Last Stage of Socialism*, London: Centre for Research into Communist Economies, 1991.

Meanwhile, Gorbachev's encouragement of glasnost in the media provoked a wide-ranging debate over economic reform. All sorts of ideas were voiced. By 1990, Soviet economists had begun openly to advocate the "destatisation" of the Russian economy, the legalization of all forms of private ownership, and the transition to a market economy.[3]

In their study of Russia's new economy, David Kotz and Fred Weir point out that the Party-state elite, which could have nipped the discussion in the bud, tolerated the free-ranging discussion. They conclude that some members of the elite quickly sensed that there might be advantages for them were the USSR to make the transition from socialism to a capitalist economy. Their conclusion is upheld by the work of Stephen White and Russian sociologist Olga Kryshtanovskaya and by Steven Solnick's study of the Communist Party's youth wing, the Komsomol. All these authors argue that the main reason why the Soviet state disintegrated was not, as many have assumed, because it was weighed down by economic stagnation and political repression (though those factors undoubtedly played a role), but because it was dismantled from within by opportunistic members of the Party-state elite.[4]

DISMANTLING THE STATE ECONOMY

Privatization of state-owned property did not become official policy until the end of 1991, when the Yeltsin leadership launched full-scale market reform. Long before that, enterprise directors, who had come over the years to feel that they possessed virtual property rights over the organizations they managed, had read the writing on the wall. Seizing on a loophole in the Law on Cooperatives that allowed firms to set up cooperatives, they spun off those sectors of their firms' activities that were potentially profitable to subsidiaries run by themselves. Thousands of such

---

3. Joseph R. Blasi, Maya Kroumova and Douglas Kruse, *Kremlin Capitalism: Privatizing the Russian Economy*, Ithaca, NY: Cornell University Press, 1997, p. 18; David M. Kotz with Fred Weir, *Revolution from Above: The Demise of the Soviet System*, London: Routledge, 1997, pp. 87-4.

4. David M. Kotz with Fred Weir, *Revolution from Above: The Demise of the Soviet System*, London: Routledge, 1997, pp. 72, 92; Olga Kryshtanovskaya, "Finansovaya oligarchiya v Rossii," *Izvestiya*, January 10, 1996; Olga Kryshtanovskaya and Stephen White, "From Soviet Nomenklatura to Russian Elite," *Europe-Asia Studies*, No. 5, July 1996, pp. 711-33; Steven L. Solnick, *Stealing the State: Control and Collapse in Soviet Institutions*, Cambridge, MA: Harvard University Press, 1998.

intra-enterprise cooperatives, many of them essentially private firms, sprang up. As Gorbachev's reforms gathered steam, enterprise directors, and Party and government officials, moved fast to ensure that they would be well placed to take full advantage of the impending changes and to appropriate any state assets on which they could lay their hands.

Their efforts were boosted by Gorbachev's decision to dismantle central controls over the economy. In 1988, firms were given the freedom to bypass the old state foreign trade monopoly and to deal with foreign partners directly. Government ministries were reorganized and consolidated into larger units. In 1990, the central planning body, Gosplan, and the system of central allocation, Gossnab, were disbanded.

THE KOMSOMOL GOES CAPITALIST

The first commercial undertakings were set up under the aegis of the Komsomol and with the blessing of Yegor Ligachev, Gorbachev's straitlaced deputy in the CPSU. Concerned about the low esteem in which Soviet youth held the Komsomol, the Kremlin tried to revitalize the organization and turn it into a voice campaigning for the interests of young people. Local branches were freed from the requirement to recruit a specific quota of new members; at the same time, they were given control over membership dues. This deprived mid-level Komsomol officials of any interest in maintaining the status quo, unfair and inefficient as many of them had long perceived it to be, and provided them with an entry to the world of business. Simultaneously, glasnost and new freedoms to travel abroad were opening the eyes of the elite at all levels to the fact that their counterparts in other parts of the world often lived far better than they did. Perceiving that, under a different system, their own living standards might improve, ambitious Komsomol officials led the way in turning themselves into a new generation of youthful capitalists.[5]

As early as 1987, Komsomol leaders began to strip the organization of its assets and to exploit gaps in the Soviet market, in particular, the almost complete absence of a service sector. Starting modestly with bars, discos, video outlets and youth employment bureaux, Komsomol officials soon diversified into a multitude of other activities of which the most lucrative, by far, was banking. Under Gorbachev, says Solnick, there were two economies, a state-controlled one and a liberalized one. Those savvy enough to play one sphere against the other stood to make huge profits. Kryshtanovskaya and White, recount, for example, that the

5. Solnick, op. cit.

Komsomol was the first Soviet institution allowed to convert paper assets into liquid cash. Thanks to this concession, Komsomol officials were able to charge a rate of up to 30 percent a day on the profits arising from such transactions. It was accordingly through the Komsomol that many members of the first wave of Soviet entrepreneurs became established. They included men such as Mikhail Khodorkovsky, who began his career as a Komsomol official at the Mendeleev Chemical Technical University and went on in mid-1998 to found Menatep Bank with sponsorship from the Komsomol Central Committee. By the early 1990s, Menatep ranked among Russia's most powerful financial groups. Kryshtanovskaya calculates that in 1995 at least 37 percent of Russia's business elite had previously worked for the Komsomol—a higher proportion than for either Party or state officials.[6]

PRIVATIZING RUSSIA'S CROWN JEWELS

High-ranking members of the elite were quick to follow the Komsomol's example and to parlay the political power they enjoyed under the Soviet regime into economic power in a new system, the contours of which were still barely defined. One of the first was Viktor Chernomyrdin, later to serve five years as Yeltsin's prime minister. In his capacity as USSR Gas Minister, Chernomyrdin launched the privatization of the gas industry and the creation of the gas giant, Gazprom. "Already in 1988," he proudly told the *Financial Times*' Chrystia Freeland, "I transformed [Gazprom] into a company and I myself left the cabinet. I was the first to do this in the [Soviet] Union. I understood even then that we had reached a dead end... I had already begun to work in the market when he [Gaidar] was still sitting in *Kommunist* and writing Party articles."[7]

The USSR Gas Ministry had had responsibility for all spheres of gas production from excavation to distribution. The company Chernomyrdin established controls one-third of the world's natural-gas reserves. A highly centralized, semi-private monopoly, it accounts for 5 percent of the Russian economy and also has extensive stakes in media and banking. Chernomyrdin, who had spent his working life in Party work and in the oil industry, became the first chairman of the board of the new concern.

---

6. Kryshtanovskaya, op. cit.; Kryshtanovskaya and White, op. cit.; David Hoffman, "Yeltsin's Pick Is Epitome Of the Hustler Generation," *International Herald Tribune*, April 1, 1998.

7. Chrystia Freeland, "First came the power, then the wealth," *Financial Times*, July 11, 1998.

Chernomyrdin ensured that Gazprom had wide autonomy, being linked to the state only by a small oversight body; after he became prime minister, his protection is believed to have enabled Gazprom to retain its monopoly status even as other raw material producers, such as the oil industry, were being broken up into separate companies.[8] There were persistent reports that Chernomyrdin held a 1 percent share in Gazprom. If true, that would have made him one of Russia's richest men; indeed, a 1997 report by the newspaper *Le Monde* put his personal fortune at $5 billion. Chernomyrdin strongly denied all these reports and Le Monde was forced to retract its account.

In August 1990, the Soviet government gave the green light to private business ownership. A group of economists, convened jointly by Gorbachev and Yeltsin—leaders, respectively, of the USSR and the RSFSR—produced a 500-Day program of radical economic reform. Gorbachev, who read the program, rejected it; Yeltsin, who did not, gave it the go-ahead. In December 1990, the Russian parliament eliminated restrictions on all forms of entrepreneurial activity.[9] Meanwhile, Yeltsin complained loudly that the Soviet government was preventing the RSFSR from implementing the 500-Day program. Yeltsin's insistence that Russia would go its own way set him on a collision course with Gorbachev. The RSFSR was not the first of the Soviet republics to assert its independence from the center but, once it did so, the USSR was doomed. Had Gorbachev been prepared to tolerate such action, other republics might have broken away without destroying the Soviet Union, but this was not the case with Russia. Those members of the Russian elite who hoped to do well out of privatization immediately switched their allegiance from Gorbachev to Yeltsin and threw their support behind his drive for self-determination.

THREE WAYS TO GET RICH QUICK

Anders Aslund, who served as an economics adviser to the Russian government between 1992 and 1994, has identified three ways in which the "new Russians" made their fortunes. Chief among them was arbitrage, which exploited the gap between the controlled prices set by the Soviet state and the prices goods could obtain on world markets. The key was

8 Valery Kryukov and Arild Moe, *The New Russian Corporatism? A Case Study of Gazprom, London: Royal Institute of International Affairs*, 1996.

9. Blasi, op. cit., pp. xv, 19.

having access to official export licenses. Officials set up their own private trading companies, bought Russian-produced oil, natural gas and metals at state-subsidized prices, and sold them on world markets at world prices. The richest pickings were to be had in 1991 and 1992, when Russian raw materials could be bought for as little as 1 percent of the world price. In 1992, Aslund claims, such deals accounted for 30 percent of Russian GDP.[10] Now one of Russia's richest men, media magnate Boris Berezovsky began his career as a highly respected academic mathematician. He made his fortune out of a car dealership with Russia's largest car producer, AvtoVAZ, which enabled him to exploit the difference between the state-set price for motor cars intended for export and the (much higher) prices such cars could fetch inside Russia. Today he controls the Sibneft oil company, part of Aeroflot, Russian Public Television (ORT), and the leading newspaper, *Nezavisimaya Gazeta*. Another of Russia's richest men, Vladimir Potanin, was working at that time in the Ministry of Foreign Trade, where his father was a highly placed official. Potanin Junior's job entailed trading raw materials for the government. When he left the government in 1991 to start his own trading company, he could rely on his contacts with Russia's biggest raw materials exporters; when, in 1993, he started his own bank, Oneksimbank, he did so with funding from the state foreign trade bank. Then Oneksimbank was one of thousands of new banks; today, it is Russia's largest private commercial bank.[11]

THE ELITE GET RICHER

During the winter of 1991-2, import subsidies proved to be another source of wealth for the well-connected. Alarmed by the prospect of widespread food shortages, the Russian government tried to encourage imports by introducing subsidies for essential foodstuffs. Importers had to pay only 1 percent of the official exchange rate for the hard currency to import such foodstuffs. However, the imported products went on sale in Russia at the market price and the importers pocketed the profit. Aslund estimates that import subsidies accounted for 15 percent of Russian GDP in 1992.[12]

---

10. Anders Aslund, "Novykh russkikh obogatili tri osnovnykh istochnika," *Finanasovye Izvestiya*, June 20, 1996; ibid., "Why the Doomsayers are Wrong about Russia," *The Weekly Standard*, December 29, 1997.
11. *International Herald Tribune*, 28 September 1998.
12. Aslund, op. cit.

While such deals were not strictly illegal, they were not precisely legal, either. The state's failure to provide the kind of protection that the new entrepreneurs needed meant that the door was opened for organized crime and fertile ground was found for the Russian Mafia.

Subsidized credits to state-owned enterprises were a third source of enrichment for the elite. Intended to support industry during the transition to the market, credits were issued in 1992 and 1993 at interest rates of up to 25 percent per year at a time when annual inflation was running at 2,500 percent. Aslund estimates that profits from these three sources amounted to a staggering 75 percent of Russia's GDP in 1992.[13]

YELTSIN LAUNCHES ECONOMIC REFORMS

On 24 August 1991, in the wake of the abortive coup, Yeltsin suspended the Soviet and Russian Communist Parties. On 28 October, Yeltsin announced that Russia was to introduce wide-ranging economic reforms, including privatization and price liberalization. At the beginning of November, he appointed Anatolii Chubais as minister of privatization. Two days later, Yeltsin banned the two Communist Parties outright. On 7-8 December, Yeltsin met his Ukrainian and Belarussian counterparts and, without bothering to consult Gorbachev, abolished the Soviet Union. In January 1992, Russia launched a program of radical economic reforms. This included the privatization of the housing and farm sectors and, in 1993 and early 1994, the use of vouchers to distribute large and medium-sized enterprises to the entire population. By the time the official process began, however, "nomenklatura privatization" had already gobbled up the crown jewels of the Russian economy and the country had already been divided into haves and have-nots. Meanwhile, farsighted communist officials had moved quietly out of their party posts and into parallel posts in local government.

One of the success stories of this period was Sergei Kirienko, who was President Yeltsin's surprise choice as prime minister when, in March 1998, the president sacked Chernomyrdin after five years in office. Kirienko lasted only five months in the job. The Russian media dubbed him "Kinder-Surpriz"—a reference to the egg-shaped German chocolates, popular in Russia, that contain a surprise toy. He exemplified the younger generation of Russian entrepreneurs who made early fortunes out of the ruins of the Soviet Union.

13. Aslund, op. cit.

SERGEI KIRIENKO MAKES HIS APPEARANCE

Born in 1962, Kirienko began his career in Nizhnii Novgorod, Russia's third city. There he trained as a shipping engineer before becoming a full-time regional Komsomol official. Just after the coup of August 1991, he shifted careers, securing a place at the Academy of the National Economy in Moscow. The institute was headed by Academician Abel Aganbegyan, an economist who had acted as adviser to President Gorbachev during the early years of perestroika. According to the *Washington Post's* David Hoffman, Kirienko was the youngest but brightest in his class, concentrating on how the banking sector could make the transition from central planning to the market.[14] Kirienko translated his ideas into practice when, in 1994, he returned to Nizhnii Novgorod to found his own bank, Garantiya. According to Gordon Hahn, his initial capital was made by buying oil low domestically and selling it high abroad. Eventually, he founded his own oil company, Norsi, while Garantiya became an "authorized" bank handling federal and regional pension funds on behalf of the Nizhnii Novgorod regional government. When his patron, regional governor Boris Nemtsov, moved to Moscow to join the federal government, Kirienko moved with him to a post in the federal energy ministry.[15]

Some members of the elite, of course, supported the economic policies of neither Gorbachev nor Yeltsin. Heads of government departments and local officials, who did not have the opportunities to enrich themselves, as did bankers and enterprise managers, put up dogged resistance. Also resisting were directors of factories in the defense sector who saw that there would be little demand for the goods they produced in a peacetime, market-oriented economy where output targets were no longer set and paid for by the state. Many of those who opposed Gorbachev's reforms in the 1980s made up the nucleus of the CPRF and its Russian nationalist allies in the 1990s.

Their opposition to Yeltsin's reforms increased as a result of the way in which privatization was carried out in the 1990s by the Yeltsin leadership. This saw the handing over of state assets into the private pockets of cronies or even members of the government, by means that were often blatantly unjust and corrupt.

---

14. David Hofmann, "Yeltsin's Pick Is Epitome Of the Hustler Generation," *International Herald Tribune*, 1 April 1998.

15. Gordon M. Hahn, "From Chernomyrdin to Kirienko," *Problems of Post-Communism*, September-October 1998, pp. 3-16.

4: The Ideology of the CPRF

Critics have accused the CPRF of being two-faced, saying that its leaders—Gennadii Zyuganov in particular—pose as Social Democrats in their dealings with the West while behaving as unreformed Stalinists at home. This criticism oversimplifies the modern communist soul, which is emotional rather than rational by nature. Zyuganov and his followers appear quite sincere in preaching things that seem, on the face of it, completely contradictory. They want to be accepted as representatives of a respected political tradition while simultaneously professing a militantly anti-Western, particularly anti-American and anti-Semitic worldview; they combine overt Stalinism with adherence to democracy and pluralism (as evidenced by their openness to all kinds of joint actions and coalitions with alien political forces inside Russia); and, finally, they mix inherent conservatism with an equally evident ability to change.

As this chapter seeks to show, the ideology of the CPRF underwent profound changes in all directions in the period following the party's formative period under Ivan Polozkov. Under Zyuganov's leadership, the CPRF came to have little in common, either politically or ideologically, with the closed sect of zealots that had been the Bolshevik Party founded by Vladimir Lenin in 1903.

Gennadii Zyuganov

Zyuganov himself is more of a nationalist than a Marxist, yet he manages to combine elements of both. He exemplifies the complex and contradictory mindset of today's Russian Communist Party, for while he was not the only person to have developed such thinking, it was he who made the political link between these ideas and the party on the ground and in the political arena. It is therefore legitimate to talk about "Zyuganovism" as an ideological and political phenomenon.

Born in 1944 into a family of teachers in Orel Oblast, Zyuganov began his career as a teacher. Joining the CPSU in 1966, he worked first in the Komsomol and then in the Party apparatus in Orel. In 1983, he moved to Moscow where he worked in the departments of ideology and propaganda of the CPSU Central Committee. He came to national prominence one month before the August 1991 putsch, when he and the ultra nationalist Aleksandr Prokhanov co-authored a manifesto entitled *Slovo k narodu* (*A Word to the People*), attacking the policies of both Gorbachev and Yeltsin.

As an ideologist, Zyuganov tends to think in terms of global categories, which perhaps explains why his ideas are often vague and why, sometimes, he does not bother to make ends meet. He differed from all other CPRF officials with whom the author met in the course of the research for this book in that the others (including Zyuganov's first deputy Valentin Kuptsov) tended to be down to earth and matter-of-fact. For example, the head of a district CPRF committee from the city of Tula, Mikhail Filshin, complained bitterly about the failure of "red" Governor Vasilii Starodubtsev to root out corruption among local industrial managers. The Governor of Amur Oblast, Anatolii Belonogov, asked rhetorically why Russia should persist with the reforms that had in the past ten years proved counterproductive from the point of view both of economic efficiency and of popular living standards. Yurii Lodkin, Governor of Bryansk Oblast, talked about the regional economy and inequality between the various Russian regions. Zyuganov, by contrast, talked about global politics. When he volunteered suggestions on how Russia should be remodeled, he did not always appear to have thought through how his proposals would work.

Elite Continuity

To understand the peculiarities of communist ideology in post-Soviet Russia, one must refer to the composition of Russia's political elite. As has already been stressed, the CPRF and Russia's smaller, splinter communist parties did not consist of "former communists" of the Central and East European type. Rather, the CPRF was formed largely of people who had remained in the Communist Party after their more daring and pragmatic comrades had gone. Unlike its Central and East European cousins (the Czech Communist Party excepted), the CPRF did not even consider removing the word "communist" from its name. Official CPRF documents and the writings and speeches of party leaders demonstrated that the CPRF in many respects evolved in a direction opposite to that taken by almost all the Central and Eastern European communist parties and even, in its final years, by the late and unlamented CPSU itself. The ideology of the CPRF was in almost all respects the opposite of everything espoused not only by Marx but also by Lenin. For example, the party jettisoned the orthodox Marxist preference for revolutionary and violent ways of coming to power. Instead, it professed support for democratic principles and a mixed market economy. It dropped its total ban on private enterprise and private property—though it maintained its anathema on the free sale of land. Proletarian internationalism was discarded in favor of a Russian nationalism that often slid over into outright xenophobia. Whereas Lenin and the Bolsheviks had been driven by their vision of some bright, yet unknown, future when they would realize "the age-old dream of all mankind," the CPRF sought inspiration in Russia's glorious past as one of the world's two superpowers and drew their strength from that common human sentiment, nostalgia. This made it possible for the CPRF to form alliances with nationalist movements with whom it shared a tendency to blame all of Russia's ills on foreign conspiracies. The party even endorsed Stalin for his alleged achievement of strengthening Russian statehood. At the same time, Zyuganov and his colleagues actively campaigned for Russia to be accepted into various prestigious international clubs, such as the Council of Europe. Such inconsistencies underlined the fact that the CPRF's policies were often more open-minded than its ideology.

Indeed, the CPRF often looked more like a right-wing party, highly suspicious of new ideas, than a left-wing party bent on revolutionary change. Originating in the chance arrangement of seats in the National Convention during the French Revolution, the term "left" is used to denote political movements campaigning for a new social order, whereas their "right-wing" opponents stand either for the maintenance of the status quo (in which case, they may be termed "conservative") or for the restoration of an earlier state of affairs (in which case the term "reactionary" is generally used). In other words, the left wing finds its inspiration in a radiant future, while the right wing harks back to a past golden age.

In contrast to the situation in most of Central and Eastern Europe, all attempts to transform the Russian Communist Party into a classic Social-Democratic party failed, and the groupings that emerged as a result of such efforts proved unable to win enough votes to secure representation in the Russian parliament. Zyuganov and his colleagues lacked the revolutionary zeal that characterizes the leaders of a true "mob party." They might perhaps be seen as the functional equivalents of former civil servants searching for a new role. The CPRF of the 1990s was a party not of former communists of the Central and East European type, nor of revolutionaries, but of unemployed apparatchiks. This helps explain why the CPRF followed a different ideological path from that pursued by the former "fraternal" parties of Central and Eastern Europe.

The CPRF nonetheless remained, throughout the 1990s, Russia's only nationally organized political party. It survived several attempts to ban its activities and close its newspapers. This apparent anomaly demands an explanation. The answer seems to be that the harsh anticommunist rhetoric employed by Boris Yeltsin and his entourage allowed the communists to capitalize on the errors of the "party of power" and the hardships suffered by the population as a result of Yeltsin's economic reforms. The lower Yeltsin's popularity in the opinion polls, the more the older and more vulnerable members of the population hankered after the "good old days." As a result, the CPRF retained its influence in the country and in the corridors of power.

Slavophiles and Westernizers

Russia's attitude to the outside world has always been complex. Russia's most densely populated regions lie in Europe and it was there that the first Russian state took shape in the ninth century AD. By the eleventh century, Kievan Rus'—as that first state was called—was one of the main centers of Christian civilization and a hub of European trade and manufacturing. But Russia sees itself as a Eurasian country and has vital trade and security interests in both Europe and Asia.

The Mongol Conquest of 1240 cut Russia off from the Western world for nearly 250 years. In the sixteenth century, when the princes of Muscovy had defeated the Golden Horde, Russia began its rapid eastward expansion across Siberia. A century later, Russia had pushed its borders to the shores of the Pacific Ocean. Today, two-thirds of Russia's territory and most of its natural wealth lie east of the Urals. Russians have traditionally been a Christian nation and their closest ethnic ties are to their fellow Eastern Slavs in Ukraine and Belarus, yet Russia is also home to some twenty million Moslems. Tatars make up the country's second largest ethnic group. "Scratch a Russian," runs the saying, "and you'll find a Tatar." In the seventeenth and eighteenth centuries, Russians commonly used the word "Europe" as shorthand for "the civilized world," yet Russians have traditionally regarded Europe with mixed emotions of envy, longing, suspicion and superiority. "In Europe," wrote Dostoevsky, "we Russians are seen as Tatars; in Asia, we are seen as Europeans."

Until the time of Peter the Great, Russia was isolated from the rest of Europe. And for all Peter's efforts to modernize his country and to transform it into a great European power, its political system remained closer to what liberal Russian intellectuals consider "Asiatic despotism" than to the western democratic tradition. With its deeply rooted tradition of authoritarian rule, Russia has, until only comparatively recently, stood apart from the European model of pluralistic democracy, the rule of law, a market economy and human rights.

The Great Debate

In the 1840s, a debate broke out among the Russian intelligentsia that continues to this day. The "Slavophiles" argued that destiny had fated Russia to follow its own path. Though the Slavophiles did not reject western values in themselves, they insisted that Russia's unique combination of semi-Asiatic roots and Orthodox religious heritage could not be reconciled with the individualistic and materialistic values of the western world. The "Westernizers," for their part, did not deny the intrinsic value of Russia's cultural heritage. But they argued that, if Russia was to overcome its backwardness and realize its potential as a great power, it must adopt some western customs and find ways of integrating with the rest of Europe. Otherwise, Russia would be condemned forever to exclusion and impotence.

Left-wing politicians in Tsarist Russia were predominantly "Westernizers" who borrowed their ideas from contemporary Western European thought. The ideas on which Lenin and his fellow Bolsheviks based the Russian Communist Party were drawn from the teachings of two German academics, Karl Marx and Friedrich Engels, who predicted the emergence of a communist society based on shared wealth and universal equality (communism); such a society would come about, Marx and Engels asserted, as a result of the inevitable uprising of blue-collar workers against their bourgeois oppressors. Lenin's party rejected all things traditional and Russian in favor of the mission of the world proletariat and the would-be global proletarian revolution. In pursuit of their global vision, however, the Bolsheviks, systematically suppressed all the institutions that Russia had in common with other European powers. These included the Christian religion, civil and political liberties, organized labor, and private property rights. As a result, Russia ceased to be one of a number of more or less similar European countries and turned into something completely different. Objectively, therefore, the extreme cosmopolitans among Lenin's party paved the way for the isolationist Russian nationalism of Stalin and future generations of Soviet leaders.

Stalin's Dream

In a sharp departure from the cosmopolitanism of Lenin's generation, Stalin abandoned the dream of "world revolution" in favor of a restoration of the Russian Empire and a creeping communist expansion, turning to the legacy of Tsar Ivan the Terrible along with that of Marx, Engels and Lenin. Misleadingly entitling itself "Marxism-Leninism," Stalinism fostered the extreme isolationism that culminated in the isolation of the communist East behind an iron curtain cutting it off from the rest of the world. Stalinism forced on its subjects both in the USSR and in other communist countries all things conservative in every field of human life, not just in politics but in the arts, literature, fashion and relations between the sexes. Yet the ideas of progress and aspiration towards that "bright future of all humanity," communism, survived in the minds of the faithful. Stalin's successor Nikita Khrushchev declared that the foundations of a communist society would begin to emerge in the USSR by 1980. Khrushchev's replacement, Leonid Brezhnev, also paid lip service to the theory. In 1976, he declared that the USSR had reached the stage of "developed socialism," meaning that the foundations of the future communist system were already in place and needed only to be "perfected," that is, improved in minor details. The concept of "developed socialism" was quietly dropped by the altogether more radical Gorbachev leadership in the mid-1980s. Today, opinion polls find that little more than a half even of the CPRF's supporters believes in the ideas of socialism or communism.

Moving from "Left" to "Right"

The emergence of the CPRF marked the culmination of the gradual process whereby Russia's communists crossed the line from "left" to "right." In the sense in which these terms were defined above, the ideology propagated by Zyuganov and his associates was reactionary, rather than conservative. It hinged on nostalgia for the lost paradise of a Golden Age identified not only with the post-revolutionary, Soviet era, but also with the pre-Revolutionary society that Lenin and the Bolsheviks destroyed. Zyuganov, for instance, depicted the March 1917 abdication of the last Russian Emperor, Nicholas II, and his younger brother, Grand Duke Michael, as a national catastrophe that deprived Russia of legitimate power. Such ideological versatility turns the CPRF into a natural political ally of all sorts of Russian nationalist, clerical and monarchist groups. According to Dmitrii Furman, "Their ideological eclecticism is the prime source of both the power of the communists and of their impotence. Power—because [such ideological flexibility] enables them to unite the oppositions of all shades of the political spectrum and to rely on all the might of Russian traditionalism. Impotence—because they are unable to offer any clear perspective and are therefore doomed to continue in their role of eternal opposition, of which they have definitely tired."

The "right-wing" character of the CPRF's ideology comes as little surprise given that the communists ruled Russia for over seventy years, during which period their once revolutionary ideology became habitual and traditional. In its conservative nature lies the key to the CPRF's electoral successes. This explains why a growing number of Russians feel nostalgia for the country's communist past, given that Yeltsin's anticommunist regime has been marked by constant failure to pay wages and social benefits.

PODBEREZKIN'S "STATE PATRIOTISM" ADDS NATIONALISM TO CPRF IDEOLOGICAL SOUP

The ideology of the CPRF is multi-layered. One layer consists of the party's official statements and program documents. Another is made up of the works of party leader Gennadii Zyuganov, who is also the party's chief ideologue. Yet another layer consists of the writings of the party's non-communist allies, such as the chairman of the "Spiritual Heritage" foundation, Aleksei Podberezkin. The ideas of Podberezkin and the CPRF's other Russian nationalist allies have shaped the CPRF's new ideology and exerted particularly strong influence on the thinking of Zyuganov himself.

Podberezkin's think-tank—the idiosyncratically named RAU (Russian-American University) Corporation and the periodicals of which he was chief editor, *Obozrevatel'-Observer* and *Dukhovnoe nasledie* (*Spiritual Heritage*)—has had an enormous impact on Zyuganov's views. Podberezkin is an advocate of the ideology of "state patriotism," which Zyuganov has developed further in his works. A staunch opponent of liberalism and of Mikhail Gorbachev's insistence on the universal validity of "all-human" (obshchechelovecheskie) values, Podberezkin has also attacked Marxism. He sees the CPRF as the only force capable of pulling Russia out of crisis "not because they are communists, but because they are great power statists (gosudarstvenniki)." Rejecting the doctrine of the messianic role of the working class, Podberezkin counterpoises Russia's intellectual, scientific and cultural achievements that will, he argues, ultimately determine the nation's significance on the global stage (a view shared by Zyuganov). Contrary to Marxist materialism, Podberezkin argues that "the idea must triumph over the instinct for self-preservation, the fear of death and the desire for gain," while "the highest spiritual and moral interests must take preference over material ones." At the same time, the crux of Podberezkin's theory of "state patriotism" consists in the priority of national and state interests and the need to defend Russian interests even at the expense of those of other nations, in particular, those of the United States. In more concrete terms, Russia's primary task is, according to Podberezkin, "the peaceful restoration of the Russian state within its natural borders which existed until 1991" (that is, until the collapse of the Soviet Union).

Nostalgia for the USSR seems to have been the only point in Podberezkin's teaching that rendered him unacceptable to the Yeltsin establishment. That apart, Podberezkin's place in the opposition was determined by his close relations with Zyuganov and, before him, with former Vice-President Aleksandr Rutskoi (in 1991-93, Podberezkin headed Rutskoi's team of consultants). All in all, Podberezkin seems to have had a moderating influence on his CPRF partners. For instance, unlike certain members of the top CPRF leadership, Podberezkin denied that his Russian nationalism was in any way influenced by racial considerations; the development of the nation state, he argued, was shaped not by race but by culture and history. It followed, he argued, that Russian national identity had nothing to do with the notorious "paragraph 5" of Soviet and Russian identity documents (which, until 1998, indicated the ethnicity of the bearer). On occasion, the very moderation of Podberezkin's views made problems for the powers-that-be, given that he was the driving force behind the establishment of the Popular Patriotic Union of Russia (PPUoR)—the communist/nationalist electoral coalition set up in 1996—of which he was a co-chairman. In that capacity, Podberezkin engineered the policy of cooperation between the CPRF and other PPUoR member-parties, on the one hand, and the Yeltsin government on the other.

Russian Orthodox Church Offers Inspiration to CPRF

Unlike that of Podberezkin, the contribution of the Russian Orthodox Church to the CPRF's ideology could not be termed moderate. Extremist members of both the hierarchy and the laity sought in the CPRF a safeguard against the penetration into Russian society of other faiths. Often monarchist and anticommunist by political affiliation, these Orthodox activists opposed the participation of the Moscow Patriarchy in the ecumenical movement and in the activity of the World Council of Churches. They found a welcome in the pages of Zyuganovite periodicals

In 1993-5, for example, Metropolitan Ioann (Snychev) of St Petersburg and Ladoga made regular contributions to such newspapers as *Zavtra* and *Sovetskaya Rossiya*. There he published his openly chauvinistic and anti-Semitic articles. Ioann reputedly owed his 1990 appointment to the diocese of St Petersburg to his stance as an anticommunist monarchist.

The British historian Wendy Slater has identified Ioann and Zyuganov as the "major ideologues of the national-patriotic coalition." Zyuganov implicitly confirmed this assertion when he acknowledged that Metropolitan Ioann's works had influenced the development of his own ideas.

On the pages of the national-patriotic press, Ioann advocated the reintroduction to Russia of absolute monarchy based on the following principles: (1) ethnic (Russian) homogeneity; (2) Orthodox Christianity; (3) unanimity (sobornost') in decision-making (that is, rejection of individualism and pluralism, both of which Ioann dismissed as Western inventions alien to the Russian soul). Ioann's efforts to reach a compromise with the CPRF created a stir when, in March 1994, *Sovetskaya Rossiya* published his article "Makers of Cataclysms." In it, the Metropolitan asserted the authenticity of the well-known anti-Semitic forgery, "The Protocols of the Elders of Zion," and accused the Jews of being responsible for all of Russia's calamities, beginning with the Bolshevik revolution of 1917.

With the Metropolitan's blessing, *Sovetskaya Rossiya* in 1994 launched a special religious supplement entitled *Rus' Pravoslavnaya* (*Orthodox Russia*). First published in 1994, the supplement continued to appear even after Ioann's death at the end of 1995. In the pages of this supplement, Russian fundamentalists tried to combine communism and Eastern Orthodoxy, producing what came to be known as "Orthodox Stalinism." The brainchild of Andrei Ryumin, editor of the miscellany *Pravoslavie ili Smert'!* (*Orthodoxy or Death!*), "Orthodox Stalinism" lauded Stalin's grudging and partial recognition of the Russian Orthodox Church in 1943. It also tried to justify Stalin's terror, including the executions of the Soviet military leadership from 1937 on, claiming that all Stalin had done was purge the Red Army of "Zionists" (code-name for Jews) such as Iona Yakir. In this, the "Orthodox Stalinists" went further than the common or garden-variety Stalinists among the CPRF leadership, who usually dismissed the terror as the "mistakes" of a great statesman.

Concept of Orthodox Stalinism

Zyuganov and the "Orthodox Stalinists" professed a common conviction that the dictator had removed all the restrictions imposed on the Russian Orthodox Church by his "Trotskyite" (i.e., "Zionist") predecessors. This did Stalin too much honor. The dictator did indeed, in 1943, release from labor camps a number of priests and bishops who had expressed themselves willing to cooperate with his regime, and he did allow the Church to resume its functions within certain very narrow limits. Over the ensuing forty-four years, however, religion remained an object of oppression in the Soviet Union; believers were discriminated against in employment and other spheres of civil activity; ruined churches were not restored. It was not until the advent of Mikhail Gorbachev and Aleksandr Yakovlev that a stop was put to the harassment of religion in the USSR. Believers were allowed to enjoy the same rights as other Soviet citizens—in particular, the right of the clergy to have access to the media—and the Church was allowed to restore old churches and open new ones.

The concept of "Orthodox Stalinism" seemed a promising ideological innovation. It would appeal to Christians who were not communists, while the idea of the Orthodox Church's supremacy appealed to many communists. Viktor Anpilov, leader of the far left "Working Russia" movement, told a press conference in January 1999 that "Working Russia" was forming an alliance with the "Officers for the Restoration of the USSR" movement and intended to erect Orthodox crosses alongside traditional communist red banners everywhere across the territory of the former USSR, from Kamchatka in the Far East to Brest on the Belarussian-Polish border. Stalin's grandson, Evgenii Dzhugashvili, and the leader of the Union of Officers, Stanislav Terekhov, were also present and appeared to share Anpilov's esteem for the Orthodox cross. The incident exemplified the disagreements on the left wing of the Russian political spectrum. On the far left, the Anpilov-Dzhugashvili bloc advocated the restoration of the Stalinist system in all its respects, including a return to state ownership of the means of production, restoration of the centrally-planned economy, and a return to the system under which the government of the country was ideally carried out by a network of locally-elected Soviets. The role assigned to the Orthodox Church was the only manifestation of modernism in the bloc's ideology.

It was also virtually the only policy that the far left shared with Zyuganov's CPRF. The turn toward the Orthodox Church was a radically new departure for the CPRF, requiring it to amend its program and statutes in order to allow religious believers to join the party. On the eve of the second round of the presidential elections in July 1996, Zyuganov visited the head of the Russian Orthodox Church, Patriarch Aleksii II, apparently to assure the hierarchy that they had nothing to fear from a possible communist return to power. The CPRF proved its loyalty by the role it played in the adoption of Russia's "Law on Freedom of Conscience." The controversial law banned missionary activity on Russian territory by all but a small group of "traditional" religions, defined as Russian Orthodoxy, Islam, Buddhism and Judaism. Among those excluded were Roman

Catholicism, Lutheranism and other mainstream Protestant confessions. The bill was drafted by members of the Duma's Committee on the Affairs of Public Associations and Religious Organizations, and introduced by its chairman, CPRF deputy Viktor Zorkaltsev. It entered into force in 1997.

CPRF Historiography and Zyuganov's "sobornost'"

Another consequence of the national-patriotic alliance was the willingness of the CPRF to recognize the continuity of Russian history before the October 1917 revolution. Soviet historiography viewed everything that preceded the Great October Revolution of 1917 as pre-history, the sole purpose of which was to prepare humanity for the arrival of communism. At first, the CPRF said its aim was to make room for a more pluralistic attitude toward the past and for less hostile treatment of historic figures who did not belong to the revolutionary or "progressive" camp. Zyuganov, for example, expressed a desire to "make peace" between the "Whites" and "Reds," that is, between the hostile camps in Russia's Civil War of 1918-22. In reality, modern communist historiography has displayed growing sympathy toward the tsars at the expense of the heroes of the Soviet period, the revolutionary intellectuals. Like their Marxist predecessors, however, the nationalist CPRF ideologists continued to interpret Russian history as a struggle between the forces of good and evil. The difference lay in the distribution of roles: Soviet historians depicted the struggle as one between good workers and peasants against bad nobles and capitalists. For Zyuganov and his allies, the heroes were the Russian military and government officials who forged a powerful centralized state and defended Russia against "cosmopolitan" forces bent on destroying the country.

Zyuganov's main contribution to this debate was his development of the idea of sobornost' (unanimity). The term is derived from the word sobor (cathedral). In its primary meaning, it describes the way in which ecclesiastical assemblies in pre-Petrine Russia adopted key decisions. Such decisions required consensus rather than a mere majority vote. In religious life, the term sobornost' (or its adjective sobornyi) is often applied to the common prayer of the Orthodox congregation. In the nineteenth century, a founding father of the Slavophile movement, Aleksei Khomyakov, reinvented the concept, endowing it with a number of new meanings ranging from "togetherness" to "symphony." Khomyakov believed that human beings could best achieve spiritual and intellectual maturity in an organic community that respected the liberty of its members and that true progress would depend not on competition (as in the West) but on cooperation. Zyuganov appears to have derived his vision of sobornost' from Metropolitan Ioann rather than from Khomyakov's works. Unlike Khomyakov, Zyuganov tends to interpret the term as "collectivism" rather than as "symphony."

ZYUGANOV'S GEOPOLITICS

A strong influence on the views of Zyuganov and other CPRF leaders was exerted by contributors to the militantly anti-Western and anti-Semitic weekly newspaper *Den'* (re-named *Zavtra* following the short-lived attempt by the Yeltsin government to shut it down after the bloody events of October 1993.) Since the early 1990s, the paper's chief editor Aleksandr Prokhanov, together with essayists Sergei Kurginyan, Aleksandr Dugin and Geidar Dzhemal, propounded a theory of "geopolitics" posited on the existence of an eternal struggle between two hostile civilizations. These were the "Atlanticist" civilization (primarily represented by the USA and Great Britain) and, opposed to it, the so-called Eurasian civilization (represented by Russia). As elaborated by Prokhanov and his associates, these concepts became extremely popular among Russian intellectuals. The founding fathers of the CPRF were the first to pick up on them. (They did so regardless of the fact that Marx and Lenin had taught the precise opposite, arguing that all the countries of the globe were bound to develop in accordance with a single set of laws of historical development and that all international conflicts were the product of competition between capitalists of various countries.) Zyuganov himself became a leading contributor to *Zavtra* and a proponent of geopolitics. Two of his books (*Za garizontom* [*Beyond the Horizon*] and *Geografiya pobedy* [*The Geography of Victory*]) were devoted entirely to geopolitics, whereas others bear the evidence of a specific geopolitical way of thinking. It would be only a minor exaggeration to identify geopolitics as the essence of Zyuganov's ideology.

The term geopolitics was coined by the Swedish political scientist Rudolf Kjellen in his book *The State as an Organism*, published in 1916. The term spread through Central Europe in the period between the two World Wars, coming into worldwide use during the Second World War. The Nazis, for instance, adopted the theories of the German scholar Karl Haushofer, who sought in his monthly journal of geopolitics, *Zeitschrift fur Geopolitik*, to give a geopolitical rationale to Germany's territorial claims. At the opposite end of the political spectrum, the British scholar Sir Halford Mackinder advanced the theory of a heartland in world politics. This heartland embraced Central and Eastern Europe and all of Germany and, according to Mackinder, it was essential that it be kept within the democratic sphere of influence. Mackinder's main works, *The Geographical Pivot of History* and *Democratic Ideals and Reality*, were published in 1904 and 1919 respectively.

Eurasianism

The geopolitics of Zyuganov, Prokhanov, Kurginyan and Dugin owes much to the influence of "Eurasianism" (Evraziistvo), an intellectual movement that emerged among Russian émigrés in the early 1920s. Its founders—Prince Nikolai Trubetskoi, Georgii Florovsky, Petr Savitsky and Petr Suvchisky—published in 1921 in Sofia a collection of articles entitled *Iskhod k Vostoku* (*Exodus to the East*). Later, the movement was supported by a number of prominent Russian exiles, among them Petr Bitsilli, Georgii Vernadsky, Lev Karsavin, Sergei Efron and the literary historian Prince Dmitrii Svyatopolk-Mirsky. The Eurasians saw Russia as a "special" civilization, neither European, nor Asian, but Eurasian. The West, they argued, had contributed positively to Russian developments in the past, but Russia's future belonged to the East. They believed in the eventual emergence in Russia of a unique culture that would unite Europe and Asia. Impressed though they were by the dynamics of the young communist regime, the Eurasians believed that the Bolsheviks would not, in the final analysis, be able to put forward a fruitful national idea for Russia. Sooner or later, Eurasianism would become Russia's leading ideology.

With its crude cartoons and tabloid headlines, *Zavtra* was a far cry from the elevated style of those scions of the Old Russian nobility who founded the original Eurasian movement. Traces of their teachings could easily be found on *Zavtra*'s pages, however. The writings of Azerbaijani author Geidar Dzhemal, a Muslim fundamentalist and admirer of the Ayatollah Khomeini, is a case in point. "Russia will become great," according to Dzhemal, "only if she unites with Islam and gives up her pathetic attempts to become a member of the 'civilized world,' which has merely downgraded her. Russia's power lies in her opposition to the West."

In conversation with David Remnick, Prokhanov reiterated his vision of Eurasianism as potentially being Russia's major ideology. He told Remnick that his greatest achievement was "helping the communists to replace their old and useless dogma with elements of nationalism that would help them build a broader political base." Prokhanov recalls, too, that the idea of uniting the "Red" communists with the "White" nationalists and forming a united opposition movement came to Zyuganov in the course of his visits to the editorial offices of Den' at the end of 1991.

In all fairness, it should be added that the sources cited in Zyuganov's works are by no means restricted to the names of those who write for such hard-line newspapers as *Den'*, *Zavtra*, *Sovetskaya Rossiya* and *Pravda*. Zyuganov also quotes such Slavophile writers of the nineteenth century as Nikolai Danilevsky and Konstantin Leontev, and the TmigrT author Ivan Ilin. Among Western writers referred to are Oswald Spengler, Arnold Toynbee and Samuel Huntington, author of *The Clash of Civilizations.* As Joan Urban and Valerii Solovei note, Huntington's article was particularly important for Russian geopolitics of the *Den'* mold, "for it enabled them to claim that even a world-class Harvard professor held that Russia represented a special civilization and that conflicts between civilizations were all but inevitable."

Zyuganovism

To judge from most of the literature published on the CPRF, Zyuganov is the leading ideologue of today's CPRF, and his ideas tend to become incorporated into the party's program documents. Surprisingly few of his ideas, however, have been incorporated into the day-to-day routine in the "red" regions.

The leaders of the CPRF customarily identify themselves as gosudarstvenniky (great-power statists). When Zyuganov published his doctoral thesis in book form, he added a subtitle reading "The Ideology of State Patriotism." Zyuganov defended his doctoral dissertation, then entitled "The Basic Tendencies and Mechanisms of Sociopolitical Change in Contemporary Russia," in the Faculty of Philosophy of Moscow State University on April 21, 1995. In the course of his presentation, members of the faculty's academic council reproved Zyuganov for the absence of the words "Lenin" and "Leninism" in his thesis. Zyuganov responded that he was not going to defend Marxist ideology since 800 million copies of Lenin's works had been published and were available in all the world's libraries.

Zyuganov first attracted nationwide attention in early 1991 with a series of articles in which he attacked Gorbachev's policy of glasnost' in the media. Glasnost', he wrote, was nothing other than "a weapon in the psychological war against the [Soviet] people." Later, criticism of Russia's highly opinionated journalism became the constant refrain of Russia's communists and their nationalist allies. Zyuganov's early works were marked with catastrophism. This was particularly evident in the collective appeal *Slovo k narodu* (*A Word to the People*), published in July 1991, one month before the attempted putsch that precipitated the collapse of the

USSR. Signed by a number of nationalist cultural and political figures, the appeal was penned by Zyuganov and Prokhanov. It called on various strata of the Soviet population—workers, peasants, academics, communists, and believers—to resist the threatened collapse of their Motherland. In time, the appeal came to be seen as an attempt to prepare the population psychologically for the ensuing putsch. In due course, some of its predictions did indeed prove to be correct, notably, the collapse of the USSR, about which the "Communists of Russia" faction in the Russian Supreme Soviet had been warning ever since the body was elected in March 1990.

ZYUGANOV'S "ATLANTICIST" SCARE

Zyuganov did not, in subsequent years, lose his inclination toward catastrophism, though he did gradually modify it as the CPRF itself grew more moderate. Zyuganov and his party did not, however, lose their tendency to view all unpleasant developments as evidence of a worldwide conspiracy against all things Russian. In 1994, for instance, Zyuganov wrote that the Anglo-American enemies of the Russian nation (the "Atlanticists") had destroyed all the pillars that ensured the strength of the Russian spirit in a deliberate attempt to turn Russia into a supplier of raw materials and cheap labor for the West. They had, he alleged, encouraged the worldwide use of the English language specifically in order to undermine Russian national identity.

The attitude of Zyuganov and the other members of the *Den'/Zavtra* geopolitical school to continental West European nations, such as Germany and France, tends to be rather sympathetic. It may not, therefore, be entirely correct to describe them as "anti-Western." But Zyuganov and his colleagues, both inside and outside the CPRF, all profess to believe the same anti-American myth, which they support by reference to various secret documents of questionable authenticity. Addressing the Constitutional Court during the hearings on Yeltsin's ban on the CPRF, for example, Zyuganov quoted excerpts from a "top secret instruction" in which US President John F. Kennedy allegedly called for the destruction of the CPSU as a means of precipitating the collapse of the USSR. Other witnesses at the hearings followed Zyuganov's lead and read out similarly sinister utterances by various American figures, for which neither independent confirmation nor any published source was offered. The best known of such quotations was an address by Alan W. Dulles allegedly made to CIA officers some time in the 1940s. Cited by many Russian communists, starting with Polozkov, the paragraph in question sounds little like the language of an American bureaucrat but is only too reminiscent of the tone and substance of the Protocols of the Elders of Zion: "Having spread chaos in the Soviet Union, we will secretly replace their values with false values, and make them believe in those false values (...) We will use all means to support so-called artists who will foster the cult of sex, sadism, and treason—in a word, every kind of immorality (...) Actively but imperceptibly, we will foster official arbitrariness, bribe-taking, and lack of principles."

In the Russian provinces, allegations of American plots against all things Russian sometimes take on particularly extreme forms. At a meeting in Tula in October 1998, for example, an aged CPRF activist alleged that Dulles dispatched no fewer than ten thousand CIA agents to Russia in the 1930s, with instructions that they should make a career in the CPSU apparatus with the aim of destroying the Communist Party from within. Through this very program, the speaker said, Aleksandr Yakovlev became a member of the Politburo dedicated to bringing down both the party and the Soviet Union.

Capitalism, Zyuganov asserts, is alien to the Russian mentality. What Russia needs now, he asserts, is a "national idea" capable of uniting the mentally healthy sections of society and achieving the resurrection of the Russian nation. Along with other Slavophile authors, Zyuganov argues that Russian history represents a synthesis of two opposing elements, Western and Eastern. It is Russia's historic task to absorb and combine within its gigantic territory all the opposing economic structures, nationalities, cultures, landscapes and climatic zones. "Russia and the USSR acted as a kind of microcosm of the entire world with all its problems, controversies and conflicts," Zyuganov wrote. Harmonizing all the controversial trends in her economic, political, cultural and spiritual life, Zyuganov went on, "Russia resolved not merely her own problems, but those of global civilization." Because of her complex nature, Russia had always "marched half a step ahead of other nations, pointing the way, or warning against approaching danger." This, according to Zyuganov, is the source of Russia's much-criticized messianism.

Zyuganov's Plan to Restore Russia

Zyuganov saw the greatest danger for Russia as lying in the attempt by unidentified "world powers" to assert control over post-Soviet territory. Russian foreign policy, in Zyuganov's view, should be aimed at stopping such attempts on the Eurasian continent. Echoing Sir Halford Mackinder's concept, Zyuganov called on Russia to restore her natural geopolitical status by ensuring her domination over the heartland (the Eurasian landmass).

Zyuganov planned to achieve this aim in three stages. The first phase would be the consolidation of all forces inside the country. According to Zyuganov, such unity would be possible only on the platform of the national-patriotic bloc. The second phase would see the reintegration of the Eastern Slavs—Russians, Belarussians and Ukrainians. While the union of Russia and Belarus got underway in the late 1990s, Ukraine remained reluctant to merge with Russia. Zyuganov believed that Ukrainian resistance could be overcome if only the Ukrainian military would favor such a move. Finally, the third phase would see the reinstatement of Russian dominance over the heartland as such. Since the resurrection of a single state (the former USSR) was not a possibility in the immediate future, Russia should aim to establish geopolitical control over the territory of the former Russian Empire/Soviet Union, rather than trying to resurrect a single state.

Translated into the language of modern politics, Zyuganov and the CPRF wanted the states that emerged from the ruins of the Soviet Union to return to the Russian sphere of influence. It might be argued that, in this respect, the communists did not differ greatly from the ruling Russian establishment, which had strenuously opposed the desire of Central and Eastern European nations such as the Baltic states to join NATO. It might also be argued that Zyuganov's claim to the "heartland" marked a certain progress in comparison with the worldviews of Joseph Stalin and Nikita Khrushchev, both of whom professed to believe that communism was the "radiant future" of all humanity and both of whom, in theory at least, sought domination over the entire globe.

What distinguished Zyuganov's ideology both from that of the foreign policy makers of the Yeltsin government camp and from that of their Soviet-era predecessors was the Slavophile myth. This myth asserted the spiritual superiority of the Russian nation with its allegedly innate collectivism and its self-proclaimed mission to counter the maritime "Atlanticist" powers. This Russian nationalism amounted to thinly veiled racism since it saw the Slavs predominantly as a racial rather than a linguistic or cultural category. Zyuganov's ideology was further distinguished by his infatuation with Stalin, whom he revered as the architect of a superpower and defender of Russia's true national interests. These features made "Zyuganovism" a less dangerous ideology than the traditional Marxist-Leninist version of communism had been in its Stalinist, Troskyite, Maoist or Latin American variety. At least at the moment, the CPRF's ideology appeared to be completely lacking that mass appeal in foreign, particularly Roman Catholic, countries, that once provoked the French philosopher Raymond Aron to dub Marxism "l'opium des intellectuels." While Marxism retained its popularity with the Western left, Zyuganov and his ilk were barely tolerated, if, indeed, considered at all.

THE CPRF'S SOCIAL AND ECONOMIC PROGRAMS

While foreign policy (in the form of Zyuganov's geopolitics) occupied a prominent place in the ideology of the CPRF, critics complained that it played too prominent a role and pointed out that the party lacked a detailed program of either social or economic policy. Here too the party's ideology was contradictory. Zyuganov said on more than one occasion that the CPRF had recognized the plurality of forms of property (that is to say, the party accepted the legitimacy of private property and had abandoned the goal of wholesale nationalization of industry and agriculture—but see below for further details of the party's position on re-nationalization). The right to private property, he affirmed, would continue to be recognized should the CPRF come to power. (Apart from anything else, that right was guaranteed by Russia's 1993 Constitution.) At the same time, the party's program stated that the CPRF would not tolerate the use of property rights for "any form of exploitation of man by man." This was the formulation that outlawed private property in the USSR until Gorbachev came to power. The clearest part in the economic section of the party's program was that which reiterated the CPRF's opposition to the private ownership of agricultural land. According to this document, Russian citizens would be allowed to buy or sell only the small plots of land used in Russia as private gardens. (This right was significant: research conducted in 1998 by the US Information Agency revealed that, as in the Soviet period, three out of four Russian citizens depended on their private plots for food.) As for agricultural land, citizens would be entitled to own, rent and inherit such property but would not have the right to sell or mortgage it. The CPRF program also promised to provide state subsidies to protect the domestic agricultural sector from foreign competition.

The CPRF opposed the privatization of state property as it was carried out in the early 1990s under the supervision of Yeltsin's privatization minister Anatolii Chubais. In the intervening period, Chubais' campaign has come under increasing criticism not only in Russia but also from Western academics. The CPRF program calls for "nationalization or confiscation of property that was appropriated illegally, in violation of national interests and the rights of workers." This point was used by Yeltsin's camp against Zyuganov during the 1996 presidential campaign. Yeltsin's economic adviser Aleksandr Livshits has acknowledged that the entire privatization campaign was carried out on the basis of presidential decrees and thereby contravened the law on privatization adopted by the Russian parliament. It followed, Livshits conceded, that all the property privatized in Russia was, technically, "appropriated against the law." Strangely enough, the CPRF has not tried to capitalize on so extraordinary a statement. The party program notwithstanding, Zyuganov seems in no hurry to modify the privatization process.

ZYUGANOV'S VIEWS ON PRIVATIZATION AND BUSINESS ACTIVITY

Zyuganov sounded quite sincere when, during the 1996 presidential campaign, he reproached his then ally, Viktor Anpilov, for urging re-nationalization. Zyuganov said that, if elected president, he would not seek to confiscate private property since such a move could unleash a "civil war." Zyuganov's refusal to advocate the reversal of privatization subsequently drove Anpilov to split from the CPRF and form his own Stalinist bloc with which to campaign in the 1999 parliamentary elections. Zyuganov's reluctance to undo the results of privatization makes the CPRF leader look more moderate than many advocates of re-nationalization, from the moderate Marxist reformer Aleksandr Buzgalin to Moscow Mayor Yurii Luzhkov. Luzhkov, who is widely perceived as being further to the right than the CPRF, has called for the confiscation without compensation by the state of inefficient industrial enterprises.

Zyuganov's cautious approach met with little support inside his own party. Gennadii Gamza, first secretary of the Amur regional committee of the CPRF and head of its whole Far Eastern organization told this author that he did not share Zyuganov's economic modernism, including Zyuganov's fascination with China's economic reforms and his insistence on their relevance for Russia. Instead, Gamza said, he himself preferred traditional Soviet-style "socialism," including state ownership of the means of production and restoration of the command economy. One of the most influential members of the CPRF Central Committee, Gamza does not belong to the category of party hard-liners. His idea of socialism is shared by many members of the CPRF, especially in the provinces. And yet, the party's program does not provide for the confiscation and re-nationalization of private property, only for property that can be proven to have been privatized by illegal means. Nor does the program call for a return to central planning, advocating nothing more radical than state monitoring of the activities of private banks and the establishment of a state monopoly on the export of certain strategic materials, natural resources and "food products in short supply."

Zyuganov's caution over the issue of confiscation seems not to derive from his economic ideas, vague as those are, but to be tied directly to two key tenets of his ideology, both of which are profoundly non-Marxist. One of these is that, for all his professed admiration for strongmen and tyrants from Peter the Great to Stalin, Zyuganov is a principled opponent of violence, revolutions and dictatorship. His favorite maxim is "Russia has exhausted its revolutionary resources." Russia, he often repeats, "would not survive another civil war," and "proletarian dictatorship would be incapable of resolving Russia's many problems." CPRF documents call for the party to engage only in non-violent, constitutional forms of political activity, ranging from participating in federal and local elections to organizing political rallies and, where necessary, workplace strikes. The party program calls, for example, for the reintegration of the Soviet Union "on a voluntary basis," which appears to be a purely Utopian aim.

The second factor underlying Zyuganov's idiosyncratic attitude to private property and commercial activity is his determination to form unions and coalitions with other players on the Russian political scene, including what he has termed "patriotically-minded businessmen." In the course of its parliamentary activities, the CPRF has repeatedly displayed its flexibility and readiness to compromise. The party's program stipulates its willingness to cooperate with other Russian communist parties and to respect their independence. The CPRF has identified itself as a true member of the Union of Communist Parties (UCP-CPSU) and voiced its confident hope that a united communist party will eventually emerge on a "voluntary basis" in a reintegrated Soviet state. The CPRF program also asserts the party's desire to cooperate with various non-communist "cultural, political, social and confessional movements, parties and organizations." This has on occasion led the CPRF into some improbable coalitions. At the end of 1994 and beginning of 1995, for example, moderates in the party leadership went so far as to suggest backing the liberal opposition leader, Grigorii Yavlinsky, as the candidate of a united opposition in the 1996 presidential election. Since Yavlinsky refused the offer, the matter went no further and it will never be known whether the CPRF leadership could have sold so bizarre an idea to party hard-liners. For public consumption, Zyuganov has ruled out an alliance with the Yabloko leader, branding him "a Harvard puppet." In reality, Yabloko and the CPRF have often cooperated in the

State Duma. They worked together, for example on the commission on Yeltsin's impeachment, initiated by the CPRF in 1998, and to secure the appointment of Evgenii Primakov as Prime Minister in September of the same year. As a rule, however, Yabloko has adopted a more uncompromising stance than the CPRF and its allies; in particular, Yabloko has consistently voted against the Yeltsin government's proposals for the federal budget.

DEMOCRACY AND THE CPRF

Aleksandr Mekhanik, leader of the reform-oriented Republican Party of the Russian Federation (formerly "Communists for Democracy") has described the CPRF as "the only party in today's Russia that is consistently democratic in its internal organization." It may be added that, at least in theory, the CPRF would like to be democratic in its dealings with the outside world as well. Although the party's record in this respect has so far appeared rather double-edged, the recognition by Party ideologues of the validity of democracy is in itself a major step forward. Lenin and his followers dismissed the "bourgeois" concept of democracy as nothing more than the hypocrisy of the exploiting classes. In his study of geopolitics, by contrast, Zyuganov identifies "the democratic idea" as one of the four basic preconditions for Russian national revival. He added:

"We must finally understand: democracy in Russia is serious and will be long lasting. It would be ridiculous to deny that the ideals of civil freedom and human rights have, in a remarkably short time, put down strong roots in our country and found a multitude of ardent supporters. It is only, thank God, through democratic mechanisms that we shall be able to find that public, sobornyi consensus on the crucial questions of our existence without which we shall never succeed in overcoming [the new] "time of troubles." Of course, a return to authoritarianism and even dictatorship is still possible on our way to revival. But it is already quite clear: Nobody will succeed in driving people back into the fetters of the command unanimity... Consequently, we must once and for all replace that non-democratic image that, out of thoughtlessness or misapprehension, has been painted of us by the patriotic opposition."

The CPRF has not always lived up to these high criteria. The Law on Freedom of Conscience, which Yeltsin was forced reluctantly to sign into law in 1997 after both chambers of the Russian parliament overruled his veto, is a particularly notorious example. Ostensibly aimed at restricting the harmful activities of foreign missionaries, the law hit Roman Catholic, Lutheran, Baptist and other churches that had existed in Russia for centuries and, above all, those Russian Orthodox congregations which did not subordinate themselves to the Moscow Patriarchate.

In other instances, policies advocated by the CPRF could be seen as more democratic than those of the existing order could. Two examples of this are the opposition's demand that government ministers be made accountable to parliament, and that political parties in the State Duma be allowed unfettered access to the electronic media. Nonetheless, some of the CPRF's conditions could not be implemented without the reintroduction of state censorship. Among them is the provision calling for outlawing "the blackening of Russian and Soviet history and of the memory and teachings of V.I. Lenin." The CPRF's program promises, too, that when the CPRF comes to power it will "halt the spread of Russophobia, Westernism, Americanism, historic Vandalism, and the cult of profit, violence and promiscuity, egoism and individualism." To uproot all of the above-listed vices, a victorious CPRF would have to resort to mass terror rather than mere censorship.

THE CPRF AND ANTI-SEMITISM

November 1998-January 1999 found Zyuganov scurrying from one Western capital to another in a desperate attempt to reassure the outside world that the CPRF was not an anti-Semitic party. The alarm had been provoked by a series of virulently anti-Semitic statements by two members of the CPRF Central Committee and was compounded by the refusal of the CPRF faction in the State Duma to pass a vote of censure against the culprits. Zyuganov's own failure publicly to rebuke the renegades added to public concern that the CPRF was turning to anti-Semitism.

On October 4, 1998, the party's aged enfant terrible, retired General Albert Makashov (who had played a leading role in the 1993 parliamentary rebellion against the Yeltsin leadership), addressed a group of striking coal miners on Moscow's Red Square. The miners had come to Moscow from the Far North of Russia to demand payment of their long overdue wages. Makashov found nothing better to tell them than that Russia was governed by "ten Yids" whom he planned soon to bring to retribution at the Lobnoe Mesto (part of Red Square where, in the Middle Ages, corporal and capital punishments were carried out). Footage of Makashov's remark was widely aired by Russian Television and provoked protests throughout Russia and the rest of the world.

Two parliamentary deputies, Jewish singer Iosif Kobzon (a close associate of Moscow Mayor Yurii Luzhkov) and film director Stanislav Govorukhin (who had been Zyuganov's close associate during the 1996 presidential campaign), immediately drafted a motion of censure condemning Makashov's outburst. Duma Speaker Gennadii Seleznev and other prominent members of the CPRF faction supported the resolution, which was, however, opposed by the overwhelming majority of the communist and nationalist factions and all of Vladimir Zhirinovsky's supporters. It was, accordingly, defeated by 121 votes to 107. Instead, on November 13, the Duma adopted a text that made no mention of Makashov but merely criticized certain unidentified deputies whose statements "did not promote friendship and mutual respect among people of different nationalities." Meanwhile, Makashov repeated his inflammatory statements at every opportunity. In the face of a rising tide of criticism, the Presidium of the CPRF Central Committee went on the counterattack, blaming the mass media rather than Makashov for promoting anti-Semitism.

Fuel was added to the fire by another CPRF maverick, Viktor Ilyukhin, a former deputy Prosecutor-General of the USSR who had taken over the leadership of the Movement in Support of the Army and Defense Industry (which had, incidentally, been founded by a person of Jewish descent, the late General Lev Rokhlin). The aim of the movement was to rally opposition to the Yeltsin government in Russia's cash-starved armed services and defense sector. In November 1998, Ilyukhin came out with a string of anti-Semitic remarks of his own, provoking a fresh wave of protest. Yeltsin issued a strong statement of condemnation, but Prime Minister Yevgenii Primakov, himself a Jew, remained silent. Media magnate Boris Berezovsky, undoubtedly one of the ten Jews Makashov had in mind, called for the CPRF to be banned. Mayor Luzhkov was forced to abandon his earlier plans of forming an electoral pact between his newly formed Otechestvo (Fatherland) movement and the CPRF.

ZYUGANOV'S RESPONSE TO CHARGES OF ANTI-SEMITISM

Zyuganov responded with a statement that the CPRF was not anti-Semitic but was opposed to Zionism. By internationalizing the issue, Zyuganov made things much worse. His statement was denounced as classic anti-Semitism by the Israeli government and condemned by the World Jewish Congress and the Council of Europe. Many western governments, including those of the USA and Great Britain, protested both to the Russian government and to Zyuganov personally. The controversy brought the CPRF to the verge of a split, since many of its members began to feel uncomfortable within its ranks. As a result of this growing unease, Makashov and Ilyukhin were excluded from the list of CPRF candidates for the December 1999 parliamentary elections. Both announced that they would instead run on the list of Ilyukhin's Movement in Support of the Army and Defense Industry.

Anti-Semitism has deep roots in Russian society and was evident among Russia's communists well before the CPRF was founded. Anti-Semitic leaflets on his behalf probably cost Polozkov the handful of votes he needed in June 1990 to beat Yeltsin in the election for Speaker of the RSFSR Supreme Soviet. David Remnick found "enough anti-Semitism on the pages of *Zavtra* to fill an issue of *Der Sturmer*." The same could be said of the mainstream newspaper of the CPRF, *Sovetskaya Rossiya*. It may however be added that anti-Semitism has never brought the CPRF anything but trouble. Jewish communists (of whom there have always been many) became afraid to attend rallies of their own party because of the abundance of neo-Nazi literature and slogans at such gatherings.

At least two of Zyuganov's books contained anti-Semitic passages, and these were skillfully used against him by Yeltsin's camp in the 1996 election. In one notable passage, Zyuganov claimed that "The ideology, culture and worldview of the Western world are becoming more and more influenced by Jews scattered around the globe. Jewish influence is growing not by the day, but by the hour. The Jewish Diaspora has traditionally controlled the financial life of the continent, and is increasing its control over Western civilization and its socioeconomic system." In another, Zyuganov alleged that "the characteristics of the 'chosen' people" were making "a decisive impact on Western consciousness." During the presidential campaign these passages were repeatedly cited in the government-controlled media which, on occasion, went on to explain to readers that the CPRF was now "a National Socialist rather than a Communist party."

Here, as in other aspects of its ideology, the CPRF's position was contradictory. Zyuganov's denunciations of Makashov's outbursts were mealy-mouthed and satisfied no one. The best that could be said of them was that they were aimed at keeping his division-ridden party from splitting at a time when the CPRF was preparing for the 1999 parliamentary elections and the 2000 presidential race. They harmed the CPRF most of all.

It was nonetheless true that the only Jew so far to have been elected a member of the upper chamber of the Russian parliament was a member of the CPRF from Amur Oblast, Pavel Shtein. Amur is a "red" region on the Russo-Chinese border, administered along traditional lines with government officials continuing to take their orders from the local communist party organization. On 7 November 1998, in the wake of the Makashov scandal, local communists gathered, as always at that time of year, to mark the anniversary of the 1917 Revolution at the local statue of Lenin. Television footage showed that the ceremony was attended by people of several different ethnic backgrounds, with a couple of Jewish faces unmistakably present. Despite the large number of anti-Semites among the top CPRF leadership, the CPRF does not, on the whole, appear to be an anti-Semitic party. Nor would it be entirely fair to claim that it preaches an anti-Semitic ideology.

CONCLUSION

Reporting on Zyuganov's visit to Paris in early 1999, a liberal Russian weekly quoted Zyuganov's French publisher as stressing the closeness of Zyuganov's ideas with those of the anticommunist Nobel prize winner, Aleksandr Solzhenitsyn. To claim an identity of views between the two men would of course be an exaggeration. Yet it would be no less inaccurate to dismiss the ideology of the CPRF as the product of a relatively limited party circle and its more or less reactionary allies. In reality, a number of the CPRF's more controversial tenets—such as its enthusiasm for geopolitics along with its belief in the allegedly unique "Eurasian" nature of Russian civilization—are increasingly widely held even by non-communist Russian intellectuals, while anti-Americanism is an almost universal sentiment among the population at large. As popular disappointment grows with the fruits of Yeltsin's political and economic reforms, the ideology of the CPRF seems destined to become more and more widely accepted among the Russian population.

Bibliography of Books by Gennadii Zyuganov

Zyuganov's ideas have been elaborated in hundreds of articles and interviews in Russian and Western media. Books by Gennadii Zyuganov include the following titles:

- *Sotsial'noe razvitie goroda i kommunisticheskoe vospitanie: problemy planomernogo sovershenstvovaniya gorodskogo obraza zhizni (Urban Social Development and Communist Education: Problems of the Planned Improvement of Urban Life)*, Moscow, Profizdat, *1982.*
- *Drama vlasti: stranitsy politicheskoi avtobiografii (The Drama of Power: Pages from a Political Autobiography)*, Moscow, Palea, *1993 (an anthology of Zyuganov's articles and speeches together with his own commentary).*
- *Derzhava (Great Power)*, Moscow, Informpechat', 1994.

- *Veryu v Rossiyu (I Believe in Russia),* Voronezh, "Voronezh" publishing house, 1995.
- *Za gorizontom (Beyond the Horizon),* Moscow, Informpechat', 1995. 2nd ed., Orel, Veshnie vody, 1995.
- *Sovremennaya russkaya ideya i gosudarstvo,* Moscow, Obozrevatel', 1995 (a collection of articles in which Zyuganov acted as chief editor and to which he contributed a long introduction).
- *Rossiya i sovremennyi mir,* Moscow, Obozrevatel' (together with the Russian-American University Corporation), 1995.
- *Rossiya pered vyborom,* Moscow, Obozrevatel' (together with the RAU Corporation), 1995.
- *Geografiya pobedy: osnovy rossiiskoi geopolitiki (The Geography of Victory: The Foundations of Russian Geopolitics),* Moscow [no publisher identified], 1997.
- *Uroki zhizni (Lessons of Life),* Moscow [no publisher identified], 1997.
- *Smysl' i delo Oktyabrya; Stat'i, issledovaniya, pis'ma (Meaning and Cause of October: Articles, Research Works and Letters),* Moscow, *Sovetskaya Rossiya*, 1997.
- *Oktyabr' i sovremennost' (October and Contemporaneity),* Moscow, Inform-Znanie, 1997.
- *Nevolnik chesti: Gosudarstvo, armiya, narod (Prisoner of Honor: State, Army, People),* Moscow, Foundation for Friendship with the Peoples of Arab States, 1997.
- *Dukhom okrepnem v borbe (Struggle Will Strengthen Our Spirit),* Moscow, Informpechat', 1998.
- *Pozitsiya KPRF v period krizisa: Avgust - Sentyabr' 1998 (Position of the CPRF during the Crisis Period: August-September 1998),* Moscow, Informpechat', 1998.

5: The CPRF at the Ballot Box

Until Mikhail Gorbachev came to power, the Soviet Union had an electoral system that its leaders claimed was more democratic than anyone else's but which, in reality, was condemned throughout the democratic world. The name of only one candidate, pre-selected by the CPSU, ever appeared on a ballot sheet. Gorbachev changed that by making contested elections the cornerstone of his reforms. His introduction to Russia and the rest of the USSR in 1989 of relatively free and democratic elections ("relatively," since Gorbachev's original concept did not envisage the creation of political parties in competition with the CPSU) was the beginning of the end for the Communist Party's grip on power.

And yet, as time passed, the various elections and referendums held in post-communist Russia facilitated the emergence of a new Communist Party—the CPRF—and enabled it to play an important role on the political scene. Skeptics argue that many of these elections, particularly those to legislatures at various levels, had little real impact on the distribution of power and the policy-making process. For the CPRF, however, the electoral process was important. Elections endowed the party with some respectability and provided it with a useful niche in local political institutions. For example, the regional committees of the CPRF (obkomy) consisted as a rule of the local CPRF representative to Russia's State Duma together with his (or, in rare cases, her) aides. If nothing else, this gave the regional CPRF organization the useful right to maintain an office in the local government headquarters.

Elections in the Soviet Period

Soviet citizens were regularly called upon to vote in regional and national elections. When they got to the polling booth, however, they were not presented with a real choice. Any candidate whose name was to be included on the ballot slip had to have received prior approval from the Communist Party and, to make doubly sure that only Party-friendly candidates were elected, all candidates stood unopposed. In theory, voters had the right to scratch the name of a candidate whom they did not support. In practice, such protests were rare and were disregarded when they took place. For this reason, western analysts sometimes used the word "selections" to describe elections in the USSR. Gorbachev's introduction of competition was accordingly one of his most radical reforms.

First "Real" Elections

The USSR's first nationally organized contested elections were for the USSR Congress of People's Deputies in March 1989. Almost 90 percent of the electorate went to the polls to elect a new national legislature. In a major departure from former Soviet practice, three-quarters of the seats were contested by two or more candidates. At that time, the CPSU was the only officially recognized political party and anyone who was anyone belonged to it. In the end, Communist Party members made up 87 percent of those elected to the Congress (compared to 71 percent in the Supreme Soviet it replaced). Party officials fared well in Central Asia. Party officials fared relatively poorly, however, in the RSFSR. In particular, the failure of fifty-eight top Party officials to win election served as the first indication of an ensuing split in the seemingly monolithic ruling party.

Elections to the RSFSR Congress of People's Deputies, and to regional and local Soviets in the RSFSR, were held during March 1990. Only a few weeks before, Article 6—which guaranteed the CPSU's monopoly on political power—had been removed from the Soviet Constitution. Although the official lists of candidates issued by the electoral authorities neglected to list candidates' political affiliations, elections in at least some Russian regions were held on what might be termed an "embryonic multi-party basis." That is to say, various political movements supported different competitors in a number of constituencies. The reform-minded "Democratic Russia" bloc of Yeltsin supporters won a landslide victory in Moscow, Leningrad and Sverdlovsk and secured about a third of the seats in the Congress as a whole. The "Democratic Russia" parliamentary faction was, nonetheless, outnumbered by that of the would-be CPRF, the "Communists of Russia" faction.

USSR and RSFSR Referendums Held

An all-Union referendum was held on March 17, 1991, in nine of the USSR's fifteen constituent republics. Gorbachev first called for such a referendum in December 1990. He did so in an effort to ward off the collapse of the Soviet Union by countering the declarations of independence issued earlier in 1990 by several Soviet republics, notably the three Baltic states, whose 1940 occupation by the Soviet army had never been recognized by the West. Other Soviet republics, including the RSFSR, were not at that time interested in independence but were bent on seeking more power for themselves at the expense of the all-Union center.

Gorbachev therefore proposed to "ask the people" to support the Union's integrity. Gorbachev's proposal was seized upon by conservatives in the Soviet parliament as an opportunity to mobilize public opinion not just for the integrity of the Soviet state but also in support of "socialism," that is, the CPSU. The question that finally appeared on the voting slips read: "Do you believe it necessary to preserve the USSR as a renewed federation of equal sovereign republics, where the rights and freedoms of a person of any nationality will be fully guaranteed?"

Six of the fifteen republics—Estonia, Latvia, Lithuania, Armenia, Georgia and Moldova—refused to conduct the referendum. However, they were small republics and 93 percent of the total Soviet population lived in the nine republics that did hold the referendum. There, 80 percent of the electorate took part, of which 76.4 percent voted "yes." In the RSFSR, turnout was 76 percent, with 71.3 percent voting in favor of a "renewed federation." Since some radical anti-Communists had campaigned against the referendum, the outcome was seen as a victory for the communist cause at that time and is often cited as such even today.

Another referendum was held in the RSFSR on March 17, 1991, the outcome of which enables us to call it one of those occasions when "both sides won." While the Gorbachev leadership sought to mobilize the "voice of the people" in support of the all-Union center, Yeltsin's team used the opportunity to strengthen its own position. They organized a companion referendum in which the population of the RSFSR was asked to approve the establishment of the post of RSFSR executive president, to be elected by universal suffrage. The RSFSR referendum was held on the same day as the all-Union referendum in hopes of counteracting resistance from pro-Communist regional authorities who might otherwise have refused to conduct such a ballot. As it was, four Russian autonomous republics (North Ossetia, Checheno-Ingushetia, Tatarstan and Tyva) refused to hold the RSFSR referendum. In other parts of Russia, however, the referendum yielded a turnout of 75 percent of eligible voters, of whom 69.8 percent voted in favor of the presidency.

The CP RSFSR called on voters to vote "yes" in the USSR referendum but rejected the RSFSR referendum as "inexpedient." Party leader Ivan Polozkov blasted the ensuing election of a Russian president as tantamount to reintroducing a "regime of personal power" in Russia and "turning away from people's democracy to a kind of monarchy." Establishing a presidency would, Polozkov predicted, "provoke a chain reaction ending in the appearance of dozens of new presidents."

Yeltsin Elected Russian President

The election of Russia's first executive president was held on June 12, 1991. As Polozkov had foreseen, it proved a grave setback to the Russian Communist Party. In theory, the CP RSFSR supported all those candidates who were CPSU members. While this excluded both Boris Yeltsin, who had left the Party a year earlier, and the unltranationalist maverick Vladimir Zhirinovsky, the Communists who stood for election spanned all points of the opinion spectrum in the CPSU at that time. They included former Soviet Minister of Internal Affairs and reform-minded Gorbachev ally Vadim Bakatin; moderate centrist and former Soviet Prime Minister Nikolai Ryzhkov; Aman-geldy Tuleev, an able administrator from Siberia's strike-ridden Kuzbass coal-mining region; and the extreme hard-line General Albert Makashov. In practice, Ryzhkov was the undoubted favorite of the Russian Communists.

With a turnout of 74.6 percent, the election was a triumph for Yeltsin, who won 57.3 percent of the vote in the first round, rendering unnecessary the need for a second ballot. Ryzhkov came in second with 16.8 percent of the vote while Zhirinovsky was third with 7.8 percent. (As an illustration of the evolution of the Russian Communist Party, it may be added that only one of the four Communists who ran in the 1991 presidential election—retired General Albert Makashov—eventually joined the CPRF. Ryzhkov and Tuleev chose instead to join the People's Patriotic Union of Russia, the electoral bloc of Communists and nationalists and Agrarians set up in August 1996, of which the CPRF was merely one of the members, albeit the leading one. Gorbachev ally Vadim Bakatin resigned from the CPSU shortly after the August 1991 coup.)

Elections in the Post-Soviet Period

The first vote in which the CPRF participated as an independent political party was the referendum called by Yeltsin during his first power-struggle with the Russian parliament, the Supreme Soviet. The referendum, held on April 25, 1993, was designed to free Yeltsin's hands in his battle with parliament. Voters were asked to answer four questions: (1) Whether they had confidence in the President of the Russian Federation; (2) Whether they had confidence in the President's social and economic policies; (3) Whether they favored early presidential elections; and (4) Whether they favored early parliamentary elections. As mentioned above, the CPRF Central Executive Committee called on the Party faithful to say "no" to the first, second and fourth question and "yes" to the third. Not surprisingly, the CPRF leaders failed to win their way with the voters on this occasion, yet their defeat was less ignominious than that of 1991. Over 62 percent of Russia's 105.5 million eligible voters took part in the referendum. President Yeltsin won 58.8 percent approval in the vote of confidence, while 56 percent expressed approval of his social and economic policies; 50.5 percent of those who voted said they favored early presidential elections, while the question about early parliamentary elections failed to win the 50 percent of the vote required to make it legally binding.

The results of the April 25 referendum did not give Yeltsin the go-ahead to dissolve the Congress of People's Deputies. He nonetheless signed such a decree on September 21, 1993. Following the firebombing of the parliament building and the arrest of leading Russian lawmakers in October 1993, Yeltsin called for yet another referendum. This one was held on December 12, 1993, at the same time as the elections to a new, bicameral Russian legislature, called the Federal Assembly. The referendum was held to approve a new Russian constitution establishing a strong presidential system in Russia. The constitution gave the president almost unlimited power over affairs of state, including the right to dissolve parliament, appoint government ministers without reference to parliament, veto laws even when they had been approved by both houses of parliament, and issue legally-binding presidential decrees.

The referendum was marred by the fact that the rules under which it was conducted violated the law on referendums as adopted by the Russian parliament in December 1990. While the law stipulated that any change of or amendment to the constitution required the prior approval of more than 50 percent of eligible voters, Yeltsin stipulated that the new constitution would be approved by a vote of 50 percent of the participants, as long as no fewer than 50 percent of eligible voters took part in the referendum. This reduced the minimum number of voters required for approval from over half to a quarter of eligible voters. And, while the law guaranteed the right of all citizens to campaign either for or against the referendum provisions, Yeltsin and his close political ally, Deputy Prime Minister Vladimir Shumeiko, forbade criticism of the draft constitution, threatening that any candidate criticizing it would be removed from the list of contestants.

According to official results, 54.8 percent of eligible voters took part in the referendum, of which 58.4 percent voted in favor of Yeltsin's new constitution. Like most of the other parties that took part in the December 1993 parliamentary elections, the CPRF called on voters to vote "no" in the referendum. Critics included virtually all the parties of democratic opposition, including the Democratic Party of Russia and the liberal Yabloko bloc led by reformist economist Grigorii Yavlinsky. In the following weeks, both western and Russian media published numerous reports alleging that large-scale fraud had taken place when the votes were counted. On at least one occasion, these allegations were upheld by a court of law. Neither the media allegations nor the court's ruling had any practical impact, however, and the constitution entered into force.

Elections to Federal Assembly

As stated above, the December 12, 1993, referendum on the new constitution was held along with elections to a new, bicameral Russian legislature, called the Federal Assembly. The lower chamber of the parliament, the State Duma, was for the first time since 1917 elected on a party basis. Half of its 450 members were elected in territorial constituencies while the other 225 were elected on the basis of party lists. A political party was required to score at least 5 percent of the popular vote to win representation in the Duma under the proportional representation system. The votes of any party attracting less than 5 percent were distributed on a proportional basis among those eight parties that did overcome the 5 percent barrier. The result was that the election was won by Russia's Democratic Choice, led by the father of Russian economic reform, Deputy Prime Minister (former acting Premier) Yegor Gaidar. In second place was the inappropriately named Liberal Democratic Party led by Vladimir Zhirinovsky. The CPRF was third, with 12.4 percent of the votes cast. This gave it 32 deputies elected on the party list; these were joined by ten communists elected in single-mandate constituencies, giving the CPRF a total of 42 deputies.

Elections to the upper chamber of the Federal Assembly, the Council of the Federation, were organized on a non-partisan basis in 1993. Each of the Russian Federation's 89 constituent republics and regions elected two senators. One of the 89, Chechnya, had by that time declared itself independent and refused to hold federal elections on its territory, meaning that Russia ended up with an upper chamber of 176 members. Most of those elected identified themselves as "non-partisan." At least thirteen, however, identified themselves as CPRF members, while others were well-known communist sympathizers.

The CPRF fared far better in the December 17, 1995, elections to the second Duma, suggesting that public dissatisfaction was growing with the Yeltsin regime. Whereas 6.7 million voters voted for the CPRF in

December 1993, two years later as many as 15.4 million (22.3 percent of those who voted) voted for the CPRF list. This allowed representatives of the Communist Party to occupy 99 of the 225 seats in the "federal" part of the State Duma. In addition, 60 CPRF candidates were elected in single-mandate constituencies. This made the CPRF the first of the four parties that overcame the 5 percent hurdle, well ahead of any other party. Together with their allies from the Agrarian Party and the nationalist "People's Power" movement, the CPRF controlled 211 (47 percent) of the seats in the second Duma.

By 1995, Yeltsin had persuaded the parliament to accept his preferred model for the upper house of the Federal Assembly, according to which the Council of Federation would not be elected directly by the population but the heads of the executive and legislature at regional level would occupy seats in the upper house ex officio. The new system did not reduce the number of CPRF representatives in the Russian Senate. On the contrary, at least 20 members of the CPRF (rather than 12 of the previous corps of Senators) secured seats in the upper house. Communists, Agrarians and their nationalist allies ended up with over 35 representatives in the upper house.

Zyuganov Loses Bid for Presidency

Contrary to the expectations of many observers, CPRF leader Gennadii Zyuganov lost the second Russian presidential election, in mid-1996, to Boris Yeltsin. Starting the year with a popular approval rating of only 6 percent, Yeltsin fought his way to a second term thanks to a skillfully run campaign that played on the population's fear of a return to communism. Television advertising, for example, contained footage of the destruction of churches by the Bolsheviks, warning that such scenes could reoccur if Zyuganov was elected president. In the first round, held on June 12, 1996, Zyuganov nonetheless secured the votes of 24.2 million participants, that is, 32 percent of the ballot. In the second round, on July 3, 1996, Zyuganov won 30.1 million votes (40.3 percent of the ballot).

Formation of the Popular Patriotic Union

Zyuganov's presidential campaign was followed by an important development that shaped future activities of the CPRF. This was the formation, in August 1996, of an electoral coalition between the CPRF and other left wing and patriotic organizations, including the Agrarian Party and the "People's Power" movement led by Nikolai Ryzhkov. Indeed, the establishment of the People's Patriotic Union of Russia (PPUoR) may have been no less significant an event for the CPRF than the party's own "founding-restoration" congress three and a half years earlier. A comparison of the two events sheds light on the policies and the ideology of the CPRF.

As detailed in Chapter 2, at its February 1993 founding congress, the CPRF rejected calls for it to become an umbrella organization of communist and left wing parties. At that time, the new party specifically chose not to ally the supposedly "red" CPRF with the various "white" nationalist groupings of great power statists (gosudarstvenniki). The reason for that decision seems to have lain less in the desire to broaden the CPRF's support on the eve of Russia's regional elections, than in the ideological transformation of the party's leaders.

Unlike the CPRF, the PPUoR had no formal membership. Nor did the deputies who were elected to parliament with PPUoR support ever form a PPUoR faction. But the existence of the bloc made it easier for the CPRF to support candidates who were not officially party members and to count on their support in time of need. Today, leaders of the CPRF as a rule cite the PPUoR rather than their own party's name in the course of any elections or vote.

Many noted observers have compared the creation of the PPUoR with earlier attempts to set up broad coalitions of communist and nationalist opponents of the "party of power," such as the National Salvation Front and Accord in the Name of Russia. However, the PPUoR seems to have been more reasonable and far less militant a body than the numerous "fronts" and "sobors" of the early 1990s. The PPUoR does count extremists among its ranks, but they do not represent the face of the new organization. With some notable exceptions, such as an overtly anti-Semitic address by a coal miner at the PPUoR's second congress, it seems to be safe to portray the PPUoR as the union of the CPRF with left-wing and Russian nationalist organizations and individuals more moderate than itself. Seen in this light, it is understandable why three prominent leaders of radical opposition organizations, all of whom had supported Zyuganov in the 1996 presidential election, refused to join the PPUoR when it was first founded. For example, deputy speaker of the State Duma Sergei Baburin was invited to join the PPUoR at the head of his Russian All-Union Sobor; Baburin refused to join the PPUoR, saying that he could not stand the domination of the CPRF apparatus over the new body. Stanislav Terekhov of the Union of Officers and Viktor Anpilov of Working Russia followed Baburin's example; they accused the PPUoR's founders of collusion with the Yeltsin regime and also refused to join the union.

The birth of the PPUoR was a logical step in a process that had a solid background in the form of the coalition of the three communist-dominated factions in the State Duma—the CPRF, the Agrarians and People's Power (Narodovlastie). Ostensibly, indeed, the CPRF did not even nominate a candidate in the Russian presidential election of 1996. Zyuganov stood as the nominee not of the CPRF but of a "Bloc of People's Patriotic Forces." Even so, the militantly anticommunist rhetoric of the Yeltsin campaign team was the most important factor in Yeltsin's unexpected electoral success (although abuse of the president's official position and some imaginative vote counting also seemed to play a part). Thereafter, the CPRF decided to downplay the "red" component during the forthcoming regional elections and to stress the theme of patriotism instead.

PPUoR's Founding Congress

The founding congress of the PPUoR opened on August 7, 1996, in the premises of the Russian parliamentary center. The 300 delegates who attended the gathering claimed to represent some 150 opposition parties and movements, but the CPRF, with its 20,000 primary cells in the provinces, was the only really strong body present. Other significant players were the All-Russian sociopolitical association "Spiritual Heritage" led by Aleksei Podberezkin, the Agrarian Party of Russia led by Mikhail Lapshin, and the "Great Power" (Derzhava) movement led by former Vice-president Aleksandr Rutskoi. Most of the rest of the participants were either completely unknown bodies, often referred to as "one-man organizations," or short-lived electoral blocs that had been set up on the eve of the 1995 parliamentary elections but had failed to overcome the 5 percent barrier.

The most striking feature at the PPUoR's founding congress was the complete absence in its documents of any mention of the word "communist" in any form. Nor could any intention on the part of the coalition's founders to reinstate socialism or Soviet rule be traced in the PPUoR's documents. Instead, the congress adopted a program that called for Russia's economy to be "socially oriented" and dedicated to the service of the majority of the country's citizens. The program promised that the PPUoR would support the armed services and the military industrial complex. It also stressed the necessity of protectionism in order to defend domestic industries and, in particular, Russia' lagging agricultural sector, against the predations of foreign products. The PPUoR's political program emphasized the intention of the founders to eliminate any possibility of violence or civil discord in Russia. The PPUoR declared its willingness to come to power by entirely peaceful means and in full accord with the Yeltsin constitution. At the same time, the body made no secret of its intention to amend the constitution in such a way as to give more say to the legislature at the expense of the executive, especially the president, whose powers under the 1993 constitution verged, at least on paper, on the dictatorial.

The PPUoR's founding congress opened with an address by the chairman of its Organization Committee, Nikolai Ryzhkov, who urged the audience to analyze the errors of their predecessors, such as the NSF or Russian National Assembly, that made them rather short-lived. According to Ryzhkov, the PPUoR's predecessors had lacked strong links between the leaders and the led. Coming to power, Ryzhkov asserted, was not an aim in itself for the PPUoR; it was more important for the PPUoR to establish mass support for a future Government of National Salvation. As Urban and Solovei note in their invaluable study of the CPRF, Ryzhkov's leadership "lent some credence to the potential viability of this new organization." In 1985-90, Ryzhkov had served as Gorbachev's Prime Minister. He was the first runner-up behind Yeltsin in the 1991 presidential election and served as leader of the People's Power faction in the Duma elected in December 1995. It seems safe to say that Ryzhkov's name gave the PPUoR a degree of respectability in the eyes of many Russians that other opposition organizations lacked.

Ryzhkov's address was followed by that of Zyuganov, who appealed to the patriotic sentiments of the audience. The aims of the PPUoR, Zyuganov stated, were shared by all of Russia and included the "reassertion of the country's independence, the preservation of civil peace, and the freedoms and rights of the individual." Spiritual Heritage leader Podberezkin followed with the assertion that the PPUoR was being established for a relatively long historic period—the coming twenty or thirty years. Its strategic aim, Podberezkin added, would be to "guide Russia into the role of world cultural and spiritual leader." The most interesting speech was, however, the address to the congress of Stanislav Govorukhin.

A famous film director and actor, Govorukhin was the author of a documentary entitled "We Can Not Live Like This Any Longer" that had played a key role in Yeltsin's election as speaker of the Russian parliament in July 1991. Govorukhin could, accordingly, be said to have made a crucial if unwitting contribution to the break-up of the USSR and the establishment of post-Soviet political systems in Russia and the other post-Soviet states. Govorukhin had been instrumental at another decisive moment when in August 1991 he rushed to Yeltsin's side and addressed rallies of coup-resisters at the Russian White House. As time passed, however, Govorukhin grew increasingly bitterly disillusioned with the ruling regime. The Yeltsin-authorized fire bombing of the Russian parliament on October 3 and 4, 1993 particularly infuriated him. Little wonder, therefore, that the documentaries Govorukhin made after the bloody events of 1993—"The Great Criminal Revolution" and "The Hour of the Rascal"—were censored for broadcast in Russia. In his address to the congress, Govorukhin warned against the presence of orthodox communists in the opposition movement and called for the creation of a "civilized and constructive opposition." The PPUoR, Govorukhin said, was not at all "a left-wing movement" but "a democratic movement." While Govorukhin's sincerity was not in doubt, he might perhaps have been better advised to seek other company for the realization of his democratic intentions.

At the congress, over 150 activists were elected to the PPUoR's Coordinating Committee, while twenty-one individuals made up the body's Presidium. Zyuganov was elected overall chairman of the PPUoR, and Ryzhkov chairman of its Executive Committee. Apart from Zyuganov, another five men—Govorukhin, Lapshin, Podberezkin, Rutskoi and Tuleev—were elected co-chairmen. (Rutskoi quit the PPUoR after being elected Governor of Kursk Oblast in November 1996.) It is worth stressing that only one of the PPUoR's seven leaders—Zyuganov—was a member of the CPRF. This answered the party's proclaimed intention on the eve of the congress to be an "equal among equals" and not to lord it over other PPUoR member-organizations. In accord with Russian law, the All-Russian public movement "People's Patriotic Union of Russia" was registered by the Ministry of Justice in October 1996.

PPUoR Election Strategy

The founders of the PPUoR made little secret of the immediate political targets of their efforts. Writing in the daily *Nezavisimaya Gazeta* on the eve of the congress, Rutskoi's former adviser, Andrei Fedorov, argued that the organization should not become a purely opposition body. The PPUoR should fight for power rather than merely against Yeltsin and Chubais, Fedorov went on. He outlined the following five points as the PPUoR's tasks: (1) Closing the gap between itself and the opposition coalition in the State Duma; (2) Rallying behind a joint candidate in each region in the course of the ensuing gubernatorial elections; (3) Preparing an effective electoral mechanism for the next parliamentary elections, due in 1999; (4) Preparing a similar electoral mechanism for the next presidential election, due in 2000; and (5) Effectively exercising power once it has been won. With hindsight, it seems worth noting that some of the five aims, listed by Fedorov, have been achieved, albeit only in part.

The second PPUoR congress opened on November 21, 1998, in the former ballroom of the Moscow Nobility's Assembly—the Hall of Columns. Following the proceedings, Zyuganov stated that the PPUoR would stand in the elections for the State Duma in December 1999, in "three columns"—that is, on the list of the CPRF proper, on the list of the hard-line Movement in Support of the Army, led by CPRF militants Viktor Ilyukhin and Albert Makashov, and on the list of Spiritual Heritage, the moderate movement headed by Podberezkin and the man who would later become Duma speaker. This seemed to many observers to indicate a split in the PPUoR's ranks at a decisive moment of its not so long history.

Between 1995 and 1997, gubernatorial elections were held in 69 regions of the Russian Federation. Candidates supported by the CPRF won 26 of these 69 contests. Of these 26 candidates, 21 had been nominated by the CPRF and its regional allies in the first round, while five were supported by the CPRF only in the second round. The campaign started rather unsuccessfully for the CPRF. The party backed candidates in ten of the 14 regions that held gubernatorial elections in 1995, but its candidates won in only two regions—Novosibirsk and Tambov Oblasts. In early 1996, a CPRF candidate ran in the gubernatorial election in St. Petersburg and lost in the first round. In the second round, however, the CPRF supported the eventual winner, Vladimir Yakovlev, and was therefore able to claim a share in his victory. Of the elections held in 52 regions in 1996 and 1997, the CPRF and its PPUoR allies ran candidates in 37, of whom 19 won.

The CPRF-PPUoR proved adept, too, at getting their candidates elected in the various local elections and Duma by-elections that are a permanent feature of Russian political life. Between 1993 and 1996, local legislatures were elected in thirty regions in the Russian Federation. The CPRF/PPUoR was successful in getting their members elected speakers in twelve of these bodies. In some local legislatures, the communist-nationalist bloc has formed factions.

The CPRF in the Regions

The importance of the regional aspect of the CPRF's activities is hard to exaggerate. The CPRF owes its strength and its very survival to the fact that it was, throughout the 1990s, the only party in Russia with a strong regional base. It was the provincial committees of the short-lived CP RSFSR and the provincial intelligentsia who preserved the party during the period when it was banned (August 1991 to November 1992). It was communists from the provinces who insisted in 1992, when the party was permitted to resume a legal existence, that the CPRF be restored in the tradition of the CPSU and CP RSFSR, rather than in the more modern way advocated by elitist comrades in Moscow and St. Petersburg. Last but not least, it was predominantly the people in the provinces who voted for the CPRF and PPUoR in national elections and who elected CPRF/PPUoR candidates in gubernatorial elections.

Geography of the Regions

The Russian Federation consists of eighty-nine component regions—known in the Constitution as "subjects of the Federation." These number twenty-one Republics, six Krais, forty-nine Oblasts, one Autonomous Oblast, ten Autonomous Okrugs, and the country's two largest cities—Moscow and St. Petersburg. In theory, all enjoy equal rights under the Constitution; in reality, some regions are more equal than others are. Furthermore, the eighty-nine include the breakaway North Caucausus Republic of Chechnya-Ichkeria, over which the federal government now has virtually no control.

Since Soviet times, the eighty-nine "subjects of the Federation" have been grouped into eleven economic zones: (1) North; (2) North-west; (3) Central; (4) Central Black Earth (Chernozyom); (5) Volgo-Vyatka; (6) Volga; (7) North Caucasus; (8) Ural; (9) Western Siberia; (10) Eastern Siberia and (11) Far East. Kaliningrad Oblast, Russia's enclave on the Baltic, forms a separate region since it is geographically isolated from the rest of the Russian Federation. However, the legacy of the Soviet period, when everything was run from Moscow, means that even today regional economic links are weak and the economic subdivisions have limited practical significance.

Political Coloration of the Regions

Politically, too, it is hard to divide the country into meaningful sub-units. Analysts often divide it into the "democratic" north and north west, that is, the regions where a majority of voters have traditionally voted for Yeltsin or for the parties and candidates that enjoyed his blessing; and the so-called "Red Belt" regions in the south and south-west of the country where voters have generally elected communist candidates. A "blue belt" of liberal regions including Novgorod, Nizhnii Novgorod, Samara, Saratov and Yaroslavl Oblasts has also been proposed. There is some truth to this schema but, as the following chapters show, Russia's political map is more complicated. In fact, few Russian regions can be painted in purely "white" or "red" terms. Taking into consideration all the ballots conducted in the given region during the 1990s, many would be better depicted in varying shades of "pink" or "cream."

The 1996 presidential election illustrates the general distribution of colors on the Russian political map. In the first round, Zyuganov won more votes than Yeltsin in forty of the eighty-nine regions. In the second round, however, Yeltsin won more votes than Zyuganov in eight of these forty regions. This was explained by the fact that, in the second round, Yeltsin won most of the votes that in the first round were cast for other contenders. The final result of the second round was, accordingly, that Yeltsin won in fifty-seven regions whereas Zyuganov won in thirty-two regions. Leaving aside the possibility that vote-rigging played any part in this outcome, these results suggest that fifty-seven regions could, in the summer of 1996, be described as "white" and thirty-two as "red," but that eight would be better described as somewhere between "pink" and "cream." While more regions were entirely "red" than were purely "white," a significant number proved reluctant to side with either of these two extremes and looked for something in between.

Formerly "White" Regions Now "Red"

One of the biggest surprises awaiting a student of elections conducted in Russia's regions since 1991 is that some of the "reddest" territories correspond with the historic sites of popular resistance to the Bolshevik regime during the Civil War of 1918-21 that followed the Bolshevik Revolution. Particularly striking is the case of Tambov Oblast in the Central Black Earth region. In 1920-22, Tambov was the site of the "Antonovshchina," a peasant rebellion against Bolshevik power. Nowadays, Tambov is a communist citadel. In 1995, CPRF member Aleksandr Ryabov was elected oblast Governor with 52.2 percent of the vote while, in the 1995 parliamentary elections, CPRF candidates won 40.3 percent of the vote in Tambov Oblast, almost twice the Russian average. In the 1996 presidential election, Zyuganov scored 62.8 percent of the Tambov vote against Yeltsin's 32.6 percent.

The interesting thing is that "red" Tambov is not an exception. The regions where the White Army was born—that is, the Kuban (Krasnodar Krai in the North Caucasus), neighboring Stavropol Krai and, to a lesser extent, the territory of the Don Cossacks in today's Rostov Oblast—were bastions of anti-Bolshevik resistance in the early 1920s but are centers of communist power today. In Omsk Oblast in Western

Siberia, Zyuganov won 47.5 percent in the second round of the 1996 presidential election, beating Yeltsin's 46.2 percent. During the Civil War, Omsk was the capital of General Kolchak's army, which opposed the imposition of Bolshevik power.

The most natural explanation for such a series of coincidences appears to be the innate conservatism of the local population. As for the members of the nomenklatura, loyalty to the ideas and values in which they were educated was more often found among provincial CPRF functionaries than among their Moscow comrades. Following the collapse of communist rule, many former members of the CPSU's regional nomenklatura proved quite unwilling to join the CPRF when it was set up in 1993. Exceptions to this rule were those officials who had been dismissed from their jobs in 1991 for cooperating with the August 1991 putsch, such as Ryabov in Tambov Oblast and Leonid Ivanchenko in Rostov Oblast. Both had been chairmen of the regional ispolkom (executive committee) before the collapse of Soviet power. More often than not, their more cautious colleagues joined the pro-government party, Our Home Is Russia (OHIR), led by Prime Minister Viktor Chernomyrdin. As a rule, such people made no secret of the fact that they remained communists in their hearts. For example, Yegor Stroev, Governor of Orel Oblast and Speaker of the Federation Council, delivered a panegyric to the CPSU when, in the summer of 1998, Zyuganov paid a visit to his native Orel. Later, he was promoted to the Politburo by Mikhail Gorbachev and given responsibility for agriculture. Stroev now enjoys the reputation of a moderate reformer. Yet, Stroev told Zyuganov that the country owed to the party all the good things in its modern history and, first and foremost, its victory in World War II.

In sharp contrast to Stroev, the governor of Ulyanovsk Oblast, Yurii Goryachev, is reputed to be a procommunist conservative, an advocate of "a gradual transition to the market economy," and a fan of food ration cards. Yet, Goryachev's party affiliation is of the same ambiguous nature as Stroev's. Ostensibly a member of OHR, Goryachev makes no secret of the fact that his true loyalty lies with the Communist Party. Moreover, Goryachev's hard-core predecessor as the first secretary of the Ulyanovsk Oblast Committee of the CPSU, Oleg Kazarov, refused to join the CPRF. Kazarov acquired notoriety as a deputy of the RSFSR Congress of People's Deputies in 1990 and early 1991, when his speeches attacked all the reformers, including Gorbachev, Yakovlev and Yeltsin. As a hard-liner, Kazarov was removed from Party office by Gorbachev. Following the collapse of the August 1991 coup, Kazarov chaired the board of the Ulyanovsk branch of the Russian Savings Bank. In December 1995, he was elected to a seat in the State Duma as an independent from one of Ulyanovsk's single-mandate districts. Today's head of the Ulyanovsk Obkom of the CPRF, Aleksandr Kruglikov, was, prior to his election, a deputy of the State Duma; in 1995 he served as an associate professor in the Ulyanovsk Institute for the Training of Public Education Personnel. The first secretary of the Orel CPRF Oblast Committee, Aleksei Zotikov, is a former professor of the Orel Institute of Culture.

Nomenklatura Background Typical for Region Functionaries

Since the departure from Nizhnii Novgorod of Boris Nemtsov, no representative of the so-called "party of power" remains in the Russian gubernatorial ranks who does not have a background in either the Party or the administrative nomenklatura (once known as "Partkhozaktiv"). In contrast, there are at least two such newcomers among those governors who are members of the CPRF—the Governor of Bryansk Oblast, former journalist Yurii Lodkin, and the Governor of Stavropol Krai, Aleksandr Chernogorov, formerly a senior lecturer at the Stavropol Legal University.

Along with representatives of the regional intelligentsia, many members of the second-ranking nomenklatura—second secretaries of the RSFSR Obkoms, City and district Party committees—joined the ranks of the CPRF when the party was set up in 1993. This helps to explain why the buildings, methods, work ethic and, above all, the personnel of the old regional and district party organizations have been safely transferred from the old CPSU bodies to the new executive organs. In terms of the modern Russian official hierarchy, "the first secretary of the regional committee of the CPRF" means a deputy of the State Duma, elected either in a local single-mandate constituency or by the CPRF party list, while the title of "the first secretary of the city committee of the CPRF" (gorkom) would be translated into modern bureaucratic Russian as an aide to a Duma deputy (alias the Obkom secretary). When the author visited such a first secretary in Pskov, she was told that Mr. Nikitin was away in his native village, helping his parents with digging potatoes.

Support for CPRF Varies by Region

Surprisingly enough, the strength and prominence of the CPRF in a given region does not necessarily correspond with the willingness of the local population to vote for the CPRF-PPUoR when elections are held. In the 1989 elections to the USSR Congress of People's Deputies, voters in the city of Leningrad (since renamed St. Petersburg) blackballed every one of the CPSU officials who stood for election. St. Petersburg voters have continued to vote that way ever since. This is so despite the fact that the CPRF was conceived, if not born, in Leningrad. It was there, in January 1990, that the Communist Initiative movement was founded with the specific aim of establishing a Communist Party of the RSFSR. The Leningrad Oblast CPRF was the first (and so far the only) regional CPRF organization to have its own Internet page.

The opposite phenomenon may be observed in the Republic of North Ossetia in the North Caucasus. There, the electorate has voted for communists in all elections and referendums without exception. The president of the republic is Aleksandr Dzasokhov, former head of the CPSU in the republic, who was elected in 1998 with 75.7 percent of the vote. And yet the CPRF itself does not have a strong presence in the republic. Few people outside the republic had even heard of the North Ossetian branch of the CPRF until it split during the January 1998 election for republic president.

Some analysts have argued that the Russian political map echoes the global pattern of "poor South versus rich North." They argued, however, on the mistaken belief that Russia's "red" south was poorer than its "white," non-communist north. But the analogy is misleading and based on the deliberately skewed structure of wages in the Soviet period. A study undertaken six months after the 1996 presidential election by Russia's State Statistics Committee (Goskomstat) found that life expectancy in the regions that voted for Zyuganov was almost four years higher on average than in those that voted for Yeltsin. While the average life expectancy for Russian males was 58.3 years in 1996, in "Zyuganov's" regions it was 61 years and in "Yeltsin's" regions it was 57.1 years. And while the average life expectancy for Russian women was 71.7 years, in "Zyuganov's" regions it was 71 years and in "Yeltsin's" it was 70.2 years. According to Goskomstat, voters in the agricultural south, where support for Zyuganov was high, tended to be healthier but older and less well educated than those in Yeltsin's industrial north. One explanation for this, of course, is the fact that three out of four Russians were, in the 1990s, dependent on the food they cultivated themselves on their land allotments and at their dachas. In such circumstances, anyone with a private plot in the fertile "Red Belt" would be likely to be better fed than an industrial worker in Russia's inhospitable far north.

Strangely enough, the CPRF often wins elections to regional legislatures in "white" regions, which do not vote for communists in either federal or gubernatorial elections, and vice versa. Two of Russia's most reform-minded regional executives were elected in regions where Zyuganov did better than Yeltsin in the 1996 presidential election. They are Semen Zubakin of the Altai Republic, the only member of Gaidar's Russia's Democratic Choice party to have won a gubernatorial election, and Nikolai Fedorov of Chuvashia.

Electoral Fraud

A problem facing any analyst of Russian politics is the fact that it would be an exaggeration to call any election ever conducted in Russia as fully free and fair. Doubts have been expressed about the reliability of official electoral returns in all elections held in Russia since 1993. Moreover, in some places they are even less fair than in others. Some may be less rigged than others, if local authorities have no vested interest. Finally, there are certain remote regions, such as the Tyva Republic, the population of which tends to vote for whoever is in power at the time of the ballot. Any categorization of regions by electoral preference is therefore likely to be no more than "relatively" accurate. Skeptics have, for example, argued, apparently with some justification, that Yeltsin would never have won the 1996 elections had they been really free and fair.

For example, official electoral returns in the breakaway North Caucasian Republic of Chechnya-Ichkeria cannot be taken with anything other than a pinch of salt. Chechnya proclaimed itself independent from Russia in late 1991 and has refused to conduct federal elections and referendums ever since. In 1994-6, the republic was invaded by the Russian army, which sought to install a puppet government headed by the former first secretary of the Checheno-Ingushetian regional Communist Party Committee. The republic was subjected to massive aerial bombardment that caused thousands of civilian casualties and a massive refugee exodus. Yet, if one is to believe Russia's Central Electoral Commission (CEC), 67.7 percent of Chechnya's eligible voters took part in elections to the federal parliament on December 17, 1995, 72.9 percent in the first round of the presidential election on June 16, 1996, and 74.3 percent in the second round on July 3, 1996. While the results of Chechnya's elections have never been officially repudiated, they have not been recognized by independent monitors, either.

Official electoral results in Russia's other North Caucasus republics—Adygeya, Dagestan, Ingushetia, Kabardino-Balkaria, Karachaevo-Cherkessia and North Ossetia—also give rise to doubt. With the exception of Adygeya, turnouts in the second round of the 1996 presidential election were higher than in the first round. And yet, in all six republics without exception, fewer people voted for Zyuganov in the second round than in the first. Only in Dagestan did the local CPRF question this unusual result. The CEC then discovered that the number of ballot-papers distributed in Dagestan outnumbered the adult population by eleven thousand. When the results were recalculated, Yeltsin's total dropped by some 4,500 votes and Zyuganov's by 11,000. The CEC punished the chairman of Dagestan's electoral commission only by reducing the size of his bonus.

Violations were reported in several other parts of Russia during the 1996 presidential election. The chairman of the electoral commission from Moscow district polling station No. 1117, Vladimir Chudin, complained to the CEC about an order he and other election officials received from their superior, territorial electoral commission chairwoman N.V. Sosnina. According to Chudin, Sosnina ordered the heads of all the district electoral commissions under her supervision to give her, along with their completed election returns, two additional blank forms, stamped and signed by all their members. The CEC ignored Chudin's complaint.

Attempts to Prosecute Electoral Fraud

Russia's Supreme Court did, however, instruct the Supreme Court of Tatarstan to prosecute officials guilty of engaging in fraud in the first round of the 1996 presidential elections. The ruling arose out of a complaint by a CPRF election monitor, Vadim Solov'ev, who uncovered discrepancies between the election returns in some republic polling stations and those in the summary table issued by the territorial commission. In one instance, Yeltsin received 23,428 votes in the initial count but 27,428 in the summary table. It turned out that 4,000 ballots had been transferred to his total from the tallies of his competitors: Zyuganov lost 1,285 votes, Yavlinsky 897, Zhirinovsky 205, and Aleksandr Lebed 1,192. Even outsider Vladimir Bryntsalov lost 13 of his miserable 64 votes. When the results were compared throughout Tatarstan, it turned out that Yeltsin had been awarded 20 percent more votes than he had really earned, whereas Yavlinsky had lost 21 percent, Lebed 27, Zhirinovsky 36, Gorbachev 42, and Martin Shakkum 50 percent. Zyuganov escaped relatively lightly, losing only 13 percent of his votes. Tatarstan's Supreme Court duly examined the issue and found that irregularities had indeed taken place. The court did not, however, mete out any punishments or try to overturn the election results.

In all fairness, it should be said that not all known instances of fraud in the 1996 presidential election went unpunished. At the beginning of 1997, Lydia Burimova, a district official from Stavropol Krai, was tried and found guilty of having tampered with the ballot in favor of Yeltsin.

She was given a suspended two-year prison sentence and required to pay a fine. The chairpersons of two local polling commissions, who were found guilty of fraud along with Burimova, were also fined. In neighboring Rostov Oblast, a city court in the town of Azov heard the case of the chairman of a local electoral commission. The chairman, identified as Denisov, was accused of submitting a fraudulent electoral report giving Yeltsin 615 votes to Zyuganov's 226, whereas the real tally was the precise opposite. He was found guilty and required to pay a fine of two million rubles. A similar attempt to prosecute five officials in Kemerovo Oblast was dismissed by the regional court on the grounds that the offense was too small to worry about.

Scare Tactics Ensure Fraud

The allegations of electoral violations that followed the 1996 presidential election differed in one small but significant detail from those that followed the December 1993 referendum on Russia's new constitution. While in 1993 violations tended to be exposed by non-communist monitors, in 1996 almost all the whistle-blowers were from the CPRF. And while CPRF monitors estimated that in 1996 Zyuganov lost about 7 percent of his votes through election fraud, the party accepted the defeat of their leader without objection, just as they had accepted the results of all the other elections and referendums held in Russia.

According to Yeltsin's entourage, the president owed his 1996 victory primarily to the support of the heads of regional administrations. Although the Law on the Election of the President stipulates that no holder of state office may campaign in a presidential election in any way, Yeltsin issued a decree after his reelection in which he thanked by name the presidents of all the republics and the governors of the regions where he had won a majority of the vote. His gratitude was not misplaced. In all the "criminal" cases detailed above, electoral officials stooped to fraud not so much because they were ardent supporters of Yeltsin, but because the heads of the regional administrations threatened to fire them if Yeltsin lost in their respective districts. At the time of the 1996 election, most of Russia's regional governors had been personally appointed by the president, not democratically elected by the population, while the heads of city and district administrations were appointed by the governor. Nor was fraud the only way in which local leaders could harm the electoral chances of Yeltsin's competitors. They could deny a candidate access to regional media. They could ensure that he was prevented from meeting with voters. Most often, they scared voters with stories that Moscow would stop paying salaries and subsidies if the local population voted against Yeltsin.

We now turn in Chapters 6-12 to a detailed examination of the performance of the CPRF in the elections held in various regions of the Russian Federation.

6: The CPRF in the Regions: The "Red Belt"

A glance at the Russian political map reveals a swath of regions in the central parts of the country that consistently vote for Communist candidates. Dubbed the "Red Belt," it is an appropriate place at which to begin an examination of the CPRF's strength in the regions.

Central Economic Zone

The strongest supporters of the CPRF are found in the Central economic zone[16]—one of the eleven economic zones into which Russia's regions are loosely divided. Even here, however, the picture is not simple. The Central zone is split into "red," "pink" and "white" regions. Forming the core of the "Red Belt" are Bryansk, Orel, Ryazan and Smolensk Oblasts, all of which belong to the Central economic zone and which are discussed in this chapter. Other member-regions of the Central zone are "pink" at best. Others—most notably Moscow City and Moscow Oblast—do not at all conform to the left-leaning inclinations of their "Red Belt" neighbors. These "white" regions will be discussed in Chapter 7.

"Red" Core

Bryansk, Orel, Ryazan and Smolensk Oblasts are strikingly consistent. Thus we find that, in the referendum of March 1991 on the introduction of an executive presidency in Russia, a majority of voters in each of these four regions voted against (that is, against the policy identified with Boris Yeltsin). In Bryansk Oblast, those supporting the idea of an executive presidency numbered only 44.4 percent, in Orel it was 46.3 percent, in Ryazan it was 49.8 percent, and in Smolensk it was 40.2 percent. For Russia as a whole, by contrast, the average was 69.9 percent. Similarly, the nationwide referendum of April 1993, in which voters were asked to choose between the president and the anti-Yeltsin parliamentary opposition, resulted in defeat for the anti-Yeltsin opposition in much of Russia, the "Red Belt" excepted. In Bryansk Oblast, only 44.2 percent voted in support of Yeltsin; the figure was 42.6 in Orel; 50.6 percent in Ryazan; and 42.8 percent in Smolensk. This contrasted with an average of 58.8 percent for Russia in its entirety.

16. The Central economic zone consists of Moscow City and Moscow Oblast in addition to Bryansk, Ivanovo, Kaluga, Kostroma, Orel, Ryazan, Smolensk, Tula, Tver, Vladimir and Yaroslavl Oblasts.

Voters in all four of the hardcore "Red Belt" oblasts voted for Communist candidates in the parliamentary elections of 1993 and 1995. In the presidential election of 1996, voters in the four core regions supported Gennadii Zyuganov against Boris Yeltsin. The governors of all four regions were elected with Communist Party support, while the speakers of the Bryansk, Orel and Ryazan regional legislatures-who acted as representatives for these regions in the Council of the Federation—were all CPRF members.

Bryansk Oblast

Bryansk is the archetypal "Red Belt" region. Situated in Russia's Central Black Earth Region, it is one of the poorest regions in the country. In April 1993, it was one of only a handful of Russian regions in which President Boris Yeltsin permitted the holding of a direct gubernatorial election. (At that time, the Russian President still appointed the chief executives in almost all of Russia's krais and oblasts.) Yeltsin's reformist protege lost the election to Yurii Lodkin, who was supported by local communists. Lodkin, who had been a Communist Party functionary in Soviet times, strongly opposed the economic program of the Yeltsin government. Bryansk was one of the small number of Russian regions where Yeltsin's dissolution of the Supreme Soviet was denounced not only by the regional Soviet but also by Lodkin. Seeking to make an example of him, Yeltsin dismissed Lodkin from his post. Local inhabitants demonstrated against Lodkin's removal and, while they were not immediately successful in securing his return to power, opposition took root. Bryansk voters overwhelmingly supported Zyuganov in the June 1996 presidential election: while Zyuganov won 48 percent of the votes in the region, Yeltsin won only 26 percent.

Meanwhile, regional politics were paralyzed by conflict. When a gubernatorial election was held in December 1996, Lodkin beat the Yeltsin-appointed incumbent by 53 percent to 27 percent.[17] The Bryansk city council restored its old name, Soviet of People's Deputies, while municipal charters were adopted that abolished direct popular election of local heads of administration. Presidential aide Aleksandr Kazakov announced that the Kremlin was willing to work with almost all of the new governors but drew the line at Lodkin. Since his election, social and economic conditions in the oblast have continued to deteriorate.[18]

---

17. *Itar-Tass,* December 9, 1996; OMRI Russian Regional Report, December 11, 1996.

18. *Moskovskiye novosti* , February 16, 1997, p 7.

Orel Oblast

Orel borders on Bryansk Oblast and is another clear member of the "Red Belt." Like Bryansk, it was in April 1993 one of the handful of Russian regions permitted to hold a direct gubernatorial election. In Orel, the Communist candidate, Yegor Stroev, a native of Orel, won the election. During the Soviet period, Stroev headed the Oblast Committee of the CPSU until 1989, when Mikhail Gorbachev brought him to Moscow as Secretary of the CPSU Central Committee with responsibility for agriculture; in 1990, Gorbachev promoted Stroev to membership in the CPSU Politburo.

Following the 1991 coup, however, Stroev avoided joining any of Russia's new Communist parties and instead went to work in a research institute in Orel. Stroev had the support of the local Communist party organization, however, when he ran in the gubernatorial election in 1993 and won 52.9 percent of the votes, while the pro-Yeltsin candidate won only 34.2 percent.[19] After his 1993 election, Stroev was one of several Communist regional leaders who opted for cooperation rather than confrontation with the federal government.[20] Stroev soon acquired a reputation as a reformer and a moderate. In 1995, Yeltsin recommended him as Speaker of the Council of the Federation, a post he has occupied ever since. When, in October 1995, he ran for reelection as Governor of Orel, he won by a landslide 97 percent (the highest percentage recorded in a Russian regional election since the Soviet era).[21] Stroev subsequently joined the "party of power," the movement "Our Home is Russia" led by one-time Prime Minister Viktor Chernomyrdin. And yet he neglected no opportunity to voice his admiration for the CPSU in public appearances, such as Zyuganov's visit to Orel in August 1998.[22] As for Orel, it remained squarely in the "Red Belt." In March 1997, the CPRF won a majority of the seats in the Orel City Soviet, while a Communist, Aleksandr Kislyakov, was elected mayor of the regional capital that same year.[23]

19. Author's interview with Aleksei Zotikov, head of the Orel Oblast Committee of the CPRF, May 13, 1998.

20. *IEWS Russian Regional Report*, No. 34, 9 October 1997.

21. *Nezavisimaya Gazeta*, October 11 and 28, 1997, and *Izvestiya*, October 28, 1997.

22. Stroev's address was broadcast by Russian TV on August 3, 1998.

23. *Moskovskie novosti*, No. 12, 1997, p. 2.

Ryazan Oblast

Located in the middle of European Russia, southeast of Moscow, the region is firmly in the "Red Belt." In the 1996 presidential election, Zyuganov won a strong margin of support in the oblast, while Communist candidates swept the board in elections to the Ryazan City Soviet. In a gubernatorial election held in December 1996, Communist Vyacheslav Lyubimov defeated the pro-Yeltsin incumbent with 58 percent of the vote.[24] A Party official in Ryazan in the 1980s, Lyubimov was a leading member of the regional CPRF organization; he deplored "shock therapy" and the free sale of land and supported the restoration of a state-run economy.

Before long, Ryazan had become the focus of a new phenomenon—the campaign of regional lawmakers for Yeltsin's resignation. In May 1998, the Ryazan Oblast Duma unanimously approved a resolution calling on Yeltsin to resign "in order to save Russia from the threat of imminent collapse."[25] Within days, the oblast Duma in nearby Yaroslavl responded with a resolution supporting the State Duma's efforts to impeach Yeltsin; their example was followed by the regional legislatures in Tula, Belgorod and numerous other oblasts, all of which called for Yeltsin's resignation.[26]

Smolensk Oblast

The short history of gubernatorial elections in Smolensk Oblast exemplifies the complex nature of the CPRF's relations with Russia's "red governors." Smolensk borders on Bryansk Oblast and was, like Orel, one of the few Russian regions where Yeltsin permitted direct gubernatorial elections to be held in April 1993. The CPRF proposed the candidacy of a local manager, Anatolii Glushenkov, a Smolensk native who had been a low-ranking CPSU official in the 1970s and later a factory manager. With Communist support and running on a platform calling for a slower pace of change, Glushenkov defeated the reformist incumbent by 41.2 percent to 30.4 percent. Communist candidates went on to score a decisive victory in local government elections in Smolensk Oblast in January 1997, winning fifteen of the twenty-five seats in the Smolensk City Duma. The Duma promptly renamed itself the "City Soviet."[27]

When, five years later, Glushenkov's term ended, the social and economic situation in the region had deteriorated. Industrial output in the

24. *OMRI Daily Digest*, December 30, 1996.

25. Russian Independent Television (NTV), May 25, 1998.

26. *Nezavisimaya Gazeta* and *Izvestiya*, July 1, 1998.

27. *Pravda*, January 14 and 15, 1997.

Oblast fell, as did agricultural productivity, plunging one in every five residents of the region below the poverty line.[28] As a result, the CPRF withdrew its support from Glushenkov, turning instead to the 45-year-old Mayor of Smolensk, Aleksandr Prokhorov. Such was the strength of Communist support among the regional electorate that all seven candidates who took part in the April 1998 gubernatorial election proclaimed themselves true Communists and publicly showed off their old Communist Party cards. Thanks to the support of the CPRF and of Zyuganov personally, Prokhorov defeated Glushenkov by 67 percent to 26.5 percent.[29]

Kaluga, Kostroma, Tula and Vladimir Oblasts

These four oblasts may be termed "pink." Although Yeltsin won a majority of votes in the 1996 presidential election in all of them, the CPRF got its revenge when, in subsequent gubernatorial elections, its candidates defeated pro-Yeltsin incumbents.

In a gubernatorial election in Kaluga Oblast in November 1996, for example, opposition candidate Valerii Sudarenkov defeated Yeltsin-appointee Oleg Savchenko with 63 percent of the vote.[30] Sudarenkov, who was backed by local communist groups, began full-time work for the CPSU in 1972. In the mid-1980s, he was first secretary of the Kaluga Oblast Committee of the CPSU; since 1993, he had been chairman of the regional legislature.

In Kostroma Oblast in December 1996, opposition candidate Viktor Shershunov defeated Yeltsin-appointee Valerii Arbuzov with 64 percent of the vote. Shershunov was backed by the local Communist Party, Aleksandr Rutskoi's Derzhava (Great Power) movement, the Congress of Russian Communities and Aleksandr Lebed's Honor and Motherland movement.[31]

Also in December 1996, CPRF member Nikolai Vinogradov defeated Yeltsin-appointee Yurii Vlasov in a gubernatorial election in Vladimir Oblast. Vinogradov, who had made his early career in the CPSU and was a member of the Central Executive Committee of the CPRF from 1993-95, won 62.2 percent of the vote to Vlasov's 27.3 percent. [32]

28. *Nezavisimaya Gazeta*, April 8, 1998.

29. *Sovetskaya Rossiya*, March 19 and May 12, 1998; *Nezavisimaya Gazeta*, April 8, 24 and 28, May 15 and 19, 1998.

30. *Itar-Tass*, November 10, 1996.

31. *OMRI Daily Digest*, December 30, 1996.

32. *Kommersant-Daily*, December 10, 1996.

In Tula Oblast in March 1997, Vasilii Starodubtsev defeated incumbent Nikolai Sevryugin, a member of Our Home is Russia who had been appointed governor by Yeltsin in 1991. Starodubtsev, a strong opponent of private land ownership, was a former chairman of a collective farm and a leader of the Agrarian Party. He had also been one of the leaders of the abortive coup that provoked the collapse of the USSR. Backed by the Agrarians and the CPRF, Starodubtsev won 62.8 percent of the vote, whereas Sevryugin came in third with a mere 4.8 percent.[33]

In at least two of these regions, the victorious "red" governors owed much of their success to the unpopularity of their predecessors, none of whom had been elected but who were appointed to their offices by presidential decree. Vladimir Oblast's Vlasov, appointed governor by Yeltsin in 1991, owed his bad reputation to his arrogance and authoritarian style. His victory was also attributed to splits in the democratic camp, which meant that no fewer than four democratic candidates ran for governor. Vladimir voters were, moreover, said to be angry about falling living standards and to have voted communist in protest.

Even more striking was Sevryugin's defeat in Tula. Sevryugin was unpopular because of the economic problems that the oblast—virtually synonymous with weapons manufacture—had suffered after Russia's market reforms began. Immensely unpopular in the Oblast, Sevryugin was arrested and charged with corruption within days of relinquishing the post of governor.[34] The exception to the trend outlined here is Tver Oblast, where the reformist governor Vladimir Platov, elected in 1995, has so far managed to resist Communist efforts to remove him from office.[35]

Central Black Earth Zone

All five oblasts of Russia's Central Black Earth economic zone—Belgorod, Kursk, Lipetsk, Tambov and Voronezh—are essentially "red" provinces. Since 1993, Yeltsin's supporters have lost every federal election and referendum in these five regions. In the March 1991 referendum on the introduction of an executive presidency, however, returns in these regions did not significantly differ from the average for Russia as a whole (69.9 percent in favor). In June 1991, when Russia elected its first president,

33. *Itar-Tass*, March 24, 1997.

34. *Interfax*, June 6, 1997; *Izvestiya*, April 2, May 15 and 30, July 9 and 27, 1998.

35. *Itar-Tass*, May 30, 1997. See also, *IEWS Russian Regional Report*, June 4, 1998.

Yeltsin came in first in each of these oblasts, with scores ranging from 61.9 percent in Lipetsk Oblast to 44.6 percent in Tambov. Indeed, he won more votes than all four Communist candidates combined. Only two years later, however, in the April 1993 referendum in which voters were asked to choose between president and parliament, Yeltsin scored a record low of 39.6 percent in Belgorod Oblast. In Kursk Oblast, he scored 42.1 percent; in Lipetsk 49.2; in Tambov 44.0 percent; and in Voronezh 49.7 percent (contrasted with an average of 58.8 percent in Russia as a whole). Then, in December 1993, a majority of voters in all Central Black Earth regions voted against Yeltsin's new constitution. Only 45 percent of voters approved it in Belgorod Oblast; 42.1 percent in Kursk; 42.4 percent in Lipetsk; 44.0 percent in Tambov; and 49.7 percent in Voronezh.

In the parliamentary elections held in 1993 and 1995, the vote for the CPRF party list in all the regions in the Central Black Earth zone was well above the average for Russia as a whole. The only exception came in 1993 in Kursk Oblast, where Vladimir Zhirinovsky's misnamed and chauvinistic Liberal Democratic Party (LDPR) swept the board. In 1995, however, the communist-led People's Patriotic Union of Russia (PPUoR) coalition scored a clear majority throughout the Central Black Earth zone. In Belgorod Oblast, for example, 36.3 percent of voters voted for the CPRF in 1995 while the left-wing parties, taken together, scored a total of 48.5 percent overall. In Kursk Oblast, the corresponding returns were 28.3 percent and 66.6 percent; in Lipetsk Oblast 29.0 percent and 50.1 percent; in Tambov Oblast, 40.3 percent and 54.1 percent; and in Voronezh Oblast, 26.8 percent and 41.7 percent.[36] Members of the CPRF or PPUoR won a majority of single-mandate seats in this zone, too. Former USSR Prime Minister Nikolai Ryzhkov, leader of People's Power, a key component of the PPUoR coalition, for example, won the single-member seat in Belgorod. The exception to the rule was Ivan Rybkin, a founder member of the CPRF who later defected to the Yeltsin camp. In December 1995, Rybkin was elected to the State Duma in a single-mandate constituency in his native Voronezh Oblast. But when, in 1996, two by-elections were held in Voronezh, they were won by moderate Russian nationalists—Dmitrii

36. Apart from the CPRF, the "left" parties in the 1995 parliamentary elections included the following: Agrarian party of Mikhail Lapshin, People's Power of Nikolai Ryzhkov and Sergei Baburin, Aleksandr Rutskoi's Derzhava, and the "Communists-Working Russia-For the Soviet Union" bloc embracing various communist groupings to the left of the CPRF, such as Tyul'kin's, Anpilov's and Prigarin's communist parties.

Rogozin, leader of the Congress of Russian Communities, and Elena Panina, leader of the Zemstvo movement (a movement organized to campaign for the reinstatement of the system of self-government that had existed in Russia in the late nineteenth century).

Belgorod Oblast

In the December 1993 elections to the upper chamber of the Russian parliament, the Council of the Federation, pro-Yeltsin candidates were defeated in two regions of the Central Black Earth zone. In Belgorod, the appointed mayor of the provincial capital, Ivan Gusarov, and the first deputy Governor of the oblast, Nikolai Melentev, lost to Aleksei Ponomorev, prorector of the Belgorod Agricultural Institute of Higher Education, and the chairman of the Oblast Soviet, Mikhail Beskhmelnitsyn, respectively. (December 1993 was the only time the members of Russia's "Senate" ran for election; thereafter, they were appointed ex officio.) The "party of power" got its revenge two years later when, in December 1995, Evgenii Savchenko distinguished himself as the only officially supported candidate to win a gubernatorial election in the entire Black Earth zone. To illustrate the complicated nature of relations between communist and anti-Communist "parties," it may be pointed out that both Ponomarev and Beskhmelnitsyn ran as independent candidates in the 1993 Senate elections. As for Savchenko, he had served in the 1980s as a secretary of the Belgorod Oblast Committee of the CPSU. Like many former Soviet officials, he quit the CPSU following the collapse of the August 1991 coup. In October 1983, Yeltsin appointed Savchenko governor of Belgorod Oblast as part of the mass replacement of those governors who had opposed the president's September 1993 dissolution of the Russian parliament.

Tambov Oblast

In Tambov, both the head of the Oblast administration Vladimir Babenko and his first deputy Lyudmila Kudinova lost in the elections to the Council of the Federation to members of the CPRF, Aleksandr Ryabov and Pavel Gorbunov. This time, it was the CPRF that avenged itself when, in December 1995, Ryabov was elected governor of Tambov Oblast. Formerly head of the Oblast committee of the CPSU, Ryabov had been elected chairman of the Tambov Oblast Soviet in 1990. He was removed from that position and charged with high treason for supporting the putschists during the August 1991 coup, though the case against him was eventually dropped for lack of evidence. Reelected chairman of the Oblast legislature, Ryabov publicly supported the Supreme Soviet when Yeltsin dissolved it in September 1993.37 He came to prominence in 1997 when, in his capacity as a leading member of the Federation Council, he launched an investigation into the appeal by then Deputy Prime Minister Boris Nemtsov to foreign businessmen to not invest in regions where gubernatorial elections had been won by Communists.[38]

Kursk, Lipetsk and Voronezh Oblasts

In all three regions, pro-Yeltsin candidates were elected to the Council of the Federation in 1993 but defeated in gubernatorial elections a few years later. However, only one of the newly elected governors was a member of the CPRF—Voronezh Oblast Governor Ivan Shabanov. In Lipetsk, the then chairman of the Oblast Legislative Assembly, Oleg Korolev, was backed in the gubernatorial election not only by the opposition but also by many Yeltsin supporters.[39] His rival, Mikhail Narolin, was elected governor in April 1993 in what was widely reputed to be a rigged ballot.[40] In December of that year, both Narolin and Korolev were elected to represent Lipetsk Oblast in the Federation Council, where Korolev subsequently served as first deputy chairman.

The October 1996 gubernatorial election in Kursk Oblast was the most dramatic event so far in the Black Earth zone. When the local PPUoR nominated former Vice President Aleksandr Rutskoi for the post, the Oblast Electoral Commission vetoed his candidacy. (Elected in 1991 as Yeltsin's running mate, Rutskoi fell out with Yeltsin and helped lead the parliamentary rebellion against the president in October 1993.) Thereupon the organizations that made up the local branch of the PPUoR nominated the leader of the Kursk Oblast committee of the CPRF, Aleksandr Mikhailov, to contest the election.[41] Just two days before the election, the Supreme Court annulled the decision of the Electoral Commission. With only one day for his campaign, Rutskoi won a landslide 77 percent of the vote.[42] Following his election, Rutskoi attempted to restore good relations with his former foes in Yeltsin's administration, provoking a corresponding deterioration in his relations with the communist and nationalist opposi-

---

37. For biographies of all Russian governors, see the site of National News Service <www.nns.ru\persons\>.
38. *Sovetskaya Rossiya*, December 6 and 25, 1997.
39. *Izvestiya*, April 14, 1998; *Sovetskaya Rossiya*, April 17, 1998.
40. *Izvestiya*, May 6, 1995.
41. *Sovetskaya Rossiya*, October 15, 1996.
42. Radio Liberty, October 21, 1996.

tion. Rutskoi refused, for example, to support Mikhailov in his campaign for election as speaker of the Kursk Oblast Duma.[43] These days, it is hard to find a member of the CPRF in Kursk who does not voice regret at having supported Rutskoi's candidacy for governor.

In the 1996 presidential election, Zyuganov won a majority of votes in all the regions of the Black Earth zone. In Kursk and Tambov Oblasts, Zyuganov's victory might be termed "absolute," as he won over 50 percent in the first round-more than the votes for all the other ten contenders put together. In the second round, Zyuganov won 58.6 percent and Yeltsin 36.3 percent in Belgorod Oblast. In Kursk Oblast, the corresponding scores were 58.9 percent to 36.2 percent; in Lipetsk, 56.3 percent to 38.6 percent; in Tambov Oblast, 62.8 percent to 32.6 percent; and in Voronezh, 57.6 percent against 37.0 percent.

VOLGA-VYATKA ZONE

Volga-Vyatka is renowned among Russia's eleven economic zones for the diversity of its component regions. The three republics and two oblasts of which it consists—namely, the Republics of Mari-El, Mordovia and Chuvashia, and the Kirov and Nizhnii Novgorod Oblasts—have little in common as regards economic development, natural resources or communications. Some scholars have claimed that the artificial composition of the zone can be justified only by the center's desire to establish an economic buffer around Russia's third largest city, the industrial giant Nizhnii Novgorod. While Mordovia's fertile soil recalls the agricultural centers of the Black Earth zone, the forested, taiga-like terrain of Kirov Oblast is more reminiscent of the Komi Republic in the north or Perm Oblast in the Urals.

This disparity carries over to the political life of the five regions that make up the Volga-Vyatka. Four of the five may be termed "conservative." In the Russian context, this translates into a strong Communist or, at times, LDPR presence. The fifth region—the economic powerhouse of the zone, Nizhnii Novgorod—served for a long time as the embodiment of Yeltsin's economic reform, a model for how reform should be implemented and a showcase for its efficiency. Though things changed somewhat with the departure for Moscow of the oblast's first governor, Boris Nemtsov, Nizhnii Novgorod still did not turn into a region of communist supporters.

43. On Rutskoi's relations with the Yeltsin administration see *Izvestiya*, November 6, 1996; *Obshchaya Gazeta* , No. 33, 1996, p. 8, and No. 45, 1996, p. 2.

Chuvashia

Chuvashia is reputed to be the "reddest" region in Volga-Vyatka and has regularly elected communist candidates. The republic takes its name from the indigenous Chuvash—a Turkic people who make up nearly 69 percent of the population, with ethnic Russians accounting for 26.5 percent. Chuvashia enjoys the reputation of a haven of good interethnic relations and, while the republic's relations with the federal authorities have occasionally been strained, separatism and nationalism have not been significant forces. This may be partly explained by the republic's lack of valuable raw materials or of an industrial base, which makes it dependent on the federal center for financial support.

Like all the republics in Volga-Vyatka, Chuvashia is a poor province. Income per capita is only a little over 50 percent of the Russian average. Just fewer than 40 percent of the inhabitants are rural dwellers, compared with 27 percent for Russia as a whole. Like the neighboring Republics of Mari-El and Mordovia, Chuvashia's industrial output in 1996 was only 30 percent that of 1990, before the Yeltsin leadership launched Russia on the road to the market.

Chuvashia nonetheless made one very notable departure from its habit of voting for communists, having on three occasions elected as its president one of Russia's most prominent reformers, Nikolai Fedorov. The ethnic composition of the republic is the probable explanation for this phenomenon: Fedorov seems to be the world's most renowned Chuvash, with the possible exception of the avant-garde poet Gennadii Aigi.[44] Elected a deputy to the USSR Congress of People's Deputies in 1989, Fedorov played a key role in the adoption of the USSR Law on the Press, which outlawed censorship. This made him the darling of Russian journalists and, consequently, a very famous person. In December 1991, he was appointed Russian Minister of Justice and became one of the most ardent reformers in Yegor Gaidar's government. He resigned in the spring of 1993 in protest against Yeltsin's threat (carried out in October) to dissolve the Russian parliament. Explaining his action, Fedorov cited his inability to influence what he called "the atmosphere of total lawlessness" prevailing in the Kremlin.

---

44. For biographies of both men, see *Kto est kto v Rossii* (*Who's Who in Russia*), Moscow, Olimp Publishing House, 1997, pp. 658-659 (Fedorov) and pp. 13-14 (Aigi). See also Yelena Dikun, "Nikolai Fedorov: A Kulak's Grandson at the Head of a "Red" Republic," Jamestown Foundation, *Prism*, January 1997.

Fedorov was elected President of Chuvashia in December 1993. He soon ran into opposition from what he complained was the republic's anti-reform legislature, chaired by CPRF member Valentin Shurchanov. In December 1995, the communist-dominated legislature held a referendum and tried to abolish the office of president of the republic. The motion was narrowly defeated and, two years later, Fedorov was reelected, winning 57 percent of the vote to Shurchanov's 34 percent.[45]

It took all of Fedorov's charisma to overcome the communist conservatism of Chuvashia's electorate. No fewer than 62 percent of republic voters voted against Yeltsin in the nationwide referendum of April 1993, in which voters were asked to choose between the president and the parliamentary opposition, while 58 percent voted against Yeltsin's new constitution on the very day that Fedorov was elected president the first time. In the 1993 elections for the Russian State Duma, 20.6 percent of Chuvashia's voters voted for the CPRF list; in the 1995 elections, the figure grew to 31.8 percent. In the single-mandate constituencies, Chuvashia's voters chose Valentin Agafonov, a member of the CPRF faction in the Duma, and prominent eye-surgeon Svyatoslav Fedorov (no relation to the republic president). Svyatoslav Fedorov was probably Russia's single most respected private entrepreneur and yet, at the same time, a member of the People's Power faction which, as mentioned above, was a key member of the PPUoR.[46]

Mari-El: Forests cover about half of the republic. Ethnic Russians account for 49 percent of the population while the indigenous Mari, a Finno-Ugric people, make up around 40 percent. The Mari have been subject to centuries of russification, and neither separatism nor nationalism is strong in the republic. Some 38 percent of the population are rural dwellers. In 1996, the average monthly wage in the republic was less than 40 percent that of Russia as a whole, while some 43 percent of the population were estimated to be living below the official poverty line.

Voting patterns in the republic, while inconsistent, seemed to represent an uneven slide toward conservatism. The electorate voted in favor of the introduction of an executive presidency in Russia in the referendum of 1991, but against Yeltsin in that of 1993. Eight months later, 52.4 percent of voters supported Yeltsin's new constitution. In elections to the State Duma in 1993, the vote for the CPRF in Mari-El was the same as the Russian average, but in the parliamentary election of 1995 it was lower

45. *Nezavisimaya Gazeta*, December 30, 1997.

46. On Fedorov's reputation, see *Obshchaya Gazeta*, No. 29, 1998, p. 6.

than the national average, at 18.5 percent against 22.3 percent. In both elections, however, the vote for the list of the CPRF's closest ally, the Agrarian Party, was considerably higher than that in Russia as a whole. As for the single-mandate half of the State Duma, in 1993 the republic was represented by a member of the pro-government Party of Russian Unity and Concord, and in 1995 by an Agrarian deputy.

In the 1996 presidential election, Zyuganov won 43.4 percent of the votes in Mari-El against Yeltsin's 24.3 percent in the first round, and 52.8 percent in the second round. At the end of 1996, the Kremlin-supported incumbent, Vladislav Zotin, was defeated in the first round of his bid to win reelection as president of the republic. Victory in the second round, held in January 1997, went to the PPUoR candidate, Vyacheslav Kislitsyn.[47]

Mordovia

The Mordovian Republic lies at the center of European Russia and straddles the railway and highway communications connecting Moscow with other parts of Russia. Geologically, the republic's territory is a continuation into European Russia of the Siberian taiga; this largely explains why many prison camps were built in Mordovia. The existence of a fast railway between the republic capital, Saransk, and Moscow prompted the Soviet leadership to construct that famous center for nuclear research, the secret city Arzamas-16, in the north of the republic. The fact that the regional economy was dominated by defense-related industry helped to explain why the socioeconomic situation in Mordovia was essentially no better than that in nearby, poverty-beset Mari-El. It also explained why communists and other radicals played a dominant role in politics. Long after the collapse of the USSR, Mordovia retained the words "Soviet" and "Socialist" in its official title, finally dropping the two words in January 1994.

Interethnic relations in Mordovia have at times been tense. Separatism has not, however, been an issue for the republic. At 30.6 percent of the population, the indigenous Mordvins, a Finno-Ugric people, are heavily

---

47. According to *Nezavisimaya Gazeta* of January 9, 1997, Kislitsyn's campaign was supported by Aleksandr Lebed. The CPRF nonetheless presented him as the PPUoR's candidate, while analysts of the Panorama research center included Kislitsyn in their list of CPRF members in the Council of the Federation (www.panorama.org/fs/sf2fkp.shtml). According to *Panorama*, both the Yeltsin side and the CPRF supported Kislitsyn in the second round, in order to ensure that his rival in that round—a member of the LDPR—did not win.

outnumbered by the 62.4 percent who are ethnic Russians. Equally important is the dominance of the republic's economy by the defense sector: military-industry managers have close ties to the federal center, on which they depend to fund the conversion of defense plants to civilian production.

In the early 1990s, Mordovia gained national prominence with the rise and fall of its first president, Vladimir Guslyannikov, a pro-reform radical and ethnic Russian who was elected president at the beginning of 1992. When, in 1990, the Mordovian parliament established the post of executive president, the job was, as elsewhere in Russia, created with a concrete candidate in mind. In Mordovia, this was the chairman of the republic's Supreme Soviet, Vladimir Biryukov. Biryukov, a Mordvin, had formerly been a republic CPSU official with responsibility for agriculture. Unexpectedly, he lost the presidential election to Guslyannikov. Guslyannikov was a leader of the local Democratic Russia movement, set up by Mordovia's urbanized Russians to counter the local communist nomenklatura that consisted largely of Mordvins from rural backgrounds. He owed his electoral success to the popularity of the "democratic" camp in the months immediately following the August 1991 coup.

A bitter struggle ensued between president and parliament. Guslyannikov fell out with the local elite when he filled key positions in accordance with his personal and political motives. Moreover, he proved incompetent and his popularity plummeted. Guslyannikov blamed the republic parliament, accusing it of resisting progressive legislation. While some analysts portrayed the struggle in nationalist terms, others saw it as a conflict between a reform-minded executive and an anti-reform legislature. It bore a striking resemblance to the contest going on at the federal level between Yeltsin and the Russian parliament.

In April 1993, the republic parliament abolished the post of executive president and ousted Guslyannikov from office, blaming him for the "failure" of economic reforms. Power passed to Biryukov—now a member of the CPRF—as speaker of the legislature. Ten days later, 61 percent of those who voted in the republic expressed lack of confidence in Yeltsin in the nationwide referendum in which voters were asked to choose between the president and his parliamentary opposition. In the national parliamentary election in December 1993, a member of the CPRF was elected in Mordovia's single-mandate constituency; in the 1995 election, however, Mordovia's voters opted for Nikolai Medvedev, a leader of the usually pro-government "Russian Regions" faction in the Duma. The vote for the CPRF list was 50 percent higher in Mordovia than the Russian national average in 1993, but only 5 percent higher in 1995. In republic legislative elections in January 1995, however, Biryukov lost control of parliament to Nikolai Merkushkin, a one-time Komsomol official who had been appointed second secretary of Mordovia's Communist Party in 1991 and who subsequently became a leader of the Agrarian Party.[48] Then, in the first round of Russia's 1996 presidential election, Zyuganov won more than twice as many votes as Yeltsin (49.7 percent against 24.3 percent); in the second round, however, the communist leader won only 47.7 percent while Yeltsin won 45.6 percent.[49]

In late 1997, Mordovia's lawmakers changed their collective mind once again and decided that the republic's leader should, after all, be elected by universal suffrage. This time, however, the establishment took the necessary precautions to secure the job for its preferred candidate—Merkushkin. Local electoral officials wiped the names of four of the six presidential hopefuls from the list of candidates. As Russian law forbids elections with fewer than two contenders, the director of a local macaroni factory was registered as Merkushkin's sole rival.[50] Among those refused registration was the leader of the republic Communist Party, Evgenii Kosterin. The CPRF protested to Russia's Prosecutor-General, but its efforts to get Kosterin reinstated were ignored and Merkushkin won a landslide 96.6 percent of the vote in the February 1998 election.[51] The election was seen as detaching Mordovia, at least temporarily, from the "Red Belt."

---

48. A detailed account of political events in Mordovian Republic may be found at the site of the National News Service (www.nns.ru). The Guslyannikov-Biryukov controversy of 1991-93 was given prominence in broadcasts of Russian television, because of the similarity of events in the republic to the conflict between Yeltsin and Russian parliament, which was underway at that time.

49. According to data released by the National News Service, a total of 690,266 people voted in Mordovia on July 3, 1996, but only 504,220 of the ballot papers—that is, 73 per cent—were regarded as valid, while18,283 were invalidated and 1,020 were left blank (www.nns.rus/voting/elects91_96.html). Taken at face value, this implies that 166,743 adult residents of the republic (almost a quarter of those who voted) went to the trouble of visiting a polling station with the express aim of pocketing the ballot paper.

50. *Sovetskaya Rossiya*, January 9 and February 10, 1998; *Kommersant-Daily*, January 29, 1998; *Nezavisimaya Gazeta*, February 14, 1998.

51. *Sovetskaya Rossiya*, January 13, 1998.

Kirov Oblast

Although the Volga-Vyatka economic zone owes its name to the ancient city of Vyatka, that city itself is one of the few big Russian cities that still retain their Soviet-era names. Vyatka was renamed Kirov in 1934, following the assassination of Sergei Kirov, the Leningrad Party boss whose death in suspicious circumstances provided Joseph Stalin with a pretext to unleash his policy of mass terror. It is still called Kirov today.

Kirov Oblast is covered with swamp forest, or taiga. Official socio-economic statistics show the region to be slightly better off than the three republics discussed immediately above, yet still well below the Russian average. Considerably higher than the national average of 82.9 percent is the 91.8 percent of the population of Kirov Oblast who are ethnic Russians. Much of the region's economic activity is concentrated in those branches of the economy hardest hit by recession, among them defense production, forestry and light industry. Agriculture is poor and relatively unimportant. Oddly enough however the Agrarian Party, the CPRF's junior partner in the PPUoR, seems to enjoy better standing than the CPRF. Conservative and quiet though the oblast is, the population has so far demonstrated no particular admiration for either democrats or communists.

The region's vote in all the federal referendums conducted in Russia was very close to the average. The largest difference was registered in December 1993, when 61.4 percent of Kirov voters voted for Yeltsin's Constitution, as opposed to 58.4 percent in Russia as a whole. In the simultaneous election to the upper house of the Russian parliament, Kirov voters elected the appointed head of the Kirov administration, Vasilii Desyatnikov, and the rector of the Kirov Institute of Socioeconomic Problems, Vladimir Sergeenkov. In both the 1993 and the 1995 parliamentary elections, the CPRF list did considerably worse in Kirov Oblast than in most of the rest of Russia—8.7 percent in 1993 and 14.8 percent in 1995. The Agrarian Party, by contrast, got twice as many votes in Kirov Oblast as it did on average in the rest of Russia. The LDPR also scored relatively well. In single-mandate constituencies, the region opted in 1993 for a member of the LDPR and an independent who later joined the pro-government "Stability" faction. Two years later, voters chose an Agrarian candidate and the above-mentioned Sergeenkov, who joined the People's Power faction.[52]

52. For an interview with Sergeenkov, see *Moscow News*, No. 38, 1996, p. 7.

In the 1996 presidential election, Yeltsin scored better than Zyuganov in Kirov both in the first round (with 31.2 percent against Zyuganov's 29 percent) and in the second round (50.7 percent against 41.8 percent). In October 1996, Sergeenkov was elected Governor of the oblast while Yeltsin's choice, Desyatnikov, was knocked out in the first round. Sergeenkov's victory in Kirov Oblast marked a turning point for the PPUoR, which began from that point on to win gubernatorial elections in various regions.

Nizhnii Novgorod

The oblast lies in the Volga-Vyatka economic zone but does not share the "conservative" inclinations of the majority of the regions in this zone. Instead, the region was the home of the once famous Nizhnii Novgorod reform experiment.

Throughout Russian history, Nizhnii Novgorod was renowned as a city of merchants. Its famous fair was held every year until 1917. During the Soviet period, however, the city was renamed Gorky and, because of its heavy concentration of defense industries, was closed to outsiders. The fair ceased to be held in 1929. It was not held again until 1991, when the restrictions were lifted and the city and region's historic name restored. In November that year, Yeltsin appointed a young local politician, Boris Nemtsov, as governor of the oblast. Yeltsin acted out of gratitude for the support Nemtsov had given him during the August 1991 coup. Nemtsov turned the region, formerly a center of the Soviet military-industrial complex, into a showcase of market reform and a symbol of a new, non-communist and democratic Russia.

Quite a number of books have been written on the reforms in Nizhnii Novgorod.[53] Nemtsov was indeed very different from other Russian governors. Unlike virtually all of them, he had never been a member of the CPSU. Unlike most of them, too, Nemtsov was young, tall, good-looking and half-Jewish. He graduated from Gorky State University with a degree in radio physics—a very different background from that of his peers, most of who were former Soviet managers. Nemtsov began his political career in 1987 as an activist in a regional environmentalist movement, opposing the construction in Gorky of a nuclear power station. In 1990, Nemtsov was elected to the Russian Congress of People's Deputies, where he became friendly with other rising leaders such as Yeltsin and Yavlinsky.

53. Boris Nemtsov, Provintsial, Moscow, Vagrius Publishing House, 1997.

Yavlinsky was the architect of the model of regional reform enacted under Nemtsov's leadership in Nizhnii Novgorod.

The economic reform in Nizhnii Novgorod differed from that of other regions in that Yavlinsky tried to make it socially oriented. An important innovation was an ambitious land reform aimed at replacing gigantic state-owned agricultural enterprises with private farms. Unlike other democratic regional leaders, Nemtsov established excellent working relations with the regional legislature and its chairman, Evgenii Krestyaninov; he also did his best to cooperate with former CPSU apparatchiks, one of whom, Ivan Sklyarov, was to become his successor as governor.

The market reforms in Nizhnii Novgorod turned the region into a pilgrimage site for Western politicians, such as former British Prime Minister Margaret Thatcher and her successor, John Major; this in turn attracted foreign investors to the region. In the end, however, Nemstov's success catapulted him away from Nizhnii Novgorod to Moscow, where he was appointed First Deputy Prime Minister. With the departure not only of Nemtsov but also of Yavlinsky, the reforms foundered. They turned out to have been too dependent on personalities. Disillusion with both the reforms and the reformers ensued. Untypically, however, it was not the gubernatorial election but the election of the mayor of the provincial capital, the city of Nizhnii Novgorod, which marked the beginning of the public's turn to the CPRF.

Support for Yeltsin's cause, as measured by the votes cast in elections and referendums, was higher, and those for the CPRF lower, in Nizhnii Novgorod than in most other regions of Russia. In 1993, both Nemtsov and Krestyaninov were elected to the Council of the Federation. Nizhnii Novgorod's single-mandate seats in the State Duma were won that year by one member of Yabloko and five independents, who later formed a faction called "Stability." Two years later, however, three of the six regional seats were won by PPUoR candidates. Among the victors was CPRF activist Gennadii Khodyrev, who acquired all-Union notoriety in the Soviet era as the head of the Gorky Oblast Committee of the CPSU, at the time when the city served as the place of internal exile for the human rights champion, Andrei Sakharov. In December 1995, on the day that the second Duma was elected, Nemtsov was elected to a second term as governor with 58.4 percent of the vote. Six months later, Yeltsin scored 51.7 percent in the presidential election in Nizhnii Novgorod against 32.5 percent for Zyuganov.

For a long time, Nemtsov was Yeltsin's darling. During Yeltsin's visit to Nizhnii Novgorod in 1994, he went so far as to indicate that he would like Nemtsov to succeed him as Russia's next president.[54] Although Nemtsov declined the honor,[55] a few months later Yeltsin introduced Nemtsov as his would-be heir to US President Bill Clinton. The idea of elevating the young governor to the top of the Russian pyramid of power resurfaced in March 1996, when Gaidar tried in vain to persuade Nemtsov to run in Russia's second presidential election.[56] Nemtsov rejected Gaidar's pressure also, but he did not resist the third such occasion a year later, when Yeltsin's daughter, Tatyana Dyachenko, along with the family's eminence grise, Boris Berezovsky, traveled to Nizhnii Novgorod with the sole aim of persuading Nemtsov to accept the post of First Deputy Prime Minister.[57] Nemtsov's appointment in March 1997 provoked general disenchantment in the region with Nemtsov and in the cause of reform.[58] In summer 1997, Nemtsov succeeded, with some difficulty, in arranging for the former mayor of Nizhnii Novgorod city, Ivan Sklyarov, to be elected governor of the region in his place. Sklyarov defeated Khodyrev in the second round of that election, in July 1997, by 52 percent to 42.2 percent. No sooner was the election over, than Sklyarov started to criticize his predecessor.[59]

The voters of Nizhnii Novgorod city vented their anger and frustration over Nemtsov's "selling them out" when, in March 1998, they elected Nemtsov's worst enemy, the dubious businessman Andrei Klimentev, as mayor in Sklyarov's place.[60] Klimentev won 34 percent of the vote, defeating Nemtsov's choice Vladimir Gorin with 31 percent and former Mayor of Nizhnii Novgorod Dmitrii Bednyakov with 24 percent. Taken together, outsiders supported by the CPRF and LDPR won 4 percent.[61] The events that followed struck a fatal blow to the tarnished image of Russian leaders as democrats and opened the way for the CPRF to return to the region. On the day the results of the mayoral election were announced, Nemtsov

---

54. Russia's Radio, August 17, 1994.
55. See the interview with Nemtsov in Nevskoe vremya (St. Petersburg), October 22, 1994.
56. *Nezavisimaya Gazeta*, March 12, 1996; *Obshchaya Gazeta*, No. 10, 1996, p. 3.
57. National News Service, <www.nns.ru>.
58. Moscow News, No. 12, 1998, p. 7.
59. Sklyarov's reaction was announced on a Russian television newscast of August 24, 1998.
60. For earlier stories on the scandal between Nemtsov and Klimentev, see *Izvestiya*, October 3, 1995; *Pravda*-5, No. 16, 1995, p. 10.
61. *Argumenty i fakty*, No. 15, 1998, p. 8.

told Russian TV that the matter [of Klimentev's election] would be settled "in full accord with Russian law."[62] Next day, the regional electoral commission annulled the election results.[63] Later the same day, Klimentev was arrested on charges of misappropriation of state subsidies.[64] Within days, Yeltsin issued a decree reprimanding Sklyarov for his "unsatisfactory work in the field of legality during the mayoral election."[65] In June 1998, Klimentev was sentenced to six years' imprisonment. The entire affair was sharply criticized by a media that had hitherto been well disposed towards Nemtsov.[66] No one seems to have believed that Klimentev's trial and appeal were fair. Klimentev became a cult figure. Since by law Klimentev was forbidden to take part in the forthcoming mayoral election, he recommended another man in his place—this was none other than Vladimir Semago, [67] the prominent "red millionaire." Semago had resigned from the CPRF faction in the State Duma on the grounds that it was not radical enough in its relations with the executive branch.[68] In the election that took place in September 1998, however, Semago came in third and left the place to the local politicians.[69]

62. *Izvestiya*, April 1, 1998.
63. *Izvestiya*, April 2, 1998; *Sovetskaya Rossiya*, April 2, 1998.
64. *Izvestiya*, April 3 and 4, 1998.
65. *Izvestiya*, April 7, 1998.
66. *Izvestiya*, April 1, 2 and 7, 1998; Moscow News, No. 13, 1998, pp. 2-3; *Obshchaya Gazeta*, No. 14, 1998, p. 1; No. 15, 1998, p. 7; No. 19, 1998, p. 4; and No. 22, 1998, p. 2.
67. *Izvestiya*, July 23 and August 12, 1998.
68. Russian television newscasts, September 16, 1998.
69. *Sovetskaya Rossiya*, September 29, 1998.

7: The "Democrats" of the North, North-West and Center

Voters in Russia's northern and northwestern zones have consistently chosen liberal candidates. So too have voters in certain regions of the Central zone. These regions are among the richest of Russia. Falling into this category are the cities of Moscow and St. Petersburg (since the nineteenth century commonly referred to as "the two capitals").

Northern Economic Zone

If any of Russia's economic zones can be depicted as predominantly "White," it must be Russia's European North. The region consists of the Republics of Karelia and Komi, the Oblasts of Arkhangelsk, Murmansk and Vologda, and the Nenets Autonomous Okrug (AO), which is administratively subordinate to Arkhangelsk Oblast. Communist candidates have lost almost all elections and referendums held in these regions, the only exceptions being the March 1991 referendum on the preservation of the USSR and several elections for single-mandate seats in Russia's State Duma.

Karelia

Renowned for its forestry and lumber industry, the Karelian republic on the Russia-Finland border is a "white spot" on Russia's political map. Yeltsin and the "democrats" have won all federal elections held in Karelia. Eastern Karelia has been a part of Russia since 1323, but western Karelia was annexed by the USSR only after the latter's victory in the Russo-Finnish War of 1939-40. Since the 1917 Revolution, the status of Karelia has changed several times; in 1923 it became an autonomous republic; in 1940, after the addition of western Karelia, it was given full union-republic status; and in 1956 it assumed its present status. Ethnic Russians comprise 73 percent of the population while Karelians constitute 10 percent.

One of only a few departures from Karelia's "white" profile came in 1994 when Viktor Stepanov, a member of the CPRF who had headed the republic under Soviet rule, was reelected prime minister (the chief post in the republic); Stepanov remained in charge of Karelia until May 1998, when he was defeated in the second round of a direct gubernatorial election by Sergei Katanandov, former mayor of the republic capital, Petrozavodsk. Katanandov, who won 50 percent of the votes to Stepanov's 43.2 percent, was backed by the local branch of Our Home is Russia and by representatives of small and medium businesses.[70] However, Stepanov had been dubbed the "favorite communist" of Russian democrats. In 1988, Yeltsin was elected a delegate of the XIX Party Conference from Karelia, after he had been blackballed in Moscow and in his native Sverdlovsk Oblast, and was said to have had a soft spot for Stepanov ever since.[71] On the eve of the decisive, second round of the gubernatorial election, Grigorii Yavlinsky called on his supporters in the region to vote for Stepanov.[72] Katanandov reportedly owed his victory to the fact that Yavlinsky's supporters ignored his call.[73] The incident serves to underline, yet again, the fact that selection of regional governors is in many regions decided more often than not on personal rather than partisan grounds.

Komi

The most striking example of anti-Communism on the part of the electorate is to be found in the Komi Republic. After Karelia, Komi was, in 1992, the second of the Russian Federation's autonomous republics to declare itself sovereign. Over half of the population is ethnic Russian, while the indigenous Komi people make up less than one quarter of the residents.

During the Soviet era, Komi's Inta, Pechora and Vorkuta coal basins had been among the most notorious centers of the Gulag, the chain of slave-labor camps set up under Stalin. This may help to explain the strength of anticommunist feeling in the region. In 1989, Komi became the first Russian region to attempt to nominate a former political prisoner, mathematician Revolt Pimenov, for election to the USSR Congress of People's deputies. At the same time, the electorate refused to elect the first secretary of the Komi Oblast Committee of the CPSU, Vladimir Melnikov.[74]

---

70. *IEWS Russian Regional Report*, No. 17, April 30, 1998; RFE/RL Newsline, May 18, 1998.

71. Boris Yeltsin, Ispoved' na zadannuyu temu (English translation: Against the Grain), Rostov-on-Don, "Inmag" Publishing House, 1990, pp. 126-8.

72. *Izvestiya*, April 22, 1998. See also the interview with Stepanov in *Izvestiya*, March 26, 1998.

73. For two rounds of the Karelian gubernatorial election see *Nezavisimaya Gazeta*, April 28 and May 19, 1998.

74. Melnikov leapt to national fame when he attacked a number of top Soviet officials, including former USSR Foreign Minister Andrei Gromyko, at the XIX CPSU Conference in June 1988 (XIX Vsesoyuznaya konferentsiya, Vol. 1, p. 270). In the meantime, Melnikov criticized Gorbachev at various CPSU Central Committee sessions and was replaced as Party boss in the republic by Yurii Spiridonov, the current Governor.

The following year, moreover, Pimenov was elected a deputy to the RSFSR Congress of People's Deputies.

In the ensuing years, the population of the republic voted for Yeltsin in all elections and referendums. This was so despite the fact that, because Komi's economy is dependent on its coal mines and these were particularly heavily hit by Russia's economic recession, the republic was a major center of industrial unrest in the 1990s.[75] In the 1996 presidential election, Zyuganov scored only 16.3 percent of the vote in the first round and 28.3 percent in the second. In both the 1993 and 1995 elections to the State Duma, the CPRF scored considerably fewer votes in Komi than its average for Russia as a whole. In 1993, 7.1 percent of the Komi electorate voted for the CPRF list, while for the Russian Federation as a whole the figure was 12.4 percent; in 1995, the CPRF's tally in Komi was 13 percent against 22.3 percent in Russia overall. In elections to single-mandate constituencies, however, the CPRF scored a rare victory when Rita Chistokhodova, an employee of the Syktyvkar City Prosecutor's Office, ran as an independent candidate but later joined the CPRF faction in the State Duma.

A gubernatorial election was held in Komi in May 1994, and Yurii Spiridonov, a former CPSU leader of the republic but one of Yeltsin's most ardent supporters, was elected head of the republic.[76] He was re-elected in November 1997 with over 60 percent of the votes, defeating Chistokhodova, who won 21.3 percent.[77]

Arkhangelsk and Murmansk Oblasts

Against this background, the voting pattern in Arkhangelsk and Murmansk Oblasts is not surprising. Unlike much of the rest of Russia, the peasants of these regions were never serfs. Moreover, both provinces have a long tradition of links with the West. Arkhangelsk—Russia's largest timber exporting port—was the first port of the Russian Empire to conduct trade with England and, later, other European countries. Murmansk is the largest city within the Arctic Circle. It is strategically important because it houses the only large Russian port that is ice-free all year, being kept open by the warm waters of the Gulf Stream and having unrestricted access to the Atlantic and other world sea routes. Founded as a supply port during the

---

75. For information on the workers' movement in Komi, see *Nezavisimaya Gazeta*, August 1, 1998.

76. See the interview with Spiridonov in *Nezavisimaya Gazeta*, June 30, 1998.

77. *Nezavisimaya Gazeta*, December 2, 1997.

First World War, Murmansk served during the Second World War as the main port for Anglo-American convoys carrying war supplies to the USSR.

Although research centers, shipyards and military industries in both oblasts were hard hit by the recession that accompanied Russia's move to the market, the CPRF has won few victories in either region. The CPRF has lost every election in Arkhangelsk Oblast save that in 1995 for single seats in the State Duma, when CPRF members won both of the seats assigned to the oblast, with one going to the region's last CPSU leader, Yurii Guskov. The CPRF was slightly more successful in Murmansk Oblast. In the 1996 presidential election, Yeltsin won 70.1 percent of the vote to Zyuganov's 21.9 percent. But, in a gubernatorial election at the end of 1996, the incumbent governor, Yeltsin-appointee Evgenii Komarov, lost by a small margin to a local factory manager, Yurii Evdokimov, whose campaign was supported by the CPRF. Evdokimov has subsequently declared his support not for the CPRF but for Yurii Luzhkov's Fatherland movement.

Nenets Autonomous Okrug

As tends to be the case in other centers of the oil and gas industry in Russia, voters in the Nenets AO have so far shown little inclination to vote for the CPRF in either presidential or parliamentary elections. Its title notwithstanding, the region is predominantly populated by ethnic Russians. The formerly nomadic Nenets people, who constitute only about 15 percent of the population of the region, live chiefly by reindeer herding. Russians live mainly in the administrative center, Naryan-Mar, and other urban areas. In elections to the State Duma, the CPRF scored only about half the average for Russia as a whole—that is, 6.5 percent in 1993 and 11.4 percent in 1995. In 1996, 18.4 percent voted for Zyuganov in the first round and 28.9 percent in the second round of the Russian presidential elections. The CPRF did not even bother to nominate a candidate for the December 1996 election for the head of the Okrug administration. Instead, the CPRF supported the incumbent, Vladimir Khabarov, who was also supported by the presidential administration. Perhaps for this reason, Khabarov lost to a well-known local businessman, Vladimir Butov.[78]

Vologda Oblast

A highly publicized corruption scandal would have discredited the ruling party in many places in the world, even in the Russian Federation. Such an

78. *Sovetskaya Rossiya*, December 24, 1996.

event seems not to have shaken the confidence of the population in Vologda Oblast. Nor does there seem to be an economic explanation for their loyalty. Famous for its church architecture and paintings, Vologda Oblast also houses a major center of ferrous metallurgy in Cherepovets, along with timber, pulp and paper production in other parts of the region. Apart from the usual problem of unpaid wages, the Oblast is particularly hard hit by unemployment. In 1996, there were as many as 31 job seekers for every vacancy in the region. Vologda residents nonetheless voted for Yeltsin and his policies in all federal elections and referendums. In the parliamentary elections of 1993 and 1996, the CPRF list got 5.2 percent and 12.1 percent respectively, less than half of the national average in both instances. In the 1995 election for single-mandate seats, a CPRF member from Cherepovets, Aleksandr Mikhailov, won one of the oblast's two mandates, but the other went to democrat Vladimir Lopatin, well-known as a radical advocate for military reform.

The victory of the "party of power" in Vologda's 1996 gubernatorial election was even more impressive. The region's first governor, Nikolai Podgornov, was not elected but appointed by Yeltsin. Following a scandal in the Moscow media, Podgornov was arrested on six charges of corruption and embezzlement, most notably, for alleged misappropriation of bread subsidies.[79] In the midst of the scandal, Yeltsin suspended Podgornov and replaced him with the former mayor of Cherepovets, Vyacheslav Pozgalev.[80] Although the social situation showed no improvement under Pozgalev and crime rates remained high, Pozgalev won a landslide 80.7 percent of the votes in the first round of the gubernatorial election held in October 1996. The candidate of the CPRF, Mikhail Beznin, a professor of the Vologda Pedagogical Institute, scored a mere 3.2 percent of the vote, while Mikhail Surov, portrayed in the media as the godfather of the local criminal underworld, got 4.2 percent.[81]

79. *Izvestiya*, July 14, August 2 and 30, September 9, 22 and 26, October 11, November 15, 18 and 21-25, December 2, 7 and 16, 1995; January 11, February 20, March 30, April 14, July 11, 1996; May 8, 1997; February 25 and 28, March 3 and 30, 1998; Moscow News, No. 8, 1996, p. 2; *Pravda*-5, No. 12, 1996, p. 5; *Literaturnaya gazeta*, No. 8, 1998, p. 4.

80. *Izvestiya*, March 26, 1996.

81. *Izvestiya*, February 18, 1998.

North-West Region

The CPRF has fared slightly better in Russia's Northwest economic zone, which includes Kaliningrad, Leningrad, Novgorod and Pskov Oblasts, and the city of St. Petersburg. (St. Petersburg is discussed separately at the end of this chapter.)

Novgorod Oblast

Novgorod, one of Russia's most ancient cities, is the only cast-iron stronghold of Yeltsin and the "democrats" in the area. Courtesy of Yeltsin, Novgorod has recently regained its ancient name of "Mr. Great Novgorod" (Gospodin Velikii Novgorod, as distinct from Nizhnii [Lower] Novgorod on the River Volga.[82] The city takes pride in itself as the birthplace of Russian statehood and the oldest center of Christianity in Russia. During the Middle Ages, it had its own system of self-government that included the right of the town assembly to elect its princes. Suppressed by Moscow's Grand Duke Ivan III in 1471, Novgorod's tradition of self-government gives modern Russians an opportunity to claim at least some democratic tradition. The CPRF has so far won neither a federal nor a local election in the Oblast. Mikhail Prusak was appointed governor of the Oblast by Yeltsin in 1991 and subsequently joined Our Home is Russia. He was elected governor in a direct election in December 1995, winning 56.2 percent of the vote and defeating six other candidates. He has made a reputation for welcoming foreign investment in the region.[83]

Kaliningrad and Pskov Oblasts

Both oblasts suffered serious economic recession in the 1990s, with industrial output standing in Pskov in 1996 at 27 percent of that recorded in 1990 and in Kaliningrad at 31 percent (the average for Russia as a whole having been 48 percent). The protest vote was therefore quite strong in both regions, and particularly so in Pskov. The CPRF, however, was not the beneficiary.

Known from 1255 to 1946 as Königsberg, Kaliningrad is a Russian exclave on the Baltic coast. A sliver of land sandwiched between Poland to the south and Lithuania to the north and east, Kaliningrad is geographi-

82. Russian TV newscasts of August 14, 1998. According to these newscasts, Novgorod was stripped of this title by Peter the Great some time after St. Petersburg was founded in 1725.

83. Author's interview with the first secretary of the Novgorod Oblast Committee of the CPRF, Valerii Gaidum, taped in Novgorod on May 14, 1998.

cally isolated from Russia proper and has no common border with any other part of the Russian Federation. The oblast was created in 1945 from the northern half of German East Prussia, which was ceded to the USSR under the Potsdam Agreement. Administratively, it was made part of the RSFSR, even though it was geographically separated from the parent republic. Under Soviet rule, almost all traces of German culture were eliminated. The region's German inhabitants either fled or were deported, and the city and its hinterland were repopulated with Russian, Ukrainian and Belarussian settlers. Today, the ethnic composition of the oblast is 80.4 percent ethnic Russian, 7.3 percent Belarussian, and 6 percent Ukrainian.

Due to its closeness with the West because of a seaport on the territory, military personnel make up a substantial segment of the population. The success of the CPRF seems nonetheless to be quite modest in the region, despite the Party's claim to be the prime defender of the country's officer corps. The vote for the CPRF party list tends to be 2 or 3 percent lower in Kaliningrad than the Russian average. A modest success was achieved in 1995, when an independent candidate, elected to represent Kaliningrad's single-mandate constituency in the State Duma, joined the People's Power faction, which is allied to the CPRF. In October 1996, the CPRF supported the winning candidate, Leonid Gorbenko, in the second round of the gubernatorial election. The CPRF could take comfort from the fact that Gorbenko defeated Yeltsin's appointee. In reality, however, the CPRF supported Gorbenko only after its own original candidate, Yurii Semenov, came in a distant third in the first round.

Pskov Oblast appears to be the only real center of dissent in the Northwest. In the Middle Ages, Pskov was one of Russia's most prosperous cities, but it was overtaken in the eighteenth century by the rise of St. Petersburg and, therefore, its economic importance declined. Modern Pskov remains a major transport hub, however, and its importance as a trading center has increased since the 1991 demise of the USSR turned Pskov into a border region. The region remains poverty-stricken, however. The per capita income in the region in 1996 was 466,000 rubles, compared to the national average of 778,000 rubles, while the average monthly wage was, at 558,000 rubles, slightly more than half the then national average of 1,061,000 rubles.

Until 1993, the residents of the region voted for Yeltsin. But during the April 1993 referendum they began to display signs of dissatisfaction with his regime. At that time, less than half of those who voted (to be precise, 49.7 percent) expressed confidence in the president. In the 1996 presidential election, Zyuganov won 30.4 percent of the votes in the first round to Yeltsin's 24.8 percent while, in the second round, Zyuganov got 48.1 percent to Yeltsin's 45.2 percent.

In parliamentary elections, the citizens of Pskov have generally preferred to vote for nationalist candidates rather than for the CPRF or the PPUoR. In November 1996, Evgenii Mikhailov became the first (and so far only) member of Vladimir Zhirinovsky's LDPR to be elected governor of a Russian region. The candidate supported by the PPUoR having been defeated in the first round of that election, the CPRF and its allies called on the party faithful to vote for Mikhailov.[84] In the ensuing months, Mikhailov turned the regional newspaper, *Pskovskaya pravda*, into the mouthpiece of the LDPR and Zhirinovsky, and this transformation has not made the local committee of the CPRF any happier.[85]

CENTRAL ECONOMIC ZONE

As seen in Chapter 6, the Central zone is split into "red," "pink" and "white" regions.[86] The "white" ones will be discussed here. The situation of Moscow City, which is a case apart from the rest of Russia, is discussed at the end of this chapter, together with that of St. Petersburg.

Five regions of the Central zone can be described as "white": Moscow City and the surrounding Moscow Oblast, and Ivanovo, Tver and Yaroslavl Oblasts. In all of them, the electorates have voted for Yeltsin and the democrats in all federal elections and for candidates enjoying the support of the Kremlin in gubernatorial elections. Tver's Governor Vladimir Platov, who was elected in a popular election in December 1995, has been generally supportive of Yeltsin and his policies. So too, despite the acute poverty and unemployment facing his region, has the Governor of Ivanovo Oblast, Vladislav Tikhomirov, who was elected governor in December 1996. The exceptions have been few and not very significant, such as the victory of a CPRF candidate in a single-mandate constituency in Ivanovo in the 1995 elections to the State Duma.

---

84. For the text of the appeal of the PPUoR to the voters of Pskov, see *Sovetskaya Rossiya*, October 26, 1996.

85. Author's interviews with the leaders of the Oblast and City committees of the CPRF, Vladimir Nikitin and Nataliya Akimova. Both were taped in Pskov on May 8, 1998.

86. The Central economic zone includes Moscow Oblast in addition to Bryansk, Ivanovo, Kaluga, Kostroma, Orel, Ryazan, Smolensk, Tula, Tver , Vladimir and Yaroslavl Oblasts.

However, neither a refusal to vote for communist candidates, nor a decision to vote for "democrats," inevitably signifies unquestioning support for the powers that be. This became clear in 1998 in Yaroslavl, hitherto reputed to be a model liberal region, when the Oblast Duma adopted a resolution in favor of Yeltsin's impeachment.[87] Interviewed by Russia's Independent Television, Zyuganov pointed out in a rather apologetic tone that neither the CPRF nor the PPUoR had a majority in the Yaroslavl legislature. Among the deputies who voted for the resolution was the Speaker of the regional legislature, Sergei Vakhrukov, who was a member of Yabloko. He and his fellow lawmakers were apparently responding to pressure from their constituents, in particular, from blue-collar workers rendered desperate by persistent wage arrears. (Workers of several Yaroslavl factories at that time rallied in front of the Russian government building in Moscow, demanding payment of wage arrears.[88])

The governor of Yaroslavl Oblast, Anatolii Lisitsyn, was appointed to his post by presidential decree in 1991. In December 1997, he won direct election to the post. For some time, acting Prime Minister Yegor Gaidar treated the region as a testing ground for monetarist reform. Gradually, however, the mounting economic and social problems facing Yaroslavl soured Lisitsyn's attitude to Yeltsin and his reforms. In August 1998, Lisitsyn became the first non-communist governor to call publicly for Yeltsin's resignation.[89]

Moscow and St. Petersburg

Russia's two "federal cities," Moscow and St. Petersburg (known between 1924 and 1991 as Leningrad, in honor of the leader of the Bolshevik Revolution) are in a class of their own. The two cities are the largest, richest and most influential of the Russian Federation's eighty-nine component regions. In the summer of 1996, the votes cast in these two cities alone were enough to win Boris Yeltsin's reelection as president. Since 1989, Communist candidates have not won a single round in any election in either Moscow or Leningrad/St. Petersburg. The importance of this fact is hard to overestimate, since the residents of their capitals almost always decide the fates of highly centralized states. The success of the French Revolution, for example, depended on the support of the

87. *Izvestiya*, July 1, 1998.

88. *Nezavisimaya Gazeta*, July 8 and 28, 1998. For actions of Yaroslavl workers, see also *Obshchaya Gazeta*, No. 32, 1998, p. 3; *Nezavisimaya Gazeta*, August 25, 1998.

89. *Nezavisimaya Gazeta*, August 29, 1998.

Parisians, while the fates of the Russian monarchy and its short-lived liberal successor, the Provisional Government, were decided by the residents of Petrograd (as the imperial capital was then called). Soviet leaders, from Stalin onward, understood this and ensured that Moscow and Leningrad received larger shares of the communal pie than other Soviet cities. Today, the inhabitants of Moscow and St. Petersburg are considerably better off than people in other parts of the country, with banks and other financial organizations that control over 80 percent of Russia's financial assets based in these two centers.

In all fairness, it should be added that St. Petersburg is much the poorer of the two. This is partly because Moscow has rapidly emerged as the national trading and financial center where foreign investors have concentrated their activities and the head offices of banks and other private enterprises have tended to establish themselves. As a result, the average monthly personal income in January 1999 was 1,097.2 rubles in St. Petersburg (or 3 percent above the local subsistence minimum) and 4,439.6 rubles in Moscow (or 325 percent above the local subsistence minimum); and the number of private cars per 1,000 residents in 1995 was 119 in St. Petersburg and 154 in Moscow.[90] Finally, that malaise of the modern Russian economy—the non-payment of wages and other benefits—is far more acute in St. Petersburg than in Moscow. Democrats have nonetheless felt stronger in St. Petersburg than in Moscow, suggesting that material prosperity, while it undoubtedly plays a role in determining how individuals vote, is by no means the only determinant of voting behavior.

Election Results in Moscow and St. Petersburg

In the March 1989 elections to the USSR Congress of People's Deputies, all local Communist Party officials lost to independent candidates in Leningrad, while at least some won in Moscow. Following the RSFSR elections of 1990, the majority of radical reformers from the Leningrad Popular Front in the Leningrad City Soviet was larger than that of Democratic Russia's representatives in the Moscow City Soviet. On the eve of the collapse of the USSR, communists suffered a symbolic defeat in Leningrad, commonly known until then as "the birthplace of the Bolshevik Revolution." On June 12, 1991, Leningrad residents took part in a local poll in which they were asked whether they wanted to keep the Soviet-era name of their city, or to restore it to the one given it by Peter the Great in

90. Data from Goskomstat, Sotsial'no-ekonomicheskoe polozhenie Rossii, yanvar'-fevral' 1999 g., Moscow, 1999.

the eighteenth century). Local communists launched a nationwide opposition campaign to the proposed change.[91] Nonetheless, 54.9 percent of voters opted for St. Petersburg, while only 42.7 percent voted to keep the name Leningrad.[92]

As for Russian parliamentary elections, only 7.7 percent of St. Petersburg voters voted for the CPRF list in the 1993 elections and 13.2 percent in 1995, while in Moscow the figures were 11 percent and 14.8 percent, respectively. No CPRF candidates were elected in either of the two cities in 1993 or 1995. In 1995, the protest vote of St. Petersburg residents benefited the democratic opposition, with Grigorii Yavlinsky's Yabloko winning the largest portion of the vote (16 percent) on the party lists and six out of eight seats in the city's single-mandate constituencies. In the first round of the 1996 presidential election, Zyuganov got 14.9 percent in both capitals. In the second round, 17.9 percent voted for Zyuganov in St. Petersburg and 21.1 percent in Moscow.

The slight preference shown by Moscow voters for the CPRF may perhaps be explained by reference to the different historical legacies of the two cities. Over the decades, Moscow housed thousands, if not millions of communist bureaucrats. As well as the employees of various government offices and the leaders of the CPSU and CP RSFSR, these included retired Party bosses from all over the former USSR. St. Petersburg's residents have, by contrast, always been intensely proud of their city's cultural traditions and cherished its reputation as Russia's "Window on the West." At the same time, communist rule took on an even more cruel and oppressive shape in St. Petersburg than in Moscow. Beginning with mass executions at the dawn of the Communist regime, when Grigorii Zinoviev was Petrograd Party boss, and continuing right up until the early 1980s, when dissidents were harshly persecuted by the Leningrad KGB, Leningrad was always a more dangerous city than Moscow for those who dared to think differently.

---

91. See, for example, Glasnost', May 27, 1991; *Pravda*, June 3, 1991; *Sovetskaya Rossiya*, June 4 and July 10, 1991.

92. *Moskovskie novosti*, No. 25, 1991, p. 6. Apart from Communists, Russian nationalists—among them probably the most famous Russian anti-Communist, the writer Aleksandr Solzhenitsyn—objected to the restoration of the city's name because of its non-Slavonic (Dutch) sound. However, the Moscow Patriarchate intervened in favor of the change, dismissing Leningrad as "a mere framework into which Saint Peter's city was forced to fit" (*Komsomol'skaya Pravda*, June 12, 1991). This intervention by the leadership of the Russian Orthodox Church is believed to have played a decisive role in the way voters cast their ballots.

Elections in Moscow Oblast and Leningrad Oblast

Outside the two capitals, and even in the suburbs of Moscow and St. Petersburg, the situation is different. In Russia's 1995 parliamentary elections, three of the eleven deputies elected in single-mandate constituencies in Moscow Oblast were from the CPRF. In Leningrad Oblast, two of the three deputies elected in single-mandate constituencies were CPRF members (including the first secretary of the Leningrad Oblast party committee, Yurii Belov), while the third, Vladimir Grigoryev, was the only deputy elected to the State Duma from the Working Russia movement—the hard-line opposition to the CPRF.[93] In the 1996 presidential election, Yeltsin won a comfortable majority over Zyuganov in both Moscow and Leningrad Oblasts. A few months later, however, Aleksandr Belyakov, appointed governor of Leningrad Oblast by Yeltsin, lost the gubernatorial election in his region to the candidate of the PPUoR, Vadim Gustov.[94]

93. For a list of deputies elected to the State Duma on December 17, 1995, see Rossiyskaya gazeta, January 6, 1996.

94. For the CPRF campaign in support of Gustov, see *Sovetskaya Rossiya*, September 24, 1996. After the event, Zyuganov called a news conference to announce the CPRF's satisfaction with the results of the gubernatorial election in Leningrad Oblast (*Sovetskaya Rossiya*, October 4, 1996).

8: The Volga Region—A Set of Special Cases

Linked by Russia's "Mother River," the Volga economic zone consists of two republics and six oblasts—the Republics of Tatarstan and Kalmykia and the Astrakhan, Penza, Samara, Saratov, Ulyanovsk and Volgograd Oblasts. Despite its highly developed industrial base and favorable climate for agriculture, the Volga region has been hurt by economic recession. Its share in Russia's industrial production is considerably lower that its share in the country's population. The decline between 1990 and 1996 was from 50 to 60 percent in industry and from 20 to 25 percent in agriculture. Except for relatively prosperous Tatarstan and Samara Oblast, the regions of the Volga zone lag far behind the Russian average on all major social indices.

With the possible exception of Samara, voters in the Volga zone are reputed to be quite conservative (in the Russian sense of the word). In the 1995 parliamentary elections, the CPRF won more votes there than the pro-government Our Home is Russia and the party of the democratic opposition, Yabloko. In the 1996 presidential election, Zyuganov won more votes than Yeltsin in five of the zone's eight regions, while in two of them Zyuganov scored almost twice as many votes as Yeltsin. It seems that the residents of the region blame Moscow for the hardships of the current economic situation.

Kalmykia

Their similarities notwithstanding, several of the regions that make up the Volga zone can be regarded as a "special case." In the case of the tiny Kalmyk Republic, its specialty lies in the portrait of a Mafia-like dictatorship commonly painted of it in the Russian media. Such an image derives from the personality of the republic's president, Kirsan Ilyumzhinov, who is routinely accused by the press of embezzling federal funds, usurping power and even of being involved in the contract killing of the editor of Kalmykia's only opposition newspaper.[95] It is beyond the scope of this study to determine to what extent such attacks are substantiated. The proven facts about Ilyumzhinov's career are as follows:

---

95. See *Izvestiya*, February 5, June 11 and 16 1998; July 17, 21 and 22, 1998; *Obshchaya Gazeta*, No. 3, 1998, p. 8 and No. 24, 1998, p. 13; *Literaturnaya gazeta* , No. 29, 1998, p. 5; *Novaya Gazeta*, No. 24, 1998, p. 3; No. 27, 1998, p. 4; and No. 30, 1998, p. 3; *Moskovskie novosti*, No. 24, 1998, p. 8; *Argumenty i fakty*, No. 27, 1998, p. 10; Sovershenno sekretno, No. 7, 1998, pp. 18-19.

A graduate of the elite Moscow State Institute of Foreign Relations, Ilyumzhinov served in 1989-90 as a manager of one of the USSR's first joint ventures. By the early 1990s, he had amassed a multi-million dollar fortune. Parlaying his personal wealth into political power, the 31-year-old businessman ran for election in April 1993 as Kalmykia's first president. Traveling the steppes in a Lincoln limousine, Ilyumzhinov promised to make all the residents of the republic as rich as himself. If he was elected, he promised every shepherd would own a Mercedes and a mobile phone.

After his election, the young president dissolved Kalmykia's Supreme Soviet. Two years later, in violation of Russian electoral law, Ilyumzhinov called a referendum extending his term in office until the year 2002. Ignoring the protests of the Central Electoral Commission, he has remained in office. It may be added that inspectors from the Russian presidential administration have alleged that federal subsidies to Kalmykia worth billions of rubles have mysteriously disappeared.[96]

Kalmykia is one of the poorest regions in European Russia. The Kalmyks are the descendants of Mongol nomads who migrated from Central Asia in the seventeenth century and settled with their camels and sheep in the Volga basin. In 1943, the entire Kalmyk population was deported to Siberia by Stalin, accused of collaborating with the occupying Nazis. About one-third of them died between then and 1957, when they were finally allowed to return home. Today, they make up 52.6 percent of the population of the republic, while Russians make up 37.8 percent. As many as 61.5 percent of the population live in the countryside. As the Kalmyks are by tradition nomadic pastoralists, the republic developed little industry. What there was has been destroyed during Ilyumzhinov's rule. According to official data, industrial output in Kalmykia in 1996 constituted only 28 percent of that of 1990, as opposed to the average decline in Russia as a whole of 48 percent.

Kalmykia's voters are noted for their anti-Yeltsin sentiment. Only 31.1 percent of them voted for Yeltsin in the presidential election of 1991 (compared to 57.3 percent in Russia as a whole). And yet, the vote for the CPRF list in the republic in the 1993 parliamentary election was 14.2 percent, that is, only slightly above the Russian average. In the 1995 parliamentary election, Kalmykia's vote for the CPRF list was 17.9 percent—considerably less than the Russian average. A pro-Yeltsin candidate was elected in the 1993 election for the republic's one single-mandate constituency. Two years later, however, the pro-government candidate was

96. See Kto est' kto v Rossii, op. cit., pp. 269-71.

defeated in Kalmykia by a member of the Agrarian Party, former Deputy Prime Minister Gennadii Kulik. Kulik's victory marked the high point for the PPUoR in Kalmykia: a few months later, Zyuganov was defeated in Kalmykia with 26.7 percent of the votes to Yeltsin's 70.3 percent. To what extent election returns in such an area may be trusted remains a mystery that may never be solved.[97]

TATARSTAN

There was little mystery, by contrast, about the reliability of the returns of the March 1996 election for the president of Tatarstan. The outcome was a foregone conclusion since the incumbent, Mintimer Shaimiev, ran unopposed and was duly reelected.[98] Shaimiev was a former regional Communist Party leader turned post-communist potentate who enjoyed strong support from the local elite. Tatarstan's Communist Party tried to have the election invalidated, arguing that the federal law on elections banned single-candidate contests. The Shaimiev camp countered that Tatarstan's electoral regulations, which allowed such contests, took precedence over federal ones. The Communists proved unable to unseat Shaimiev. Three months later, fresh allegations of vote rigging were voiced over the outcome of the 1996 Russian presidential election in Tatarstan. In that election, Yeltsin won 38.3 percent in the first round and 61.4 percent in the second, while Zyuganov got 38.1 percent in the first round but only 32.3 percent in the second.

Tatarstan has an active CPRF organization led by its prominent first secretary, Aleksandr Salii. The party has nonetheless failed to achieve any significant electoral success in the republic. Apart from doubts about the accuracy of the vote count, there are a number of other reasons why Tatarstan's residents might wish to avoid arousing the wrath of Moscow with a protest vote. Tatarstan is a relatively prosperous region, thanks to its oil wells and pipelines, natural gas and petroleum production. Accordingly, the republic suffered less than other parts of Russia from the economic decline that has afflicted all of Russia's regions from 1989 onward. In 1996, Tatarstan's industrial output was 66 percent what it had been in 1990—less steep a decline than that registered in many other parts of Russia.

---

97. See, John Morrison, "Fraud Said To Mar Elections In Russian Backwater," Reuters, July 19, 1996

98. NTV, *Interfax*, March 24, 1996.

Equally important, Tatarstan succeeded in negotiating privileged status for itself through the bilateral power-sharing treaty that it signed with the Russian Federation in 1994. Unorthodox though this treaty was, it satisfied Tatarstan's insistence that it was a sovereign state and enabled Shaimiev to find the middle ground between the two extremes of opinion in his republic, where Tatars make up 48 percent of the population and ethnic Russians 45.5 percent, and where a vocal Tatar nationalist movement has repeatedly called for Tatarstan's secession from Russia. This would be a particularly drastic development in view of Tatarstan's strategic situation in the heart of Russia.

The skill with which Shaimiev picked his way through Russia's political minefields made him one of the country's most respected regional leaders.[99] He does not, however, appear to be much more of a democrat than Kalmykia's egregious President Ilyumzhinov. Formerly first secretary of the republic committee of the CPSU, Shaimiev was elected to the USSR Congress of People's Deputies in 1989 and the RSFSR Congresses of People's Deputies the following year. In both bodies, he proved a staunch advocate of the Party line and a critic of Yeltsin. In 1990, Shaimiev was elected chairman of Tatarstan's Supreme Soviet. Legally forbidden as a state official to combine a position in the Soviet structure with a leading position in the CPSU, Shaimiev relinquished his Party post. He provides a classic example of those former Party officials who moved seamlessly from high office in the CPSU to state employment (or, as seen in Chapter 3, to the new world of business). The prevalence of such officials accounts for the high degree of elite continuity characterizing today's Russia and marking it out from much of post-communist Eastern Europe.

Unlike the leaders of the Baltic states and Chechnya, Shaimiev did not wish to sever ties with Russia; his main aim was to secure local control over Tatarstan's abundant natural resources. He accordingly took care not to frame Tatarstan's dispute with Moscow in nationalist terms and to avoid exacerbating ethnic tensions.

From their positions in the Russian parliament, Shaimiev and other republic leaders saw to it that Yeltsin was allowed, in his capacity as president, to replace only the leaders of Russia's oblasts and krais, and not those of the republics. This widened the gap between the various constituent provinces. The autonomy that the republics enjoyed turned some of them—Kalmykia, Mordovia and others—into quasi-feudal princedoms.

---

99. For biography of Shaimiev see Kto est' kto v Rossii, op. cit., pp. 711-12.

Tatarstan had been the seat of the Kazan Khanate until its conquest in 1552 by Ivan the Terrible and its incorporation into Russia. The Tatars tried on numerous occasions to throw off Russian rule, but their efforts to regain independence were ruthlessly suppressed. During the Soviet era, Tatarstan's leaders deeply resented the fact that their territory only had the status of an autonomous republic within Russia, rather than that of a Union republic. They campaigned hard, but unsuccessfully, to raise Tatarstan's official status during the adoption of Stalin's constitution in 1936, during the 1950s, and again during discussions on the 1977 "Brezhnev" constitution. Not until the breakup of the USSR were they finally able to negotiate a higher status for their republic and to win recognition of the sovereignty to which they believed they were entitled.[100]

Tatarstan's electorate is a classic example of the conformist vote. Tatarstan refused to conduct the 1991 referendum on the introduction of an executive presidency in Russia, but in all other referendums the vote for proposals promoted by the powers-that-be has been consistently higher in Tatarstan than in Russia in general. To be precise, 87.5 percent of Tatarstan's voters voted for the preservation of the Soviet Union (contrasted with 71.3 percent in the RSFSR as a whole); 66.4 percent said they trusted Yeltsin more than the Supreme Soviet (contrasted with 58.8 percent in the Russian Federation as a whole); and 74.8 percent voted for Yeltsin's constitution (contrasted with 58.4 percent in Russia as a whole). Considerably fewer votes than average were cast for the CPRF list in Tatarstan in the elections for seats in the State Duma in 1993 and 1995: 9.4 percent and 15.4 percent, respectively. All of the CPRF candidates who competed in Tatarstan in 1993 and 1995 for single-mandate seats in the State Duma lost either to pro-government candidates or to their future political allies from the Agrarian or People's Power factions in the Duma.

Astrakhan Oblast

In sharp distinction to the two above-mentioned republics, in Astrakhan it is not the election returns but the official statistics on social and economic conditions that have to be taken with a pinch of salt. A considerable if, by definition incalculable, share of the population's income is generated in the shadow economy through sturgeon poaching and caviar smuggling.[101]

100. Mansur Khasanov, "The Making of the Statehood of Tatarstan: Stages and Prospects," Prism, 12 March 1999.

101. See, for example, *Izvestiya*, September 9, 1997.

Situated on the wide Volga delta and the Caspian shore, Astrakhan Oblast is famous for the high quality of its fruit and vegetables, which could surely be sold to gourmets for high prices if only the art of marketing were more highly developed in Russia. Outside the floodplain and delta, however, the land is arid and used only for cattle and sheep herding and salt extraction. Until its conquest by Ivan the Terrible and its incorporation into Russia in 1556, Astrakhan was the center of a Tatar khanate. Today, 72 percent of the population are ethnic Russians, 12.7 are ethnic Kazakhs and only 7.2 percent are Tatars.

Like other agricultural centers, Astrakhan is regarded as a "pink," or pro-Communist region, even though the color does not seem to be very intense. True, Zyuganov scored 47.8 percent of the vote in Astrakhan in the 1996 presidential election as against 46.9 percent for Yeltsin in the second round. Moreover, Astrakhan is represented in the Council of the Federation by the speaker of the oblast legislature, who is a member of the CPRF. Yet the CPRF/PPUoR has not done especially well in other elections in the region. In the various referendums held in Russia, Astrakhan's voting results have been quite close to the average for Russia as a whole. In the parliamentary election of 1993, the vote for the CPRF list in Astrakhan amounted to 16.6 percent—4.2 percent higher than the national average in 1993, while in 1995 Astrakhan's vote was 24.1 percent—1.8 percent higher than the Russian average. Astrakhan's representative in the single-mandate part of the State Duma, Vyacheslav Zvolinsky, was supported by the PPUoR in the course of his campaign. The same Zvolinsky stood in the gubernatorial election in Astrakhan Oblast in December 1996, and again enjoyed the support of the PPUoR.[102] However, Zvolinsky lost to the pro-government incumbent, Anatolii Guzhvin, with 39.8 percent of the vote against Guzhvin's 52.5 percent. Again, it should be noted that Astrakhan's gubernatorial election was not a clear-cut case of "democrats versus communists." Guzhvin had made his career in the Komsomol and served as second secretary of the Astrakhan Oblast Committee of the CPSU until the August 1991 coup. Appointed regional Governor by Yeltsin at the end of that month, Guzhvin tried to avoid antagonizing Moscow lest he lose his new job. On the eve of the 1995 parliamentary election, he became the leader of the Astrakhan branch of Our Home is Russia.[103]

102. See *Izvestiya*, December 3, 1996.
103. For Guzhvin's biography see the National News Service website.

VOLGOGRAD OBLAST

In comparison with the idyllic pink of Astrakhan, Volgograd Oblast is as red as the ripe tomatoes or the watermelons that grow on the fertile lands of the Volga basin. It has been governed since December 1996 by Nikolai Maksyuta, a communist with twenty years in the Party, who formerly chaired the Volgograd city Soviet. He defeated the Yeltsin-appointed incumbent, Ivan Shabunin, by 50.9 percent of the vote to 44.2 percent.[104]

The region is noted for the unusual level of activism of various communist and nationalist organizations. The Volgograd branch of the CPRF is particularly influential, claiming over 20,000 CPRF members, which makes it one of the largest regional organizations in Russia. Its first secretary, Alevtina Aparina, is an energetic lady, well known at national as well as regional levels in her capacity as chair of the State Duma's Committee on the Affairs of Women, Family and Youth. Apart from the CPRF and other "traditional" communist movements, the region is famous for the presence on its territory of an exotic variety called the Party of Communists "Vsevolod Unity" (Edinenie Vsevolod), whose ideology consists of Lenin hero-worship mixed with a schismatic Christianity bearing the marks of theosophy and other Eastern cults.[105]

The Oblast Committee of the CPRF (Obkom) plays a role reminiscent of the classical communist period, when CPSU committees supervised all the activities of state and government bodies on their territory. In other regions where CPRF members have won gubernatorial elections, the Obkom generally keeps a low profile. In Volgograd, however, Aparina's committee is said to exert considerable influence over the governor's policies, including personnel appointments. On occasion, Obkom intervention has provoked international tension. This was the case during the summer of 1998, when the Volgograd Deputy-Governor Vasilii Galushkin, tried to revoke a Russo-German agreement relating to a memorial cemetery for German soldiers killed in the Battle of Stalingrad.[106] Galushkin was reacting to a campaign in the local media by communists and World War Two veterans. Activists of the Volgograd PPUoR have also campaigned for Volgograd to resume the name, Stalingrad, which it bore between

104. NTV, December 30, 1996.

105. The state-run channel of Russian television, RTR, devoted an hour's program to the PKVU in its "Top Secret" series, broadcast on February 28, 1998. See also *Nezavisimaya Gazeta*, January 27, 1998.

106. *Nezavisimaya Gazeta*, August 21, 1998; *Obshchaya Gazeta*, No. 34, 1998, p. 7.

1925 and 1961.[107] The campaign, which was approved in a vote by twenty-four of the twenty-five members of the Obkom, is generally seen as an attempt to rehabilitate Stalin himself.[108]

Against this background, it comes as little surprise that residents of Volgograd Oblast vote communist. However, this has not always been the case. In the early 1990s, they voted for Yeltsin. In 1991, for instance, as many as 72.8 percent of the electorate voted for the introduction of an executive presidency in Russia. Later that year, 55.7 percent voted for Yeltsin in Russia's first presidential election; and in the referendum of April 1993, 53.7 percent of the electorate cast their ballots in favor of the President. The public mood in Volgograd changed during 1993 and has since grown increasingly critical of the Yeltsin leadership. Support for the CPRF kept pace with this change of heart. In December 1993, 51.3 percent of Volgograd voters rejected the Yeltsin Constitution. In the parliamentary elections held at the same time, 14.4 percent voted for the CPRF list while two independent candidates and two members of other opposition parties—the Agrarians and Yabloko—won Volgograd's four single-mandate seats. Two years later, almost twice as many voters (28.1 percent) chose the CPRF list while the single-mandate seats were won by three members of the CPRF and one by an Agrarian. In July 1996, Zyuganov won 50.5 percent of the Volgograd vote in the presidential election against 44.2 percent for Yeltsin.

Electoral dynamics in Volgograd Oblast suggest that historical and psychological motives play an important but not decisive role in how people vote. True, the intense local patriotism and pride felt by the population in their region's role in the Second World War seemed to incline them in favor of the communists. But the fact that similar procommunist sentiments are common to other agricultural regions hit, like Volgograd, by falling living standards, suggests that the issue of living standards may be an even more influential factor accounting for the popularity of the CPRF.

PENZA OBLAST

In September 1998, the regional statistics department announced the collapse of the economy of yet another "red" spot in the Volga zone, Penza Oblast.[109] Although agriculture and food processing are major economic activities in the region, the consumption of meat products in

107. *Nezavisimaya Gazeta*, August 11, 1998.
108. *Sovetskaya Rossiya*, September 26, 1998
109. *Izvestiya*, September 5, 1998.

Penza Oblast fell by about 20 percent within the space of a year because of the drop in the population's purchasing power. Deadbeat local enterprises were unable to contribute to the local pension fund. In September, half of the region's retirees received pension payments that had been owed to them since June, while the other half received nothing at all. These facts suggested that the election seven months earlier of a "pragmatic" and "impartial" manager as governor of this "red" region had not improved the social and economic situation in the oblast.

Like voters in neighboring Volgograd, the residents of Penza Oblast voted for Yeltsin as president in 1991. In March 1991, 65.8 percent of them voted in favor of an executive presidency for Russia, while 61.3 percent voted for Yeltsin in the first presidential election a few months later. The change of heart came earlier in Penza than in Volgograd, however. This is understandable, given that Penza suffers from severe soil erosion and is therefore poorer than Volgograd. Per capita income in Penza in 1996 amounted on average to 393,000 Rubles a month (compared to 476,000 Rubles in Volgograd), while the average monthly salary in Penza was 438,000 Rubles and 649,000 Rubles in Volgograd. Already in the April 1993 referendum, 54.7 percent of Penza's voters expressed no confidence in the president, while 56.6 percent said they did not trust his social and economic policies. In December 1993, 60.1 percent of voters voted "no" when asked whether they approved of the new Russian constitution. The CPRF scored much better in Penza than in most other regions in both the 1993 and the 1995 parliamentary elections. In 1993, 20.8 percent of Penza voters voted for the CPRF list, and in 1995 the figure was 37.3 percent. In both cases, the militant CPRF activist, Viktor Ilyukhin, won one of Penza's two single-mandate seats in the State Duma. The other went to a Yabloko deputy in 1993 and to an Agrarian two years later. In the 1996 presidential election, Zyuganov was victorious in Penza Oblast, winning 50.0 percent in the first round and 58.9 percent in the second.

Penza Oblast was one of a handful of regions permitted by Yeltsin in 1993 to hold direct gubernatorial elections. In April 1993, Anatolii Kovlyagin, a career CPSU official and Penza native who had served first as Second Secretary of the Penza Oblast Obkom and later as chairman of the Oblast Soviet's Executive Committee, but who had resigned from the CPSU following the August 1991 coup, ran against the Yeltsin-appointed incumbent on an anti-Yeltsin platform, advocating a slower pace of reform. Kovlyagin had the backing of a variety of political parties, including the Communist Party, and was elected with 70 percent of the vote. Two years later, in 1995, Kovlyagin became a member of the leadership of Our Home is Russia.[110] During his tenure as governor, he acquired a reputation for phrase mongering and disgraced himself with the protectionism and the favoritism of his economic and personnel policies.[111] When the second gubernatorial election was held in April 1998, Kovlyagin suffered major humiliation, winning only 13 percent of the vote. Vasilii Bochkarev, head of administration in a district of Penza, won with 58 percent of the votes.112. Bochkarev's trump card was the fact that wages, pensions, and child allowances were being paid on time in the district he managed—the only place in Penza Oblast where this was the case. Bochkarev reportedly owed this miracle to his control of the central market in Penza city.[113]

SAMARA OBLAST

Samara Oblast is a major industrial powerhouse in the mostly agricultural Volga zone. World War II and the presence of abundant petroleum and natural gas deposits in the oblast prompted great industrial development, especially oil refining, petrochemicals, and a broad range of engineering in towns along the Volga. A huge hydroelectric station was built on the Volga in the 1950s. In 1970s, FIAT built a large automobile plant, AvtoVAZ, in the town of Tolyatti. Space and aviation construction industries also found their place in the region. Such industries were hit in the 1990s by Russia's economic crises. AvtoVAZ, for example, is producing 125,000 motor vehicles a year instead of the 748,500 originally envisaged.[114] While there have been protests in the region, however, the CPRF has not so far been the main beneficiary. Samara Governor Konstantin Titov, formerly Deputy-Chairman of Our Home is Russia, became the most outspoken critic of his former party boss, Prime Minister Viktor Chernomyrdin, in the Council of the Federation.[115]

In spite of the presence in Samara Oblast of a strong and militant CPRF organization, led by Duma deputy Valentin Romanov, the party's electoral success in the region has so far been modest. Voting in the vari-

110. Kovlyagin voiced his opposition to the Gaidar reforms in a long article published in *Literaturnaya gazeta*, No. 35, 1997, p. 5

111. *Obshchaya Gazeta*, No. 14, 1998, p. 12. For an earlier report on corruption and power abuse in Penza Oblast, see *Izvestiya*, December 18, 1997.

112. *Izvestiya*, April 14, 1998.

113. See *Izvestiya*, August 3, 1997.

114. *Nezavisimaya Gazeta*, June 25, 1998.

115. The session on Chernomyrdin in the Russian Senate was broadcast by the RTR on September 6, 1998.

ous referendums has been close to the average for the rest of Russia. Support for Yeltsin in the 1991 presidential election was 10 percent higher than the average. The CPRF party list won 16.4 percent of the votes in Samara in 1993 and 22.3 percent in 1995. Yet, while all five deputies elected to Samara's single-mandate seats in 1993 joined various pro-government factions in the Duma, two years later three of them represented the CPRF, one the Agrarian Party and two Our Home is Russia. The three CPRF deputies included Romanov and the notoriously anti-Semitic retired army general, Albert Makashov. In the 1996 presidential race, Yeltsin won 51.9 percent of the votes in Samara as opposed to Zyuganov's 42.7 percent. And, in December 1996, Titov defeated Romanov in the first round of the gubernatorial election with 63.4 percent against 29.9 percent.

SARATOV OBLAST

The September 1996 victory of Dmitrii Ayatskov in the gubernatorial election in Saratov Oblast was seen as a major breakthrough in the "red belt" of communist-dominated regions. In an interview that he gave to a Moscow newspaper during his campaign, Ayatskov said that punching a hole in the "red belt" was the main aim of his campaign.[116] In the event, Ayatskov defeated the candidate of the CPRF, Anatolii Gordeev, with 80.2 percent of the vote against 16.1 percent. The result struck a mortal blow to the local committee of the CPRF, the last island of organized opposition to the authoritarian Ayatskov, who had already managed to assert control over the regional legislature and the local media since Yeltsin appointed him governor in April 1996. To a large extent, Ayatskov owed his electoral success to the unpopularity of his predecessor, Yurii Belykh, who had served as governor until Yeltsin replaced him with Ayatskov.[117]

Saratov Oblast encloses the territory of the former Volga German Autonomous Soviet Socialist Republic, which was abolished by Stalin, allegedly for security reasons, in 1941. The region is rich with resources that ought to make it quite prosperous. Its fertile soil makes it a prime agricultural area while the presence of natural gas and some petroleum have stimulated the growth of oil refining, the chemical industry and engineering. In the early 1980s, Saratov claimed the highest per capita income in the Volga economic zone. By the late 1990s, however, the aver-

116. Komsomol'skaya *Pravda*, April 12, 1996.

117. "Saratovskaya oblast v iyule," Politicheskii monitoring IGPI, August 21, 1996.

age salary in Saratov Oblast was about half the Russian average, while the subsistence wage was equal. Once a major agricultural center, Saratov has been forced to import basic foodstuffs, such as bread and milk, from other Russian regions.

This deterioration of living standards has on occasion prompted local residents to resort to a protest vote. In 1991-93, Yeltsin won all the referendums held in Saratov Oblast, though his majority in this region was sometimes lower than the average for Russia as a whole. In the 1991 presidential election, 55.7 percent of Saratov voters chose Yeltsin. In elections to the Duma, the CPRF list won 15.3 percent in 1993 and 28.3 percent in 1995, which was 3 percent and 5 percent higher than the average, respectively. This increase in the protest vote was also reflected in the voting for Saratov's four single-member constituencies in the State Duma. In 1993 the CPRF candidate, Gordeev, won one of the region's four single-mandate seats in the Duma. Two years later, however, three of the four were won by the PPUoR—one by an Agrarian, one by a member of People's Power and one by a CPRF member. This last was Oleg Mironov, currently Russia's ombudsman, who owed his victory to the joint efforts of the CPRF and Yabloko, both of whom were eager to prevent the election of another candidate, the extreme Russian nationalist Nikolai Lysenko. Last but not least, Zyuganov scored 50 percent in the 1996 presidential election in Saratov Oblast as opposed to 44.1 percent scored by Yeltsin.

Ulyanovsk Oblast

Lenin's native Ulyanovsk (formerly Simbirsk) Oblast may be dubbed "an especially special case" among the Russian regions. It is reputed to be "red" in a very special way—not merely because of its tendency to vote for communists but because, perhaps even more importantly, it served as a test case region that was for several years spared the rigors of economic reform. Following the August 1991 coup, Yeltsin was forced by public pressure in the region to appoint as governor the former First Secretary of the Ulyanovsk Oblast Committee of the CPSU, Yurii Goryachev. Goryachev advocated a "gradual transition to the market."[118] To this end he maintained fixed prices on rent and on staple goods such as bread and milk. The region's chief claim to fame became its retention of that Soviet-era holdover, the ration card. Goryachev could not, however, prevent the privatization of local industries, such as the giant

118. *Moskovskie novosti*, No. 39, 1996, p. 7.

"Aviastar" aviation factory. These enterprises are currently at a standstill. They are not paying wages to their employees, taxes to the regional budget, or dues to the Pension Fund.

Because their founding father had been born there, Soviet leaders regarded Ulyanovsk Oblast as their equivalent of the Holy Land. Accordingly, they were generous with investments in local industries. To this day, Ulyanovsk belongs to the minority of relatively prosperous Russian regions that do not receive federal subsidies but, on the contrary, make a net contribution to the federal budget. Needless to say, Ulyanovsk voters tend to vote for the CPRF. The pressing problem of unpaid wages and pensions has, moreover, opened the way for the establishment in Ulyanovsk Oblast of a powerful workers' movement in which the local CPRF organization and its leader, Aleksandr Kruglikov, have played an active role. In the fall of 1998, the movement organized a number of actions around a purely political demand—the impeachment of President Yeltsin. The organizers relied on the support of Goryachev who, regardless of his formal membership of the leadership of Our Home is Russia, described himself as still "a Communist in my heart."[119]

While Yeltsin came in first in the 1991 presidential election in Ulyanovsk Oblast, his score of 52.8 percent was below the average 57.3 percent. Two years later, 52.1 percent of Ulyanovsk voters expressed their lack of confidence in Yeltsin in the April 1993 referendum. Yeltsin's new Constitution was approved in Ulyanovsk Oblast in December 1993 with a bare 51.2 percent of the vote. The CPRF list won about 50 percent more votes than the all-Russia average in the 1993 election to the State Duma, but independent candidates won all single-mandate seats. The losers were independents too, since the 1993 parliamentary elections in Ulyanovsk Oblast were fought on an entirely nonpartisan basis, at least as far as the single-mandate seats were concerned. Nor did the CPRF allocate a single seat for an Ulyanovsk representative in the "party list" half of the first Duma, although it did so for many other regions. Two years later, the situation was different. As many as 37.2 percent of the voters of Ulyanovsk voted for the CPRF list in December 1995, while Goryachev's hard-core predecessor in his capacity as regional CPSU boss, Oleg Kazarov won election to the Duma in a single-mandate constituency. In the 1996 presidential election, Zyuganov won nearly twice as many votes as Yeltsin—that is, 45.8 percent to 23.8 percent—in the first round. In the second round,

119. *Sovetskaya Rossiya*, August 1 and September 3, 1998.

the gap narrowed slightly, Zyuganov's majority being 56.3 percent against Yeltsin's 37.8 percent. And, despite all the reports of the voters' procommunist sentiments, Goryachev defeated Kruglikov to win reelection as governor in December 1996.[120]

120. OMRI Daily Digest, December 30, 1996.

9: The Urals

For a long time, the Urals region was regarded as the cradle of democracy simply because Yeltsin had been born there. In reality, at least one oblast in the Urals economic zone (Kurgan) belongs to the "red belt," while another (Orenburg) is decidedly "pink." Overall, political developments in the region's two republics (Bashkortostan and Udmurtia), five oblasts (Chelyabinsk, Kurgan, Orenburg, Perm and Sverdlovsk) and single autonomous okrug (the Komi-Permyak AO) are fairly typical of those in Russia as a whole.

Bashkortostan

Elections in the Republics of Bashkortostan and Udmurtia have tended to be marred by instances of abuse. This was particularly flagrant in Bashkortostan, where in 1998 President Murtaza Rakhimov ignored repeated orders from Russia's Supreme Court to run for reelection in an open, competitive election. Rakhimov seemed however to enjoy the protection of President Yeltsin—apparently as a reward for the pressure Rakhimov put on the electorate of his republic to vote for Yeltsin in the 1996 presidential election. A former director of the Ufa oil refinery, Rakhimov had been elected speaker of the Bashkortostan Supreme Soviet in 1990. In November 1993, he was elected president of the republic.

The Bashkirs are a Turkic people of mixed origin, including Mongol and Finno-Ugric elements. In the thirteenth century, the Golden Horde conquered their territory; later, it came under the control of the Kazan khanate. It was incorporated into Russia in 1557.

As in many other parts of the former USSR, Stalin drew the present borders of the republic more or less arbitrarily. He ensured that the Bashkirs were from the beginning a minority in their own republic. Today, Bashkirs make up only 23 percent of the population, while ethnic Russians constitute 39 percent and Tatars nearly 29 percent.

Like neighboring Tatarstan, Bashkortostan has highly developed agricultural and industrial sectors. The republic is rich in mineral resources. It produces iron and steel and is a major oil-producer and oil-refiner with a sophisticated petrochemical industry. Bashkortostan has a network of oil refineries, linked by pipeline both to its own oil fields and to those of Tatarstan, which does not have the advantage of its own refineries. The republic is also noted for its horse-breeding and bee-keeping.

In the early 1990s, Bashkortostan's leaders waged a determined struggle with the federal government over autonomy. In defiance of Moscow, they declared sovereignty over the republic's natural resources. The republic's leaders realized however that, while they wanted to secure economic autonomy, Bashkortostan was surrounded by Russia on all sides and was dependent on it for communications, defense and pipelines. Political separatism was never seen as a viable option.

Elections in Bashkortostan

In the early 1990s, Bashkortostan had the reputation of being a "red" region. In April 1991, 54.4 percent of the voters in the republic had approved the introduction of a presidency in Russia, while 45.9 percent voted for Yeltsin in the presidential election later that same year. In both cases, the pro-Yeltsin vote was considerably smaller in Bashkortostan than the average for Russia as a whole. On the eve of the April 1993 referendum on confidence in Yeltsin and his policies, Rakhimov (who was at that time chairman of Bashkortostan's Supreme Soviet) publicly predicted that Yeltsin would lose the vote. "New people and [new] presidents who—unlike Boris Yeltsin—respect their people, should come to power in Russia," said Rakhimov, adding that Yeltsin was the leader of the radical democrats rather than the "father of the entire nation."[121] When the votes were cast, 57.7 percent of Bashkortostan's voters voted no confidence in the Russian president, while 61.4 percent indicated that they had no trust in his economic policies. Eight months later, 58 percent of voters in Bashkortostan voted against the Yeltsin constitution.

In the 1993 elections to the State Duma, 15.1 percent of Bashkortostan's voters voted for the CPRF, while in 1995 the percentage was 25.5—slightly higher than the Russian average on both occasions. The leader of the CPRF in the republic, Valentin Nikitin, was elected a Duma deputy on the party list in 1993, and he was reelected in a single-mandate constituency two years later. A watershed occurred between the first and second rounds of Russia's 1996 presidential election. In the run-up to the first round, Rakhimov and the republic administration did everything in their power to secure Yeltsin's victory. Rakhimov personally campaigned on Yeltsin's behalf in no fewer than thirty-nine districts. Zyuganov nonetheless won the first round of the election by 41.9 percent against 34.2 percent for Yeltsin. Rakhimov responded with a public pledge that, in the second round, returns in Bashkortostan would be "diametrically opposite."[122] So they indeed proved: in the second round, Yeltsin

121. As quoted by the National News Service <www.nns.ru>
122. *Izvestiya*, June 27, 1996.

won 51 percent against Zyuganov's 43.1 percent. How Rakhimov foresaw such a change in the mood of the electorate remains a mystery. But the Kremlin rewarded Rakhimov's loyalty not only by actively supporting his bid for reelection in 1998 but also by allowing Rakhimov to violate the law in order to keep his job. The Supreme Court three times ruled that the actions of Rakhimov's supporters in the course of his second presidential campaign had been illegal. On all three occasions, the republic leadership ignored the rulings of the Supreme Court. The offending actions had included bringing the date of the election forward to ensure that polling took place before Rakhimov attained the age of 65 when, by law, he would no longer have been eligible to stand. Next, the Electoral Commission refused to register all but one of those desiring to run against Rakhimov. Pretexts were found to shut down several of the republic's independent newspapers and a television station in order to prevent negative reporting.[123] Finally, suspicions were aroused when the Electoral Commission printed three times as many ballot papers as there were voters. The Russian Supreme Court annulled the outcome of the presidential election in Bashkortostan but, as usual, Rakhimov and his team ignored its ruling.[124]

UDMURTIA

By comparison with Bashkortostan, the Republic of Udmurtia seems law-abiding. By any normal standard, however, its record is less than squeaky clean. In 1996, Udmurtia plunged into a conflict typical of many Russian regions—a power struggle between the republic leadership and the mayor of the provincial capital, Izhevsk. The conflict erupted after the republic ruled that the administrators of Udmurtia's towns, cities and rural districts were to be appointed by the republic authorities rather than, as up until that time, popularly elected. Russia's Constitutional Court ruled the republic's law unconstitutional and, while the republic authorities tried for a while to ignore the court's ruling, eventually they capitulated.[125] In the April 1998 elections for heads of local government, all but one of the leaders of the cities, towns and districts of the Udmurt Republic were reelected to their previous offices.[126]

---

123. *Novaya Gazeta*, No. 1, 1998; *Literaturnaya gazeta*, No. 39, 1998, p. 8.
124. *Izvestiya*, April 8, 1998, June 25 and September 3, 1998; *Argumenty i fakty*, No. 24, 1998, p. 10.
125. *Obshchaya Gazeta*, No. 44, 1996, p. 2, and No. 48, 1996, p. 8; *Moskovskie novosti*, No. 48, 1996, p. 6; *Nezavisimaya Gazeta*, April 10, 1998; *Izvestiya*, April 14, 1996.
126. *Nezavisimaya Gazeta*, April 22, 1998.

As in Bashkortostan, the titular nationality is a minority in Udmurtia, comprising 31.3 percent of the population. Ethnic Russians make up 59.5 percent and Tatars 6.5 percent. The predominance of ethnic Russians may be explained by the fact that Udmurtia was a center of the Soviet machine-building industry, with as many as 60 percent of the republic's enterprises belonging to the military-industrial complex. The Kalashnikov rifle—probably Russia's most famous military invention—was created in Udmurtia where its inventor, Mikhail Kalashnikov, still lives.

Neither the end of the Cold War nor the collapse of the Soviet empire seems to have inspired Udmurtia's gunsmiths to vote for communist candidates. This fact alone gives lie to the Marxist doctrine that interests rather than ideas determines human behavior. In 1991, 67.2 percent of Udmurtia's voters voted for the introduction of an executive presidency in Russia, while 51.9 percent voted for Yeltsin in the ensuing presidential election. In the referendums conducted in 1993, 55.9 percent of Udmurtia's voters expressed confidence in the Russian president and 57.5 percent voted in favor of the new constitution. In the parliamentary elections of 1993 and 1995, the vote for the CPRF party list was lower in Udmurtia than in Russia as a whole—11.1 percent in December 1993 and 14.9 percent two years later. In the single-mandate districts, two independent deputies were elected on both occasions to the republic's seats in the State Duma. The chairman of the republic committee of the CPRF, Nikolai Sapozhnikov, was elected a deputy of the State Duma on the party list, but Sapozhnikov is a moderate communist, an advocate of small business who is on record as stating that he does not expect to see the victory of communism in Russia in the foreseeable future.[127]

CHELYABINSK OBLAST

Chelyabinsk Oblast is a major industrial center. Until 1992, the region was closed to foreigners because nuclear weapons were produced on its territory.

Yeltsin was initially very popular in Chelyabinsk. In March 1991, 81.69 percent of local voters voted for the introduction of the executive presidency, while 77.2 percent voted for Yeltsin in the presidential election in June of that year. In two referendums conducted in Chelyabinsk Oblast in 1993, 71.5 percent expressed confidence in Yeltsin and 77.2 percent approved of the new constitution. In elections to the State Duma,

127. For an interview with the leader of Udmurtia's CPRF, see *Moskovskie novosti*, No. 39, 1998, p. 8.

votes for the CPRF list in Chelyabinsk Oblast amounted to little more than half the national average—7.5 percent in 1993 and 14.7 percent in 1995. No CPRF candidates were elected to the region's single-mandate constituencies on either occasion.

Regional Governor Petr Sumin was, however, a strong opponent of reform, even though he was not a member of the CPRF. A former Komsomol and Party official, Sumin had been elected chairman of the Chelyabinsk Oblast Soviet in 1990. In August 1991, Sumin declined to side either with Yeltsin or with the organizers of the coup. At the end of 1991, accordingly, Yeltsin appointed as governor not Sumin but Vadim Solovev, who had until then chaired the Chelyabinsk City Soviet. Yeltsin's choice was not popular with the local population. In March 1993, the oblast Soviet called a gubernatorial election. Although the local court overruled the decision, the election went ahead and Sumin won.[128] Yeltsin thereupon decreed the election invalid; but the local authorities ignored his decision, with the result that the oblast had two heads of administration for the following six months. Furthermore: Russia's Supreme Soviet and Constitutional Court endorsed Sumin's election. Only Yeltsin's crushing victory over the parliament in October 1993 prompted the authorities in Chelyabinsk to implement the president's decree. Yeltsin's action did not make Solovev any more popular than before. In December 1996, a coalition of opposition parties, including the CPRF, nominated Sumin their candidate in the forthcoming gubernatorial election.[129] Sumin defeated Solovev in the first round by 53 percent against 15 percent.[130]

Kurgan Oblast

Kurgan Oblast is the red spot of the Urals. This is not surprising, given that Kurgan is mostly an agricultural region. Agricultural machinery, medicines and a wide range of foodstuffs are produced there and 45.2 percent of the population lives in the countryside.

Kurgan nonetheless belongs to that category of "red" regions that supported Yeltsin in the initial stages of his career. As many as 71.6 percent of Kurgan voters supported the introduction of the executive presidency in March 1991. Three months later, 52.3 percent voted for Yeltsin

128. *Itar-Tass*, 12 April 1993; and *Komsomolskaya Pravda*, September 11, 1993.

129. The CPRF daily, *Sovetskaya Rossiya*, devoted two of its six pages to Sumin in its December 15, 1996 issue.

130. *Nezavisimaya Gazeta*, December 25, 1996.

to be president. In 1993, 50.3 percent expressed confidence in the president and 57.2 percent voiced approval of Russia's new constitution. In both the 1993 and 1995 parliamentary elections, the vote in Kurgan Oblast for the CPRF list was close to the national average—12.6 percent in 1993 and 22.2 percent in 1995. In single-mandate constituencies, Kurgan elected a member of Zhirinovsky's Liberal Democrats in 1993 and a People's Power supporter in 1995. In the 1996 presidential election, Zyuganov won 37.5 percent of the votes in Kurgan in the first round, as opposed to 29.3 percent for Yeltsin, while in the second round Zyuganov won 50.2 percent and Yeltsin 43.4 percent. Last but not least, CPRF member Oleg Bogomolov was elected as Oblast governor in December 1996. Bogomolov's predecessor, Anatolii Sobolev, who had been appointed governor by presidential decree, came in third.

Orenburg Oblast

This oblast is located on the divide between Europe and Asia. It differs from many of its Urals neighbors in that its terrain is not mountainous but consists mainly of steppe land. The territory was originally home to several nomadic tribes. The Russian state took control of the region in the sixteenth and seventeenth centuries, when it became the home of the Ural Cossacks. In the eighteen century, the region was the center of the famous rebellion of Cossacks and peasants led by Emelyan Pugachev. Today, the oblast is one of Russia's most important industrial and agricultural regions. Its economy is dominated by gas production. Heavy industry is highly developed. Much of the region is steppe and was not put to the plow until the Virgin Lands campaign of the 1950s.

In October 1991, President Boris Yeltsin appointed a moderate reformer, Vladimir Yelagin, as oblast governor. At the time of his appointment, Yelagin was first secretary of the RSFSR Komsomol; previously, he had headed the Orenburg committee of the All-Union Komsomol. In sharp contrast to the CP RSFSR, which opposed both Gorbachev's and Yeltsin's reforms, the RSFSR Young Communist League (RSFSR Komsomol) was set up in 1990 as a group of Yeltsin fans and supported him from the time of its creation until it was disbanded following the August 1991 coup. Yelagin remained loyal to Yeltsin ever after. In June 1993, for instance, Yelagin denounced the plan for a Urals republic put forward by Governor Rossel of Sverdlovsk Oblast, arguing that such an entity would undermine the integrity of the Russian Federation. Later that same year, Yelagin supported Yeltsin in his bloody conflict with the Russian parliament. In December 1995, Yeltsin rewarded Yelagin's loyalty by including Orenburg in a handful of Russian regions permitted to hold a direct gubernatorial election. Yelagin had agitated for the election, hoping it would give him greater leverage when dealing with Moscow, and he was duly elected governor with 58.8 percent of the vote.

On other occasions, voting in Orenburg Oblast has been similar to that in Kurgan Oblast, as outlined above. In March 1991, 71 percent of Orenburg's voters approved the introduction of an executive presidency; 57.2 percent of them voted for Yeltsin in the first round of the Russian presidential election later that year. In 1993, 50.1 percent said "yes" when asked in the referendum whether they trusted the Russian president, while 58.4 percent approved of the new constitution. In the 1993 and 1995 parliamentary elections, 13.2 percent of Orenburg's voters voted for the CPRF list in 1993 and 23.6 percent in 1995. In the single-mandate districts, one Agrarian, one Yabloko candidate and one member of the CPRF were elected to the State Duma in Orenburg in 1993; in the election two years later, all these deputies were reelected.

In 1996, Zyuganov won 53.9 percent of the votes in the presidential election in Orenburg Oblast, while Yeltsin scored only 40.8 percent. In March 1998, the CPRF achieved modest success in the elections for seats in the regional legislature, winning 17 of 43 seats in the Orenburg Oblast Legislative Assembly.[131] The success of the CPRF in this south Urals region may to some extent be explained by public rejection of the abuse of power allegedly carried out by local authorities. At one point, for example, sixty workers of the local electricity station complained about Orenburg Mayor Gennadii Donkovtsev, who had reportedly not only stopped paying pensions and child allowances but raised rents and income tax rates in order to fund his election campaign.[132] Some credit was doubtless also due to the efforts of the regional CPRF leader, Yurii Nikiforenko. A teacher of history and social science, Nikiforenko owed his political experience to his activities as a deputy of the regional Legislative Assembly. A highly prolific journalist, Nikiforenko was elected a deputy of the State Duma on the CPRF party list, where he became a hardworking and very active parliamentarian.[133]

---

131. *Sovetskaya Rossiya*, March 15 and 26, 1998.

132. For the text, see *Argumenty i fakty*, No. 35, 1998, p. 1.

133. See "Federal'noe Sobranie: Sovet Federatsii, Gosudarstvennaya Duma," Spravochnik, 2nd edition, Moscow, Informatsionno-ekspertnaya gruppa Panorama, 1998.

Perm Oblast

Like Yeltsin's home territory of Sverdlovsk Oblast, two other Urals regions—Perm Oblast and the Komi-Permyak Autonomous Okrug which is administratively subordinate to it—are generally seen as being pro-reform. The CPRF's electoral chances in these two regions were considered to be so low that the communist-patriotic opposition did not bother to run a candidate in the 1996 gubernatorial elections in either region. The degree of similarity between the two is striking, given that Perm Oblast is a highly industrialized and relatively well-off region, while Komi-Permyak AO is poor, with the average monthly wage in the AO constituting less than a half of that in Perm Oblast. While the oblast is home to several major oil- and gas-processing centers and machine building, aviation and chemical plants, timber is virtually the only industry in the AO. The titular nation, the Komi-Permyaks, constitutes 58.9 percent of the population of the AO and lives mostly in the countryside.

Political developments in the two regions are similar. They differed only during Russia's first presidential election in June 1991, when in Perm Oblast 71.1 percent of voters voted for Yeltsin compared to only 40.6 percent in the AO. Two years later, 71.1 percent in Perm Oblast expressed confidence in Yeltsin compared to 62.1 percent in the AO, while 79.8 percent in the oblast approved the new Russian Constitution compared to 81.4 percent in the AO. In the elections to the State Duma in 1993, 6.9 percent voted for the CPRF list in the oblast and 6.8 percent in the AO. In 1995, 11.1 percent of electors voted for the CPRF list in the oblast and 12.3 percent in the AO. In 1996, Yeltsin outdistanced Zyuganov for the presidency with 70.8 percent against 23.6 percent of the votes in Perm Oblast, and by 62.8 percent against 32.6 percent in Komi-Permyak AO.

The heads of both regions' administrations, originally appointed by presidential decree, won direct gubernatorial elections in their respective regions. In November 1996, Nikolai Poluyanov was elected governor of Komi-Permyak AO with 69.6 percent in the first round. In December of the same year, Gennadii Igumnov won 42.4 percent in the first round, and 64.6 percent in the second round of the gubernatorial election in Perm Oblast.

Sverdlovsk Oblast

Straddling the border between European Russia and Asia, Sverdlovsk is a major industrial center and a source of almost every kind of hard currency-earning raw material, including half of Russia's copper, semi-precious stones, nickel and timber. Its main industry is heavy engineering, of which the greater part is given over to weapons production.

Sverdlovsk residents pride themselves on their radicalism and independence and consider themselves "a special type of Russian." In the 1980s, the region's name became synonymous with all things democratic and market-oriented simply because it was the birthplace of Yeltsin. Yeltsin served as first secretary of the Sverdlovsk Oblast Communist Party until, in the mid-1980s, he was elected from a local constituency to the RSFSR Congress of People's Deputies. Six years later, Yeltsin returned to the city to announce his intention to run for a second term in office. Sverdlovsk became the only region in Russia proper where the electorate voted against the integrity of the Soviet Union in the all-Union referendum of March 1991. On that occasion, only 49.3 percent of Sverdlovsk voters voted in favor, while 85.95 percent voted for the introduction of an executive presidency. In the June 1991 presidential election in Sverdlovsk, a record number of 84.8 percent voted for Yeltsin, and 84.4 percent expressed confidence in him as their president in the referendum of April 1993. A few months later—in December 1993—79.8 percent of Sverdlovsk voters approved the constitution that made the president virtually the absolute ruler of Russia. Yeltsin's triumph was particularly significant since it occurred immediately after the love affair between Yeltsin and his fellow-countrymen had suffered its first major blow.

The Saga of Eduard Rossel

Following the August 1991 coup, Yeltsin appointed Eduard Rossel as governor of Sverdlovsk Oblast. Born in one of Stalin's prison camps, Rossel was descended from Germans who settled in the Volga region in the eighteenth century. He and Yeltsin had known one another since 1977 through their common involvement in the construction industry, and Rossel supported Yeltsin during the latter's conflict with Gorbachev.

Keen to raise his region's status, Rossel asked local residents to support the transformation of Sverdlovsk Oblast into a Urals Republic with the same privileges as Russia's ethnically based republics. He did this by placing an additional question on the April 1993 referendum. When it came to the vote, 80 percent of voters voted in favor of the republic. In October, the oblast Soviet issued a declaration establishing a "Urals Republic" on the territory of the oblast. Yeltsin responded by issuing a decree dissolving the self-proclaimed republic, sacking Rossel as governor and appointing Aleksei Strakhov in his place.[134]

---

134. Radio Rossii, November 10, 1993.

The local population met Rossel's ouster with outrage. One month after his dismissal, he was elected speaker of the oblast legislature. He remained popular and continued to campaign for enhanced status for the region. The Rossel controversy did not, accordingly, bring any benefit to the CPRF in the region. In the 1993 elections to the State Duma, a mere 5.8 percent of Sverdlovsk voters voted for the CPRF list, while in 1995 the figure was only slightly higher, at 8.2 percent. No member of the CPRF was elected on either occasion to represent any of Sverdlovsk's seven single-mandate constituencies. In the first round of the 1996 presidential election, Yeltsin won 59.5 percent in the first round to Zyuganov's 11.7 percent, and against 11.7 percent in the first, and 76.9 percent against 17.9 percent in the second round.

Meanwhile, Rossel had returned to power. In August 1995, President Yeltsin permitted, "by way of exception," the holding of a gubernatorial election in Sverdlovsk Oblast. Rossel came in first among nine candidates in the first round of the election and beat Strakhov by a two-to-one margin in the runoff. Rossel quickly mended his fences with the center, declaring publicly that he would press for more economic independence and a greater share of tax revenues for his region, but would not resume his campaign for an independent Urals Republic.[135] Since then, Sverdlovsk has won broad concessions from the center in a bilateral treaty signed in January 1996, the first such treaty with a federal component other than a republic.

135. *Itar-Tass*, August 26, 1995.

10: The North Caucasus

In theory, the North Caucasus economic zone consists of seven republics and three predominantly ethnic Russian regions, all lying between the Black, Azov and Caspian Seas. In practice, however, one of the republics—Chechnya—has been independent of the Russian Federation de facto (though not de jure) since the end of 1991. The only federal election held in Chechnya that is relevant from the point of view of this study is, therefore, the presidential election of June 1991, in which 76.7 percent of the voters in the republic voted for Yeltsin. No federal election was held in the republic in 1993. And, while the returns of the 1995 parliamentary election and the 1996 Russian presidential election are still included in official reference books, there is little doubt that the relevant electoral returns were the product of pure fantasy.

The tensions, killings and kidnappings, connected to ethnic and religious disputes, in particular the aftermath of the Chechen war of 1994-96, rather than the activities of federal political parties such as the CPRF, were what made news in the North Caucasus. The region may nonetheless be characterized as essentially "red" according to the voting patterns of its various components. The only exceptions to this are those republics whose native populations fall into the category of "punished peoples." These are nations whose members were forcibly deported, men, women and children, by Stalin in the 1940s and who were allowed to return home only in the 1950s, after the old dictator was dead.[136] Apart from the Chechens, this category included the Ingush, Karachai and Balkar peoples. The residents of the relevant republics do not vote for either the CPRF or the PPUoR.

Adygeya

The Republic of Adygeya appears to be the quietest among the North Caucasus republics, rarely appearing in the news. One explanation for the peace and quiet in this region may be its ethnic composition. Today the indigenous Adygei—who, until the Soviet period considered themselves, the Cherkess and the Kabardins to be a single Circassian people—make up only 25.2 percent of the population. Ethnic Russians, by contrast,

136. See Robert Conquest, The Nation Killers: The Soviet Deportation of Nationalities, New York, N.Y.: Macmillan, 1970; Isabelle Kreindler, "The Soviet Deported Nationalities: A Summary and an Update," Soviet Studies, July 1986, pp. 387-405.

account for 64.9 percent. Surrounded on all sides by Krasnodar Krai, Adygeya is the smallest in area of Russia's twenty-one republics. It is a predominantly agricultural region, growing fruit to produce wine, juice and preserves. By 1996, the industrial output in the republic had fallen by 76 percent in comparison with that of 1990. As in all the republics of the North Caucasus, unemployment was a major problem.

Like most of Russia's agricultural centers, Adygeya belongs to the "red belt" of territories that tend to vote for communists. In the referendum of April 1993, 56.1 percent of its voters expressed no confidence in President Yeltsin. In December of the same year, 61.1 percent of voters rejected the Yeltsin constitution. And whereas Yeltsin won 51.2 percent of the votes in Adygeya in the 1991 presidential election (6.1 percent below the national average), in the 1996 election Zyuganov won 51.5 percent compared to 20 percent for Yeltsin in the first round, and 60.5 percent compared to 34.5 percent in the second. In the elections to the State Duma, the CPRF list won 28.9 percent of the votes in Adygeya in 1993 and 41.1 percent in 1995. Local CPRF activist Grigorii Senin failed to win the republic's sole single-mandate seat in 1993 but won it in 1995.

Adygeya's President Aslan Dzharimov belongs to the Gorbachev generation of regional Party leaders. He was elected first secretary of the Adygeya CPSU Committee in January 1989 and a deputy of the USSR Congress of People's Deputies a few months later. He defended Gorbachev's "centrist" line in both capacities, and quit the CPSU in August 1991. He was elected president of Adygeya in January 1992, winning 69.4 percent of the vote in defeating five other contenders. He was reelected president in 1997 with 57.9 percent. He owed reelection partly to the fact that the opposition vote was split between two local communists.[137]

DAGESTAN

In sharp contrast to the situation in peaceful Adygeya, Dagestan is the center of armed conflicts between representatives of different ethnic and religious groups. Lying at Russia's southernmost point, Dagestan has enormous ethnic diversity, being home to a larger number of ethnic groups than any other region in Russia. Power struggles in this republic tend to be resolved by guns, not by the ballot box.[138] In any case, election returns in Dagestan are reputed to be less than reliable.

---

137. See *Sovetskaya Rossiya*, January 14, 1997.
138. See Igor Rotar, "In Dagestan, War Declared On The Mafia," Jamestown Foundation, *Prism*, October 2, 1998.

Eleven nationalities are officially designated as indigenous to Dagestan. Taken together, "Dagestanis" make up 77.8 percent of the population and ethnic Russians 8.2 percent. Among the indigenous nationalities, mountain peoples predominate, with Avars, Dargins, Lezgins and Laks being the most numerous. The Turkic-speaking Kumyks and Azerbaijanis live in the lowlands, as do the Russians, many of who describe themselves as Cossacks. The Terek Cossacks have lived since the sixteenth century in the north of the country. Meanwhile, Lezgins inhabit the mountains in the south of the republic, on the border with Azerbaijan.

Dagestan is rich in oil and natural gas. There are also deposits of coal, iron ore, and nonferrous and rare metals. Industries include machine building, the production of building materials, winemaking and food processing. However, one should perhaps use the past tense when describing Dagestan's industries. Industrial output in 1996 was a mere 16 percent of that of 1990.

Elections revealed that there was considerable public disillusionment with Yeltsin in the republic. In April 1991, 70.6 percent of Dagestan's voters voted for the introduction of the presidency, as advocated by Yeltsin's supporters, and 65.9 percent of them voted for Yeltsin in Russia's first presidential election a few months later. In April 1993, a record 85.8 percent of voters voted "no" in the referendum on confidence in the president, while 79.1 percent voted "no" in the referendum on the new Russian constitution in December of the same year. In the 1993 parliamentary elections, the CPRF party list won an absolute majority of 54 percent of the vote. Contrary to the trend observed in other Russian regions, in Dagestan support for the CPRF fell between the 1993 and 1995 elections. In the 1995 parliamentary elections, the CPRF vote fell to 43.6 percent. While this was almost twice as much as the national average of 22.3 percent, it was lower than the returns of two years earlier. The main winners appeared to be the government parties, Our Home is Russia, which won 14.6 percent, and Russia's Democratic Choice, which won 13.5 percent in 1995 (up from a mere 2 percent in 1993).

The official returns of the 1996 presidential election caused many eyebrows to rise in disbelief. According to the official report, the attendance in Dagestan was 69 percent in the first round and 74 percent in the second. According to the same reports, moreover, 511,202 persons (63.2 percent) voted for Zyuganov in the first round, and only 401,069 (44.3 percent) in the second. What prompted over 110,000 voters to change their minds in the course of seventeen days remains a mystery.

The CPRF does not, however, appear to be very influential in Dagestan. The party did not manage to get any of its candidates elected to either of Dagestan's two single-mandate seats in the Duma. Instead, the Islamic fundamentalist Nadirshakh Khachilaev filled one of them.[139]

Dagestan is one of a small number of Russian republics whose chief executive is not elected by universal suffrage. Instead, the chair of the State Council typically plays the role of chief executive in such republics. This system is favored in those republics characterized, like Dagestan, by extreme ethnic diversity. Throughout the 1990s, the post of chairman of Dagestan's State Council was held by Magomedali Magomedov, a former CPSU official elected to chair the republic's Supreme Soviet in 1983.[140] and reelected in July 1998.[141] Following the assassination in August 1998 of Mufti Saidmuhammed-Hadji Abubakarov, however, the republic capital became the site of mass rallies during which armed Muslim demonstrators called for Magomedov's resignation and for Dagestan to have a popularly elected president.[142] While it remains to be seen whether Dagestan will move to a presidential system, it is unlikely that anyone elected to such a post would be a member or supporter of the CPRF.

Ingushetia

The Ingush Republic may by contrast be termed virtually "communist-free." Stalin's 1994 deportation of the entire Ingush nation to Kazakhstan appears to be the main but not the only reason for Ingush unwillingness to vote for the CPRF. Until the collapse of the USSR, this territory in the northern foothills of the Caucasus Mountains formed part of the Republic of Checheno-Ingushetia. But, whereas the Chechens opted for independence in 1991, the Ingush preferred to remain within the Russian Federation. As a result, a separate Ingush Republic was formed in 1992. Ingush loyalty was rewarded by the establishment of a tax haven in the republic in the form of a "free economic zone." In subsequent years hundreds of Russian firms registered themselves in the Ingush Republic. This did not bring prosperity to the region, however. Throughout the

139. Rishulsky visited Dagestan in September 1998 as a member of a parliamentary delegation and reportedly played a helpful role in calming unrest provoked by the Mufti's assassination. See *Nezavisimaya Gazeta*, September 4, 1998.

140. For a biography of Magomedov, see National News Service <www.nns.ru>

141. *Nezavisimaya Gazeta*, July 3, 1998.

142. See *Nezavisimaya Gazeta*, September 8 and 9, 1998.

1990s, the Ingush were embroiled in a violent territorial dispute with the neighboring Republic of North Ossetia. This created pressing refugee problems in both republics.

Ingushetia has a uniquely homogeneous population, of which 99.4 percent are Ingush. The society of this Muslim mountain people is based on clan and tribal relations. Traditionally, the chief occupations of the Ingush were farming in the lowlands and cattle raising in the mountain areas. Petroleum drilling seems to have been the only industry ever developed in the region. In 1996, 19.9 percent of the Ingush were unemployed, with the number of unemployed people per vacancy standing at 383, that—is, 38.3 times higher than the average for Russia as a whole.

Yet another factor contributing to the reluctance of the Ingush to vote for communist candidates was the influence of republic President Ruslan Aushev. Aushev's background was similar to that of Chechnya's first president, General Jokhar Dudaev, and very different from that of other North Caucasus leaders. Unlike the majority of his fellow presidents, Aushev never served as a professional Communist Party official. A commander of a motor-rifle brigade, Colonel Aushev was awarded the highest Soviet military decoration—the golden star of Hero of the Soviet Union—for his bravery in the 1980-87 Soviet-Afghan war. Elected a deputy of the USSR Congress of People's Deputies, Aushev was promoted to the rank of Major General by one of his many admirers, Mikhail Gorbachev. Aushev became the hero of Russian reformers thanks to his peacemaking role in conflicts such as the October 1993 confrontation between Yeltsin and the RSFSR parliament and the Chechen war.[143] While it would be wrong to call him a democratic ruler, Aushev nonetheless nurtures vaguely liberal convictions. The inconsistency of his views has been reflected in various votes in his republic. The returns of elections and referendums in the Ingush Republic demonstrate, more clearly than those from any other Russian region, that the CPRF-PPUoR is not necessarily the primary benefactor of any protest vote against the Yeltsin regime.

Ingushetia registered a record low level of confidence in Yeltsin and his policies in the April 1993 referendum, when no fewer than 96.63 percent of Ingush voters voted no confidence in the Russian president, and 97.14 percent voted no confidence in his social and economic policies. The vote reflected public wrath over the Yeltsin government's decision to side with North Ossetia in its war against Ingushetia.

---

143. See Kto est kto, op.cit., pp. 35-37.

In the referendum of December 1993, a majority of 56.9 percent approved Russia's new Constitution. On the same day, 6.4 percent (about half the Russian average) voted for the CPRF list in elections to the State Duma, while an unusually high 71.1 percent cast their ballots for a marginal party, the Democratic Party of Russia. Even fewer people—5.1 percent—voted for the CPRF in the December 1995 parliamentary election, the principal benefactor on that occasion being Our Home is Russia, which scored 34.1 percent. In the 1996 presidential election, Yeltsin won an easy victory over Zyuganov. In a mystery reminiscent of what happened in Dagestan, attendance in the second round of the presidential election in Ingushetia was 13.3 percent higher than it had been in the first round. Surprisingly, 24.9 percent (19,653 individuals) voted for Zyuganov in the first round, but only 15.5 percent (14,738) in the second.

Aushev was elected president in February 1994, winning 94.2 percent against a local collective farm director. He was convincingly reelected in March 1998, when his main contender was a man of national prominence, the prosecutor Isa Kostoev who had brought to justice Russia's best-known serial killer. Despite Kostoev's appeal, Aushev won 66.5 per and Kostoev only 13.3 percent of the vote.[144]

Kabardino-Balkaria

Valerii Kokov ran the Kabardino-Balkar Republic throughout the 1990s. Formerly first secretary of the Kabardino-Balkar Oblast Committee of the CPSU, Kokov stepped sideways in 1990 to become Speaker of the republic Supreme Soviet. He was dismissed from that post after he sided against Gorbachev during the August 1991 putsch, but in January 1992 he was elected to his first term as republic president, collecting 88.9 percent of the vote against three other contenders.[145] And yet, when his first term of office expired in January 1997, Kokov violated federal law by standing for reelection unopposed. In a result that reminded observers of the Soviet past, turnout was 97.5 percent and Kokov won 99.4 percent of the votes.[146]

Like so many of Russia's regions, Kabardino-Balkaria is a rich land with poor inhabitants. The territory is blessed with abundant mineral resources and, prior to Yeltsin's reforms, mining played a major role in the local economy. Sheep and cattle are raised in the mountains and the breed-

144. *Nezavisimaya Gazeta*, March 3, 1998; *Sovetskaya Rossiya*, March 3, 1998.
145. For a biography of Kokov, see National News Service <www.nns.ru>
146. *Itar-Tass*, January 13, 1997.

ing of Kabardin horses is still carried on. In addition, the region has traditionally been one of Russia's most famous resort and tourism centers.[147] But, the republic was hard hit by the ethnic and economic upheavals of the 1990s. By 1996, industrial output in the republic was only 26 percent that of 1990, while the average salary was only about half the national average.

The republic takes its name from two indigenous ethnic groups who, together with ethnic Russians, make up the bulk of the population. Kabardins make up 48.8 percent of the population, Balkars 9.3 percent and Russians 33.8 percent, many of the Russians being of Cossack descent. However, the Kabardins and the Balkars make uneasy bedfellows and the republic has been on the verge of splitting in two ever since December 1991, when the Balkar minority voted to secede. They have since made three unsuccessful attempts to declare self-rule.

The republic electorate sided with Yeltsin in all the federal referendums except for the one in April 1993, when only 35.8 percent expressed confidence in the Russian president. In December 1993, however, almost twice as many (63.3 percent) voted in favor of the Yeltsin constitution. This was close to the 63.9 percent of those who had voted for Yeltsin in the 1991 presidential election. As for parliamentary elections, 20.1 percent voted for the CPRF list in December 1993 and 23.7 percent in December 1995. No CPRF candidates were elected to the republic's single-mandate seat in the State Duma. In 1996, Yeltsin won 63.6 percent of the votes in the second round of the presidential election against Zyuganov's 33.2 percent.

KARACHAEVO-CHERKESSIA

Situated in the northern foothills of the Caucasus Mountains, the republic takes its name from two indigenous ethnic groups who, together with an ethnic Russian plurality of 40.6 percent, make up the bulk of the population. The Karachai, who constitute 33.7 percent, have little in common culturally or linguistically with the Cherkess, who constitute 11.0 percent. This has prompted frequent calls for an independent Karachai republic.

Karachaevo-Cherkessia was the last of Russia's republics to elect a president. Until 1999, it was governed by Vladimir Khubiev, who was in power in one capacity or another for twenty years.[148] Appointed first secretary of the Karachai-Cherkess district committee of the CPSU in the

147. *IEWS Russian Regional Report*, Vol. 3, No. 23, 11 June 1998.
148. For a biography of Khubiev, see National News Service <www.nns.ru>

1970s, Khubiev engineered the territory's secession from Stavropol Krai in 1991 and was appointed head of the regional administration by Yeltsin, who in 1995 reconfirmed Khubiev in office by decree.

When a presidential election was finally held in the spring of 1999, the Karachai candidate, former Russian Army Ground Forces commander Vladimir Semenov, won 75 percent of the vote, while the Cherkess candidate, Stanislav Derev, won only 20 percent. This result provoked angry street protests by Derev's supporters, who alleged that the vote had been rigged and demanded that the Cherkess territory be allowed to break away and return to the jurisdiction of Stavropol Krai. The Russian Supreme Court annulled the result of the presidential election in Karachaevo-Cherkessia in July 1999.

The majority of the population lives on the northern plains, which are in intensive agricultural use. Most industry is concerned with processing farm produce. Ostensibly, the average monthly wage is slightly over a third of the average for Russia as a whole, but it also has to be borne in mind that wage and pension arrears in this region amount to as much as a year. Meanwhile, the media portray the republic as a center of corruption, intrigue and police abuse.[149] The explosive mix of social problems has put the republic firmly in the "red belt." In 1997, the CPRF helped organize a public appeal to the republic's Supreme Court for the head of the republic to be elected by universal suffrage.[150] Even though the Supreme Court ruled in favor of a general election, it was April 1999 before the election was finally held.[151] After the first round, Stanislav Derev, the Cherkess mayor of the republic's capital, emerged in the lead with 40.1 percent of the vote. Second was Vladimir Semenov—former leader of the Russian military's ground forces and a Karachai—with 17.9 percent. The run-off in May 1999 ended in a shambles. There were widespread reports of fraud. No official results were announced, but unofficial ones gave the victory to Semenov.[152]

Like other North Caucasian republics, the voters of Karachaevo-Cherkessia sided with Yeltsin in the referendum and presidential election of 1991 but changed their minds in the ensuing two years. A mere 25.9 percent of voters expressed confidence in Yeltsin in April 1995, while only

149. *Obshchaya Gazeta*, No. 22, 1998, p. 5.

150. Russian television newscasts, September 16, 1998.

151. *Nezavisimaya Gazeta*, January 21, 1997; *Moskovskie novosti*, No. 19, 1997, p. 2.

152. NTV, May 23, 1999; The Jamestown Foundation, *Monitor*, May 24, 1999.

28 percent approved his new constitution in December of the same year. In elections to seats in the State Duma, 38.6 percent of the republic electorate voted for the CPRF list in 1993, and 40 percent in 1995. As for the republic's single-mandate constituency, an independent candidate was elected in 1993 and a CPRF candidate, Mikhail Yakush, in 1995.

The results of the 1996 presidential election were shrouded in the same mystery in Karachaevo-Cherkessia as in other North Caucasian republics. According to the official record, Zyuganov won 55.4 percent of the votes in the first round, against 25.8 percent for Yeltsin, but in the second Zyuganov got only 46.1 percent against 49.9 percent. This implies that 117,677 individuals voted for Zyuganov in the first round and only 101,379 a month later, even though turnout for the second round (219,958) was slightly higher than it had been for the first (208,000).

NORTH-OSSETIA

The Republic of North Ossetia-Alania is a predominantly Christian enclave among the largely Muslim republics of the North Caucasus. It is also reputed to be a communist stronghold, though on occasion the behavior of North Ossetia's voters has been the opposite of that in other republics. Ossetians constitute 59.3 percent and Russians 30.6 percent of the population. The Ossetians, a people of mixed Iranian-Japhetic origin, claim descent from the warlike Alans, an ancient nomadic people believed to have been descended from the Scythians and the Sarmatians. Universal respect for the military is probably the most striking feature of Ossetian tradition even today. The Alans mixed with the indigenous inhabitants of the North Caucasus to form today's Ossetians. Driven out of the fertile plains of southern Russia by Turkic and Mongol invaders in the thirteenth century, they took refuge in the Caucasus Mountains. Some settled on the northern slopes of the mountains, while others crossed over into the South Caucasus where they came under strong Georgian influence.[153]

Traditionally, the main occupation of the Ossetians was livestock breeding. Apart from the economic recession affecting Russia in general, today's North Ossetia has suffered from the ethnic conflicts plaguing the Caucasus region. Its bitter territorial dispute with Ingushetia in the early 1990s was followed by sporadic outbursts of violence. North Ossetia has also hosted refugees who fled its sister republic, South Ossetia, which had, as part of Georgia, become foreign territory when the USSR broke up in

---

153. *Encyclopedia Britannica*, 15th ed.; M.N. Guboglo and Yu. B. Simchenko (eds.), "Ethnographic Dictionary: Ossetians," Soyuz, No. 19, 1991, p. 19.

1991. Thousands of South Ossetians fled northward during their republic's attempt to assert its independence from Georgia.

In contrast with other republics, North Ossetia did not support Yeltsin in the earlier stage of his career. Later, however, it demonstrated a degree of conformism. In April 1991, the Ossetian authorities refused to conduct the referendum on the introduction of an executive presidency. In the June 1991 presidential election, 41.9 percent of North Ossetian voters supported former Soviet Prime Minister Nikolai Ryzhkov, who was backed by the CP RSFSR, whereas only 27.3 percent supported Yeltsin. On that occasion, North Ossetia was the only region west of the Urals that voted against Yeltsin.[154] In the referendums of April and December 1993, the republic's electorate sided with Yeltsin: 63.3 percent of North Ossetians voted "yes" in the referendum on confidence in the president and 53.1 percent voted in favor of the new constitution. In the December 1993 parliamentary election, 36.1 percent (almost three times the national average) of North Ossetia's voters voted for the CPRF list. Two years later, the CPRF list won 51.7 percent in the 1995 election to the State Duma in North Ossetia. On both occasions, the republic's former Communist Party boss and erstwhile member of Gorbachev's Politburo, Alexander Dzasokhov, won over 50 percent of the votes in the election for North Ossetia's single-mandate constituency. Each time, Dzasokhov ran as an independent candidate. After 1995, however, he joined the Duma's procommunist People's Power faction.

The 1996 presidential election was marked in North Ossetia by the same phenomenon as other North Caucasus republics. That is, a suspiciously large number of voters defected from Zyuganov's to Yeltsin's camp between the first (June) and second (July) rounds of the contest. Oddly enough, this did not prevent Zyuganov from emerging ahead in both rounds, scoring 62.3 percent against Yeltsin's 19.3 percent in the first round and 52.8 percent against Yeltsin's 43.0 percent in the second.

North Ossetia's first president was Akhsarbek Galazov, who had succeeded Dzasokhov as Party first secretary when the latter moved to the Politburo, and who had subsequently shifted sideways, as many canny Party leaders did, in 1990 to chair the republic's Supreme Soviet. Galazov

154. Yeltsin won fewer votes than did any other of the six contenders in five regions of Russia. Except for North Ossetia, all were situated in Siberia. They were Kemerovo Oblast, which voted for its own governor, and three tiny and remote territories—Gorno-Altai Republic, Tyva Republic and the Aga Buryat Autonomous Okrug

was elected president in January 1994. The second election for the president of the republic, held in January 1998, was an example of Russian-style democracy. Galazov was challenged for the post on this occasion by Dzasokhov, who won 77 percent of the vote against Galazov's 10 percent. To be fair, it should be added that neither of the two candidates belonged to the category of unrefined Party hacks. Prior to his election as Party first secretary, Galazov had been rector of the North Ossetian State University. Dzasokhov was a former Soviet Ambassador to Syria who quit his job as republic Party first secretary when, in June 1990, Gorbachev elevated him to the CPSU Politburo with responsibility for foreign policy.

North Ossetia's 1998 presidential election split the hitherto strong and disciplined CPRF organization in North Ossetia since its leader, Sergei Topchiev, also contested the election. In the event, half of the CPRF's district committees supported Dzasokhov and the other half backed Topchiev. As a result, Topchiev won about 3 percent of the vote, seriously damaging the CPRF's electoral capability in this "red" region.[155]

Cossack territories

The ethnic Russian regions of the North Caucasus—Krasnodar Krai, Stavropol Krai and Rostov Oblast—form the historic lands of the Don and Kuban Cossacks. For centuries, their fertile lands have produced the bulk of the grain, fruit, vegetables, tobacco and wine consumed in Russia. Large numbers of cattle, pigs and poultry are raised there. Oil and natural gas are exploited in Krasnodar and Stavropol Krais. Krasnodar Krai contains Russia's three most strategically vital oil-exporting Black Sea ports—Novorossiisk, Tuapse and Sochi. Rostov Oblast has major ports at Rostov-on-Don and Taganrog as well as a network of industrialized cities and important coal mining districts and is Russia's largest producer of agricultural machinery. Volgodonsk on the River Don is home to Atommash, a large factory producing atomic reactors. The regions also contain a string of spa and resort towns that have in the past provided crucial direct links between local leaders and the powers-that-be in Moscow. In Krasnodar Krai, such holiday centers include Sochi, Anapa, Gelendzhik and Tuapse; in Stavropol Krai they number Kislovodsk, Yessentuki, Pyatigorsk and Mineralnye Vody.

Krasnodar Krai

The Cossacks were among the first victims of the Bolshevik regime. As early as 1919, they were subjected to Lenin's policy of "razkazachivanie"

155. *Nezavisimaya Gazeta*, January 20, 1998.

(de-Cossackifization). This proved a mixed blessing for the CPRF and PPUoR in the region. Along with Leningrad/St. Petersburg, Krasnodar turned out to be a major intellectual center of the CPRF, home of such party theorists and ideologists as Professors Ivan Osadchii and Mikhail Posol, to whose intellectual input the CPRF owed much of its revival in its present form. While Yeltsin won all of the referendums conducted in Krasnodar in 1991 and 1993, he did so by a considerably smaller majority than the national average. By the same token, 45.9 percent of Krasnodar's voters voted for Yeltsin in the June 1991 presidential election; while this was higher than the vote for any other contender, it was lower than Yeltsin's national average of 57.3 percent. In the 1993 and 1996 elections to the State Duma, 16.8 percent of Krasnodar's voters voted for the CPRF list in 1993, and 24.4 percent in 1996, these results being above the national averages of 12.4 percent and 22.3 percent in both instances. No communist was elected in 1993 to any of Krasnodar's single-mandate constituencies. Two years later, however, the PPUoR achieved its first major victory when it won all of Krasnodar's seven single-mandate constituencies, three of them going to the CPRF, three to People's Power, and one to the Agrarians. In the first round of the 1996 presidential election, Zyuganov won 39.4 percent against Yeltsin's 26.3 percent; in the second round, Zyuganov won 51.5 percent against Yeltsin's 43.9 percent.

In December 1996, Nikolai Kondratenko won election as governor of Krasnodar Krai with 82 percent of the votes. Kondratenko, head of the Kuban Agricultural Institute and an able administrator, was elected with the backing of the PPUoR. However, Kondratenko's obsession with the alleged existence of a worldwide Zionist conspiracy against all things Russian turned him into one of the country's most hated figures and threatened to embarrass the CPRF and its allies.[156] During the 1996 presidential election, for example, Kondratenko acted as Zyuganov's agent in Krasnodar. However, he criticized Zyuganov for the absence from the latter's program "of the pressing problem of the need to fight Zionism."[157]

Kondratenko had been a protege of Ivan Polozkov when the latter was first secretary of the Krasnodar Krai CPSU Committee. In 1987, he was elected chairman of the Krasnodar Krai Soviet.[158] In that capacity, he published several articles in local newspapers in which he claimed that

---

156. For the text of Kondratenko's address to the youth of Krasnodar, see *Pravda-5*, No. 15, 1998, pp. 6-7.

157. *Obshchaya Gazeta*, No. 43, 1996, p. 8.

158. For Kondratenko's biography, see National News Service <www.nns.ru>

between 70 to 90 percent of the officials who had ruled in Russia since 1917 belonged to what he called the "Zionocracy."[159] In August 1991, Kondratenko cooperated with the Moscow coup plotters. Following the collapse of the coup, Kondratenko was fired from his post and charged with high treason. The charges against him were later dropped and Kondratenko set up his own nationalist movement in Krasnodar Krai, called Otechestvo [Fatherland] (no relation to the movement of the same name founded by Moscow Mayor Yurii Luzhkov at the end of 1998).

Kondratenko's anti-Semitic speeches were attacked almost daily in the Moscow media. However, being one of the most notorious figures in today's Russia did not seem to harm Kondratenko in the eyes of the local populace. In the November 1998 elections to the Krasnodar Krai Duma, Kondratenko's Fatherland won forty out of the fifty seats; the remaining ten seats went to supporters of the moderate mayor of Krasnodar city, Vladimir Samoilenko.[160]

ROSTOV OBLAST

As a rule, the top leadership of the CPRF avoids disputing election returns. It made an exception, however, for the gubernatorial election held in Rostov Oblast in September 1996. At a specially convened news conference the following month, Zyuganov and Kuptsov questioned the accuracy of the official returns.[161] According to the official results, Yeltsin's appointee, Vladimir Chub, had defeated the head of the Rostov Oblast Committee of the CPRF, Leonid Ivanchenko, by 62.2 percent to 31.6 percent. According to the CPRF leaders, however, voting had been marred by many violations pointing to the likelihood of fraud. The State Duma issued a statement citing examples of violations and fraud and detailing independent testimony concerning discrepancies between the actual vote and the official protocols.[162] Ivanchenko went to court to appeal against the results. Even the secretary of the Central Electoral Commission, Aleksandr Veshnyakov, suggested that the court might annul the election result. However, in February 1997, the Rostov Oblast Court rejected Ivanchenko's case. Russia's Supreme Court similarly rejected his appeal in May of the same year.[163]

159. Excepts from Kondratenko's articles and his addresses to the sessions of the Krasnodar Krai Soviet were reprinted in *Literaturnaya gazeta*, No. 22, 1991, p. 5.

160. NTV "*Segodnya*" and the Radio Liberty "Liberty Live," November 23, 1998.

161. For a detailed report on the news conference see National News Service, op. cit.

162. *Pravda* Rossii, May 20, 1997.

In spite of the presence of a powerful regional CPRF organization, the residents of Rostov Oblast have so far shown little inclination to vote for the CPRF or the PPUoR. In that respect the Don Cossacks differ from their Kuban and Stavropol brethren. The highly developed nature of industry in Rostov Oblast and the consequently high level of urbanization of the local population may perhaps explain this phenomenon. In any case, Rostov voted for Yeltsin in both the 1991 and the 1996 presidential elections. In 1991, Yeltsin won 53.5 percent of the votes in the region, while in 1996 he won 50.7 percent to Zyuganov's 44.2 percent. In the parliamentary elections, 17.3 percent voted for the CPRF list in Rostov in 1993, and 27 percent in 1995. On both occasions, the CPRF won two of Rostov's seven single-mandate seats in the State Duma.

Recently, as Russia's economic crisis has begun to bite deeper, the CPRF has become a little more successful in Rostov. In June 1997, CPRF member Nikolai Kolometsev, a blue-collar worker from the Rostov Agricultural Machinery Factory (Rostselmash), won a by-election for a Duma seat previously held by one of Yeltsin's closest associates, Sergei Shakhrai.[164] In March 1998, the CPRF won 25 percent of the seats in the regional legislature.

STAVROPOL KRAI

The sharing of a border with the rebel Chechen Republic turned Stavropol Krai into a battlefield of the Chechen war.[165] The need to protect the local population from terrorist raids and kidnappings forced the Kremlin into mutual cooperation with the region's "red" governor, Aleksandr Chernogorov.

Chernogorov represents a new generation of CPRF activists. Elected governor in November 1995, he had no previous managerial or apparatus background other than a few months as a CPRF backbencher in the State Duma. Prior to that, the 36-year-old Chernogorov had worked as senior lecturer in the Stavropol Legal University. Save for his relative youth, Chernogorov's background was not untypical for a regional CPRF functionary; only rarely, however, did the party nominate a university lecturer for a governorship. Chernogorov won the election with 55.1 percent of the votes, defeating the incumbent governor, Petr Marchenko, who scored 40.2 percent. This was a real triumph for Chernogorov, since Marchenko

---

163. *Izvestiya*, May 8, 1997.

164. *Sovetskaya Rossiya*, June 3, 1997.

165. See, for example, *Nezavisimaya Gazeta*, November 21, 1997.

had high-level support in Moscow and was backed by such prominent Russian politicians as Aleksandr Lebed and Vladimir Zhirinovsky, who visited the region to campaign for Marchenko in person.[166]

On all other occasions, the vote in Stavropol Krai has been similar to that in Krasnodar. In both regions, the population voted for Yeltsin in the referendums. In the 1991 presidential election, Yeltsin won 46 percent of the vote in Stavropol; this was considerably less than the national average but still more than any other candidate. In the 1996 presidential election, however, Zyuganov won 43.9 percent in Stavropol to Yeltsin's 22 percent in the first round, and 54 percent to Yeltsin's 40.9 percent in the second. In the parliamentary elections, 12.4 percent of Stavropol voters supported the CPRF list in 1993 and 28.8 percent in 1995. In Stavropol's single-mandate constituencies, three independent candidates and one Agrarian were elected to the State Duma in 1993. Two years later, the PPUoR won all four of the region's single-mandate constituencies, three of them going to the CPRF and one to the famous film director, Stanislav Govorukhin, who ran as a member of People's Power. After Chernogorov was elected governor, another CPRF member, Valerii Khmyrov, won the by-election for his seat in the State Duma.

Shared tasks are not, however, the only reason prompting Moscow to try to do business with the CPRF in Stavropol. It is a fact that many of those Stavropol residents who are disappointed with Chernogorov's performance are turning not to more moderate parties but to the extremist Russian National Unity. This organization, seen by many as neo-Nazi in character, has been gaining strength in Stavropol Krai, where entire villages have reportedly joined the ranks of the swastika-bearers.[167]

166. See *Nezavisimaya Gazeta*, November 16, 1996; *Kommersant-Daily*, November 19, 1996.
167. See, for example, *Izvestiya*, August 13, 1998.

11: Siberia

Western Siberia

The electorate in Western Siberia seems to have been the most rational in all of Russia. The difference between "red" and "white" regions within this economic zone can be measured in barrels of oil and natural gas. The "white," or non-communist regions are Tomsk Oblast, which serves as the headquarters of the Eastern Oil Company, and Tyumen Oblast, which includes the Khanty-Mansi and Yamalo-Nenets Autonomous Okrugs, which are particularly rich in oil and natural gas resources. "Red" and "pink" spots on the political map include the Altai Republic, Altai Krai, and the Kemerovo, Novosibirsk and Omsk Oblasts.

The "Reds"

Altai Krai and Altai Republic

Both Altai Krai and the Altai Republic belong firmly to Russia's "red belt." They lie in southern Siberia, on Russia's borders with China and Mongolia. Until July 1991, the Altai Republic was officially called the Gorno-Altai Autonomous Oblast and was administratively subordinate to Altai Krai. Both regions are predominantly agricultural, though the Krai is also a center of military production and houses a large number of alcohol and hard liquor factories, while a major gas-producing company, Gorno-Altaigas, is based in the Republic. Ethnic Russians predominate in both regions, making up 90.3 percent of the population of the Krai and 63.4 percent of the Republic, while the titular Altai people constitute 30.6 percent.

While the population of both regions voted in favor of the institution of an executive presidency in Russia in March 1991, Yeltsin himself scored fewer votes in the presidential elections there than he did in Russia as a whole. In the 1991 referendum, 69.5 percent in the Krai voted for the introduction of the presidency and 52.4 percent in the Republic. In the 1991 presidential election, Yeltsin won 46.4 percent of the vote in the Krai (considerably less than his national average of 57.3 percent). The Gorno-Altai Autonomous Oblast was one of only four Russian regions where Yeltsin received fewer votes (22.4 percent) in the 1991 presidential election than the 32 percent scored by the candidate favored by the RSFSR CP, Nikolai Ryzhkov. Five years later, Zyuganov won 55.5 percent compared to Yeltsin's 38.6 percent in the Krai and 51.7 percent against Yeltsin's 43 percent in the Republic.

In the referendum of April 1993, those saying they trusted Yeltsin were a minority in both territories: 47.7 percent in the Krai and 48.4 percent in the Republic. A few months later, however, voters in both regions approved the new constitution, with 51.2 percent in Altai Krai and 56 percent in the Altai Republic voting for the document. The CPRF was unsuccessful in the 1993 parliamentary elections: in both territories, the vote for the CPRF list was lower than the national average (9.9 percent in the Krai and 11 percent in the Republic). Two years later, however, the vote was above the national average (26 percent in the Krai and 25.9 percent in the Republic). Altai Krai has four single-mandate constituencies. In 1993, three of these were won by members of the Agrarian Party and one by a member of Russia's Democratic Choice. In 1995, three of the seats were won by PPUoR candidates—two of them from the CPRF and one from the Agrarians—while the fourth successful candidate joined the mostly pro-government Russian Regions faction in the State Duma. The Republic has only one single-mandate constituency. In 1993, the republic's first deputy Prime Minister, Mikhail Gvozdilov, won this; in 1995, it went to a member of Yegor Gaidar's Russia's Democratic Choice, Semen Zubakin.

The results of the gubernatorial elections held in these "red" regions reveal the ambiguous attitudes toward the CPRF held by local residents.

In the fall of 1996, Communists and Agrarians in Altai Krai formed an electoral bloc in anticipation of the gubernatorial election scheduled for the end of the year.[168] Called "For Real People's Power, Civic Peace and Workers' Interests," the bloc campaigned on behalf of Aleksandr Surikov, former director of a regional construction company who, at the time of the campaign, held the post of Speaker of the regional legislature. In a run-off election in December, Surikov defeated the incumbent, Lev Korshunov, who had been appointed by Yeltsin in 1994. No sooner was he elected, however, than Surikov warned the employees of the regional apparatus against combining their official work with activities in political parties. The secretary of the Altai Krai Committee of the CPRF reacted angrily to Surikov's attempt to form a non-partisan team, calling him "a turncoat, careerist and political Judas."[169] In the Council of the Federa-

168. See *Sovetskaya Rossiya*, October 17, 1996.
169. *Kommersant-Daily*, March 21, 1997.

tion, Surikov nonetheless proved to be an outspoken critic of Viktor Chernomyrdin's government and swelled the ranks of the procommunist opposition.[170]

One year later, in December 1997, Duma deputy Zubakin was elected president of the Altai Republic, defeating the candidate favored by the Yeltsin administration by a triumphant majority of 74 percent. This made Zubakin the first member of Gaidar's party to win a gubernatorial election.[171] However, Zubakin confounded expectations that he would continue with the economic reforms advocated by Russia's Democratic Choice. Instead, he discredited himself by interfering in the by-election for his former seat in the State Duma in an effort to secure the election of Andrei Vavilov, former first deputy Finance Minister. Vavilov was widely suspected of wanting a seat in parliament for the sake of the immunity from criminal prosecution that went with it, since his name figured in at least four corruption cases being investigated in Moscow.[172] Apart from routine attempts to manipulate the local media, Vavilov's campaign was marked by violations that would be prosecuted in any democratic country. Among them were the activities of the "People's Houses"—offices of the proreform coalition established at taxpayer's expense in various parts of Russia by Yeltsin's former chief-of-staff, Sergei Filatov.[173] In the Altai Republic, the "People's House" offered a choice of a free meal or fifty rubles in cash to anyone who promised to vote for Vavilov.[174] Zubakin's involvement in these attempts to influence the vote handed victory to the PPUoR, which had been unusually inactive during the gubernatorial

---

170. See *Moskovskie novosti*, No. 51, 1996, p. 6.

171. See *Nezavisimaya Gazeta*, December 16, 1997, and January 16, 1998.

172. One of these cases was described in detail in *Nezavisimaya Gazeta*, September 18, 1998.

173. For more on the "People's Houses," see *Obshchaya Gazeta*, No. 37, 1996, p. 8. According to this report, Filatov set up as many as four hundred "People's Houses" in seventy-eight regions and arranged their financing from the state purse.

174. Vavilov's campaign earned much unwanted publicity for Zubakin both in the republic and at the national level. The Moscow daily, *Nezavisimaya Gazeta*, reported on the campaign in no fewer than eight issues: March 18 and 31, April 3, May 28 and 30, June 2, 19 and 20, 1998. See also *Obshchaya Gazeta*, No. 20, 1998, p. 7, and No. 22, 1998, p. 7; and *Sovetskaya Rossiya*, June 2 and 20, 1998.

175. In its report on the forthcoming gubernatorial election, the Moscow CPRF newspaper did not even reveal which candidate the CPRF-PPUoR was supporting; see *Sovetskaya Rossiya*, October 14, 1997.

election.[175] As a result, the alliance managed to secure the election of Mikhail Lapshin, a founding member of the CPRF who had gone on to become leader of the Agrarian Party. Lapshin defeated Vavilov by 42 percent against 40 percent.

Kemerovo Oblast

The CPRF sociologists, Sergei Vasil'tsov and Sergei Obukhov, identify Aman-Geldy Tuleev as the most popular governor in Russia.[176] In spite of the lack of independent data, there seems to be little doubt that Tuleev is indeed extremely popular in his poverty-stricken region. Site of the Kuznetsk coal basin coal basin—Russia's largest coal-producing region—Kemerovo Oblast is also called the Kuzbass and contains 27 percent of Russia's coal deposits. The once-rich region is one of the most urbanized in Russia. In 1989, it was the birthplace of the independent Soviet labor movement. The miners' strike started in protest against the shortage of goods—soap, in particular—in the shops. Their action was a first blow in the process that ultimately brought about the collapse of the Soviet Union, the fall of Gorbachev and Yeltsin's rise to power.[177]

Once a center of the pro-reform movement, the Kuzbass is now a center of opposition. Kemerovo Oblast turned into a "red" region some time between 1993 and 1995 as its industries sank into deep depression and local people withdrew their support from the reformers. Today, Kuzbass miners block railroads and organize hunger strikes in support of their demands for Yeltsin's resignation. The main problem was that, as state subsidies fell, the local cost of producing a cubic meter of coal exceeded world prices. By 1997, coal production had fallen to about half the level of the preceding decade.[178]

As the region with Russia's highest level of overdue wages and pensions, the Kuzbass is an exception to the paradoxical rule of Russian politics, according to which poorer regions do not normally vote communist. According to numerous reports, desperate workers in Kemerovo Oblast have committed suicide in the most heart-rending circumstances; organizing collective explosions or throwing themselves in front of trains, while pensioners have been reduced to searching for food in garbage bins because their pensions have not been paid for months.[179] In the period from

176. See *Sovetskaya Rossiya*, February 12 and July 2, 1998.

177. Roxburgh, op. cit., pp. 147-8.

178. Reuters, October 18, 1997; *Delovye lyudi*, No 74, February 1997.

179. See, for example, *Izvestiya*, December 11, 1996 and April 1, 1997.

March 1994 to November 1996, male life expectancy fell by nine years, from 63 to 54 years.[180]

Regional politics in the early 1990s were marked by a bitter power struggle between the speaker of the regional legislature, Aman Tuleev, and the Yeltsin-appointed governor, Mikhail Kislyuk. During the August 1991 coup, Kislyuk took part in the defense of the White House in Moscow. Yeltsin rewarded him by appointing him oblast governor, passing over Tuleev, who had supported the coup.[181] As governor, Kislyuk proved a poor administrator and no democrat. Tuleev used his post as speaker of the oblast legislature as a base from which to confront Kislyuk.

In the early 1990s, Yeltsin had been immensely popular in Kemerovo Oblast. In March 1991, 70.2 percent of the region's electorate voted in favor of the introduction of an executive presidency. Within months, however, Kemerovo voters had nominated Tuleev to fight in the June 1991 presidential election and collected the 100,000 signatures required by law for a candidate to enter the contest. In the election, Tuleev won 44.7 percent of the votes in the Kuzbass, against 39.6 percent for Yeltsin.

Kislyuk remained in power for six long years, during which he managed to unite against himself virtually all shades of political opinion in the region.[182] At first, Kislyuk's personal unpopularity did not influence popular attitude toward the Moscow democrats. In the April 1993 referendum, 52.6 percent of Kemerovo's voters expressed confidence in Yeltsin. The miners continued to support Yeltsin in his autumn 1993 clash with the Russian parliament, during which Tuleev was one of Yeltsin's most outspoken critics; busloads of miners arrived in Moscow in October 1993 to rally in support of the president. Two months later, 62.3 percent of Kemerovo voters supported Yeltsin's constitution. The same day as the referendum, Tuleev was elected to the Council of the Federation with 80 percent of the Kemerovo vote. In the elections to the State Duma, only 9.6 percent of the participants voted for the CPRF list in Kemerovo Oblast and no CPRF member was elected for seats in the Duma in 1993.

By December 1995, the number of communist supporters in the Kuzbass had increased fivefold to 48.1 percent. In the elections that month to the Russian parliament, three of the four deputies elected to Kemerovo's single-mandate constituencies were members of the CPRF. While not for-

180. *Izvestiya*, December 3, 1996.

181. Kto est kto, op. cit., p. 646.

182. See the letter of the Kemerovo leader of Russia's Democratic Choice to the editor of *Izvestiya* in *Izvestiya*, June 27, 1995.

mally a Communist Party member, Tuleev was ranked third on the CPRF list for the December 1995 parliamentary elections and supported Zyuganov's presidential bid in 1996. During that election, Tuleev acted as Zyuganov's double, withdrawing his candidature in Zyuganov's favor on the eve of the election. Zyuganov accordingly won 51.5 percent of the Kemerovo vote against Yeltsin's 41.5 percent. In an effort to co-opt him, the Yeltsin government made Tuleev a government minister with responsibility for relations with the CIS. The attempt was not a success. When, in August 1997, the parties and groups that had supported Zyuganov joined together in the PPUoR, Tuleev was elected co-chair of the new electoral bloc. And when elections were held to the Kemerovo Oblast Duma in December 1996, Tuleev's supporters won all the seats. Aleksandr Filatov, a member of the CPRF, was elected speaker.

A gubernatorial election was scheduled for October 1997. By that date, only two Russian regions—Kemerovo and the Republic of Karachaevo-Cherkessia—were still governed by officials who had not been elected but had been appointed by Yeltsin. In July 1997, amid allegations of corruption, Yeltsin fired Kislyuk and replaced him with Tuleev. In October, the latter kept his post when he was elected Governor with a majority of 94 percent. Tuleev, who promised to make it his priority not only to pay wage and pensions arrears but also to encourage small-scale private enterprise, continued to enjoy the CPRF's support in his new capacity. When the first secretary of the Kemerovo Oblast Committee of the CPRF, Teimuraz Avaliani, began to criticize Tuleev for his alleged loyalty to Yeltsin, the CPRF leadership replaced Avaliani. A new committee of the CPRF was set up in Kemerovo, which, in turn, elected a new first secretary. At the ensuing plenum of the CPRF Central Committee, Avaliani lost his Central Committee membership as well.[183]

Novosibirsk Oblast

Developments in neighboring Novosibirsk, another "red" region, were less dramatic than those in Kemerovo, but the pattern was essentially the same.

Apart from the regional capital of Novosibirsk, which is the largest city in western Siberia and its principal cultural and educational center, towns in the oblast are small and the economy is almost wholly agricultural. Most of the fertile steppe land is under cultivation. The city of Novosibirsk was founded in 1893, at the crossing point of the projected

183. See *Nezavisimaya Gazeta*, June 25, 1998 .

Trans-Siberian-Railroad and the navigable Ob River. Industrially, it is highly developed. Metallurgy and engineering predominate, The oblast also has a high share of defense industry; this having been especially stimulated during World War II, when factories were evacuated to the region from European Russia.[184] To the south of the city lies Akademgorodok ("Academic Town"), a satellite city that houses most of the specialist research institutes of the elite Siberian branch of the Russian Academy of Sciences.

The fundamental sciences were particularly hard hit in 1991-98, when scientists with world reputations faced the option of either emigrating or earning their living as taxi-drivers or shuttle-traders. The lack of finance that starved both science and industry in Russia determined political developments in Novosibirsk Oblast.[185] Returns in successive elections in the region manifest the slow but steady decline in public approval of Yeltsin's policies.

Initially, there was high support for the reformers in the oblast. In March 1991, 71 percent of residents voted for the establishment of an executive presidency, while 57 percent voted for Yeltsin in the June 1991 presidential election in Novosibirsk Oblast. In the referendum of April 1993, 54.6 percent of Novosibirsk's inhabitants expressed confidence in the Russian president. The tide began to turn in September 1993 when oblast governor Vitalii Mukha, former head of the Novosibirsk Oblast Committee of the CPSU, loudly condemned Yeltsin's decision to disband the Russian parliament and local Soviets. Following the crushing of the parliamentary revolt, Yeltsin fired Mukha and replaced him with Ivan Indinok. Like Tuleev, Mukha was not a member of the CPRF but enjoyed the party's support.

Nonetheless, 51.5 percent of Novosibirsk voters cast their ballots in December 1995 in favor of Yeltsin's new constitution. In the elections to the Council of the Federation held at the same time, the winners in Novosibirsk Oblast were Governor Indinok and Aleksei Manannikov, a member of the radical Democratic Russia movement. In elections to the State Duma, votes for the CPRF in Novosibirsk Oblast were slightly below the national average—11.4 percent in December 1993 and 21.3 percent in December 1995. The CPRF put forward no candidates for the

184. EWI Russian Regional Investor, 18 February 1999.

185. See, for example, an open letter to Yeltsin signed by 93 members and corresponding members of the Russian Academy of Sciences from Novosibirsk; *Sovetskaya Rossiya*, June 25, 1998.

region's four single-mandate constituencies in 1993. The seats were won by centrist candidates, of whom the most prominent was Social Democrat Vasilii Lipitsky. In December 1995 all four candidates nominated by the CPRF in the single-mandate constituencies lost. Two of the seats, however, were won by members of parties allied to the CPRF, notably the chairman of the Duma's Agrarian faction, Nikolai Kharitonov.

In December 1995, a gubernatorial election was held in the oblast. Moscow supported the incumbent Indinok, while the CPRF campaigned for Mukha. Mukha defeated Indinok with 54 percent of the vote. In the June 1996 presidential election, Zyuganov won 48.9 percent of the votes in Novosibirsk Oblast to Yeltsin's 43.7 percent, with 6.8 percent voting against both candidates. Zyuganov's victory symbolized the region's shift into the "red belt." In elections to seats in the regional Duma, conducted in December 1997, the "Victory" bloc of local CPRF and Agrarian activists won 20 of the 49 seats.[186] And, on the eve of the fateful financial crisis of August 17, 1998, the heads of 36 district Soviets in Novosibirsk Oblast signed a collective appeal calling for Yeltsin's resignation.[187]

Omsk Oblast

By comparison with "red" Kemerovo and Novosibirsk, Omsk Oblast is a "pink" region. Agriculture dominates the region's economy and the towns, apart from the city of Omsk itself, are small food-processing centers. The city was founded in 1716 on the Irtysh River as a fortress for the Siberian Cossacks guarding Russia's southern border. From the seventeenth century on, Omsk was a place of exile for revolutionaries, including the Decembrists and participants in Polish uprisings against Czarism. The building of the Trans-Siberian Railroad in the 1890s led to Omsk's rapid commercial development. During the Civil War of 1920-22, Omsk was the capital of General Kolchak's anti-Bolshevik army. Industry received a boost during World War II, and since that time the population of Omsk City has more than trebled. Pipelines from the Volga-Urals and West Siberian oil fields supply the refining and petrochemical industries, which produce synthetic rubber and tires. Engineering, especially the production of agricultural machinery, is also significant.[188]

Political developments in Omsk Oblast reveal the same pattern of gradually growing public disillusionment with Russia's reformers as that seen in Kemerovo and Novosibirsk.

---

186. See *Sovetskaya Rossiya*, December 23, 1997.

187. For the text and signatures, see *Sovetskaya Rossiya*, August 15, 1998.

188. *IEWS Russian Regional Report*, No. 18, 1997.

In March 1991, 66.6 percent of the regional electorate voted in favor of establishing an executive presidency in Russia. Three months later, 53.3 percent voted for Yeltsin in the first Russian presidential election. In April 1993, 56.1 percent expressed confidence in the Russian president, while 57.8 percent approved of the new constitution a few months later. At 13.9 percent, the vote for the CPRF party list in Omsk Oblast was slightly above the national average in 1993 but, at 16 percent, considerably below the average in 1995. Two independent centrist deputies and one prominent opposition leader, the founder of the People's Power faction Sergei Baburin, were elected to the oblast's single-mandate constituencies in 1993. Two years later, all three deputies joined the People's Power faction in the State Duma. Also, in December 1995, incumbent Yeltsin-appointee Leonid Polezhaev was elected governor of the oblast. Six months later, however, Zyuganov won 47.5 percent of Omsk's votes in the June 1996 presidential election, narrowly defeating Yeltsin who scored 46.2 percent in the oblast.

The "Whites"

Tomsk Oblast

The city of Tomsk was founded in 1604 as a Cossack fort. Like its neighbors, the oblast is rich in natural resources. Forests are among its most significant assets, though much of the territory consists of taiga and is inaccessible. The severe continental climate has stunted the development of agriculture, which is why agriculture takes up only about 7 percent of the oblast's total area and is largely concentrated in the southeast. Fur trapping and fishing are important in the forested north.[189] Some 75 percent of urban dwellers live in the city of Tomsk, where all the significant industry is concentrated. Other towns are small. Chemical and oil industries are the most developed, followed by machine building. In the early 1980s, the oblast became a center of oil and gas exploitation. The offices of some major oil and gas companies, including a branch of the mighty monopoly Gazprom, are situated in Tomsk. While the region suffered a fall in industrial output in the 1990s, its decline was lower than for most of the rest of the country.

Until December 1997, when seven candidates supported by the CPRF-PPUoR, were elected to seats in the Tomsk City Duma,[190] the communists enjoyed little support in this region. In March 1991, 74.6 percent

---

189. *IEWS Russian Regional Report*, No. 20, 1997.
190. See *Sovetskaya Rossiya*, December 23, 1997.

of Tomsk residents voted for the introduction of an executive presidency in Russia; 61.1 percent of them voted for Yeltsin as president in June 1991; 66.8 percent expressed their confidence in the president in April 1993; and 68.5 percent approved Russia's new constitution in December 1993. The Yeltsin-appointed incumbent, Viktor Kress, easily won election as governor in December 1995, garnering 52 percent of the vote in the first round. The following year, Yeltsin won 59.2 percent of the votes in the presidential election to Zyuganov's 33.7 percent.

In the parliamentary elections, 10 percent voted for the CPRF in 1993 and 18.8 percent in 1995, while members of Russia's Democratic Choice were elected to the oblast's single-mandate Duma seats on both occasions. Despite the reluctance of Tomsk residents to vote for the CPRF, three prominent Tomsk communists were elected to the State Duma in 1995 on the CPRF list. All three were chosen, however, not because of their regional roles but because they were active in the CPRF at the national level. They were Viktor Zorkaltsev, former first secretary of the Tomsk Oblast Committee of the CPSU (1986-90), currently chair of the Duma's Committee on Public Associations and Religious Organizations; Vadim Filimonov, chair of the Duma's special Commission on the Impeachment of the President; and Aleksandr Pomorov, deputy chair of the Duma Committee on Conversion, who had succeeded Zorkaltsev as Tomsk Obkom secretary in 1990-1. Zorkaltsev and Filimonov belonged to the moderate wing of the CPRF and were noted for their record of cooperating with representatives of the liberal Yabloko faction in the Duma.

Tyumen Oblast

Tyumen Oblast stretches from the Ural Mountains in the west toward the lower reaches of the Yenisei River in the east and from the Kara Sea in the north to the Kazakhstani border in the south. The sparsely populated northern parts of the oblast are occupied by the Khanty-Mansi Autonomous Okrug (AO) and the Yamal Nenets AO. The Khanty-Mansi AO accounts for a third and the Yamal-Nenets AO for a half of the territory of the oblast.[191] In one of the anomalies in which the Russian constitution abounds, the two AOs are described both as being independent entities and as being subordinate to Tyumen Oblast.

Tyumen Oblast is Russia's largest producer and exporter of oil. On paper, it is Russia's richest region, with industrial output one-and-a-half

191. EWI Russian Regional Report, No. 39, 1998.

times larger than that of Moscow City.[192] In reality, it is one of Russia's most deprived regions, with one of the lowest standards of living in the Russian Federation.[193] This has fuelled local anger and prompted calls for regional autonomy. The oblast's anomalous administrative structure has also created secessionist movements in the two AOs. The south of the oblast with the administrative capital Tyumen, situated on the Trans-Siberian Railroad, has relatively well-developed industry and infrastructure. But the oblast's wealth is generated in the AOs. Yamal-Nenets holds 89 percent of Russia's gas, Khanty-Mansi 53 percent of Russia's oil, while the rest of Tyumen Oblast has only small amounts of these resources. Were the oblast to split up, the Khanty-Mansi AO would be Russia's richest region, the Yamal-Nenets AO would be in fifteenth place, and rump Tyumen' Oblast would drop to fiftieth place.[194]

Supposedly the homes of native Siberian nations, the two AOs are predominantly populated by ethnic Russians. The indigenous Khants, Mansi and Nenets make up only a tiny proportion of the population even in the AOs that bear their names. The Khants and the Mansi together make up only 2 percent of the population of the Khanty-Mansi AO, while the Nenets constitute 1.1 percent of the population of the Yamalo-Nenets AO. The indigenous peoples complain that their traditional habitats and lifestyles are threatened by the development of the Russian oil industry. The social situation in these regions, which was never good, deteriorated still further in the late 1990s as a result of the global fall of oil prices and the Russian financial crisis of August 1998. In October 1998, Russian Public Television reported that one out of every 42 women who gave birth in Tymen Oblast had left her new-born baby in the maternity ward, since she did not have enough money to care for the child. A doctor from the Tymen orphanage told ORT that people in the region were so poor that they had stopped adopting babies.[195] According to another Russian TV report, only one out of every six 19-year-old men was considered fit enough to do his military service, with the remaining five found to be suffering from drug addiction, malnutrition, mental instability or tuberculosis.[196]

---

192. *Izvestia*, October 8, 1996.

193. Michael J. Bradshaw, "Siberia Poses a Challenge to Russian Federalism," *RFE/RL Research Report*, No. 41, October 1992, pp. 6-14.

194. OMRI Regional Roundup, October 9, 1996.

195. Russian Television (*ORT* "Vremya" newscast), October 12, 1998.

196. *ORT*, October 16, 1998.

Elections in Tyumen Oblast have often been tainted by the activities of local criminal gangs, including instances of violence against rival candidates.[197] Until 1998, however, the regional voting record was very favorable for the Yeltsin team. In the March 1991 referendum on the introduction of an executive presidency, 73.9 percent of Tyumen voters checked "yes"; in Khanty-Mansi the vote was 80 percent and in Yamalo-Nenets it was 79 percent. In the presidential election of June 1991, 56.3 percen voted for Yeltsin in Tyumen; in Khanty-Mansi the vote was 68.7 percent and in Yamalo-Nenets it was 67.9 percent. In the April 1993 referendum on confidence in the Russian president, 58.4 percent voted in Yeltsin's favor in Tyumen; in Khanty-Mansi the figure was 83.2 percent and in Yamalo-Nenets it was 82.8 percent. In December 1993, 67.8 percent approved Yeltsin's new constitution in Tyumen; the figures in Khanty-Mansi and Yamalo-Nenets were 81.8 percent and 80.3 percent, respectively. In the parliamentary elections, 11 percent voted for the CPRF list in Tyumen Oblast in 1993 and 15.4 percent in 1995; in Khanty-Mansi the corresponding figures were 4.6 percent and 8.0 percent, while in Yamalo-Nenets they were 4.0 percent and 5.6 percent.

In gubernatorial elections conducted in both AOs in October 1996, the CPRF did not even bother to put up candidates to challenge the respective incumbents, Yurii Neelov and Aleksandr Filipenko. Both were elected, Neelov with 68.9 percent of the votes and Filipenko with 71.5 percent. In the gubernatorial election in Tyumen Oblast, the first secretary of the oblast committee of the CPRF was eliminated in the first round in December 1996. In a runoff in January 1997, the incumbent, Yeltsin-appointee Leonid Roketsky, won with 58 percent of the votes.[198]

Despite the generally anticommunist tenor of the vote in this part of Russia, the CPRF has not been entirely without representation. The director of Gazprom's branch office in Yamalo-Nenets AO, Sergei Korepanov, a member of the CPRF, was elected to the Federation Council in March 1994. By the end of his tenure, the law on the body's composition was changed and seats in the upper chamber have since December 1995 been reserved for the heads of the executive and legislature in each of the subjects of the Russian Federation. In 1996, Korepanov was elected speaker of the Yamalo-Nenets AO Duma and resumed his responsibilities in the

197. See, for example, *Obshchaya Gazeta*, No. 47, 1997, p. 7

198. For the election in Tyumen Oblast see *Izvestiya*, October 8 and December 17, 1996, and *Obshchaya Gazeta*, No. 43, 1996, p. 8. For lists of the CPRF nominees in gubernatorial elections, see *Sovetskaya Rossiya*, November 14, December 10 and 24, 1996.

Federation Council as representative of Yamalo-Nenets.[199] His colleague in the Russian Senate, the speaker of the Khanty-Mansi AO Duma, Sergei Sobyanin, is one of the youngest and best educated pro-market reformers in the chamber.[200]

EASTERN SIBERIA

The eighteenth century scholar, Mikhail Lomonosov, predicted with the characteristic optimism of his era that Russia's rich would grow up with Siberia. A hundred years later, a liberal historian facetiously suggested that the conquest of Siberia in 1584-1727 had fatally skewed the course of Russia's future development. Instead of developing their own domains, successive Russian rulers had relied on the seemingly inexhaustible resources of that vast continent and launched Russia on the path of extensive rather than intensive development. In reality, Russia did not become particularly rich as a result of centuries of exploitation of Eastern Siberia, while regions of this economic zone—Irkutsk and Chita Oblasts and the Republic of Tyva—today have the highest mortality rates in all of Russia. Monitoring by Russia's Ministry of Social Protection has revealed dramatic regional variations in the incidences of poverty. In the third quarter of 1996, for example, as many as 73-90 percent of households in such Eastern Siberian regions as Buryatia, Tyva and Chita Oblast were said to be living below the official poverty line.[201]

With the exception of the two great centers, Krasnoyarsk and Irkutsk, Eastern Siberia remains the most mysterious part of the Russian Federation. Ostensibly, only two regions of Eastern Siberia voted for Zyuganov in the 1996 presidential election. And yet, the faint flavor of a secret communist presence appears to lie hidden between the lines of the region's election results.

The "Reds"

Buryat territories

The "reddest" spots on the East Siberian map are three territories which are today split up between three separate federation subjects, but which in

199. See "Regiony: Spravochnie svedeniya o sub'ektakh Rossiiskoi Federatsii," Moscow, Informatsionno-ekspertnaya gruppa Panorama, 1997, pp. 270-1.
200. See Sobyanin's interview with the sociologist Olga Kryshtanovskaya in *Argumenty i fakty*, No. 30, 1998, p. 4.
201. Monitoring *sotsialno-economicheskogo potentsiala semei*, third quarter 1996, Moscow: Ministry of Social Protection and Goskomstat, 1996.

1923-37 constituted a single entity: the Buryat-Mongol Autonomous Soviet Socialist Republic (ASSR). These three regions are the Republic of Buryatia, the Aga Buryat AO (now subordinated to Chita Oblast) and the Ust' Orda Buryat AO (now part of Irkutsk Oblast).

These territories are the homeland of the Buryats, descendants of nomadic Mongol tribes who settled around Lake Baikal in the middle of the first millennium AD. China ceded them to the Russian Empire in 1689. The Buryats put up strong resistance but their revolts were firmly suppressed by Cossack troops. In 1937, Stalin split Buryat-Mongolia into three administrative units in order to ensure that the Buryats did not dominate the region around Lake Baikal. This secured Russian control of the strategically important regions of Irkutsk (a transport hub) and Chita (strategically vital for the projection of Russian military power east of Lake Baikal).

Today's Republic of Buryatia occupies only part of the historic homeland of the Buryats, who make up less than a third of the republic's total population. The three territories share no common border and Buryat leaders complain that, as a result of Stalin's machinations, Buryats living in the two AOs were robbed of their right to a common national existence. Ethnic, linguistic, cultural and economic ties between the members of the divided nation were all weakened by the split.[202] However, local authorities have never come up with any proposals for administrative or territorial reform. This comes as little surprise, given that the two top figures in the republic leadership—Buryatia's president Leonid Potapov and parliamentary speaker Mikhail Semenov—are both ethnic Russians (though Potapov was born in Buryatia).

Buryatia's rich mineral resources include gold, tungsten, molybdenum, nickel, aluminum, iron, manganese and coal. Though the republic has some of Russia's richest mineral deposits and is one of Eastern Siberia's largest energy producers, it is not industrially highly developed. Fishing (on Lake Baikal), stock-raising, horse-breeding, fur farming and hunting are the chief agricultural activities.[203] The Trans-Siberian Railroad and part of the Baikal-Amur Railroad (BAM) cut across the republic.

The Ust Orda Buryat Autonomous Okrug is entirely enclosed within Irkutsk Oblast. The Buryats live mostly in the rural areas, while the urban population is mainly Russian. Coal mining and timber working are well developed; oil and gas fields have been discovered but remain unexploited.

---

202. See the article on Irkutsk Oblast in www.nns.ru/regiony/irkut4.html
203. *IEWS Russian Regional Report*, No. 21, 1997.

Only 5 percent of the population are employed in industry, with the rest engaged in such agriculture as pig husbandry and dairy production.[204] As for the Aga Buryat AO, it is entirely enclosed within Chita Oblast. Its economy is essentially pastoral, and large herds of cattle and sheep are maintained.[205]

Elections in the Buryat Territories

The Republic of Buryatia was the only Russian region whose population rejected the introduction of an executive presidency in the March 1991 referendum, with 39.8 percent voting "aye" and 56.9 percent "nay" in response to the proposal. Voters in the AOs voted, like most other Russian citizens, in favor—56.9 percent in Aga Buryat AO and 58.5 percent in Ust Orda Buryat AO. Yeltsin received less than half of the votes in all three regions in the 1991 presidential election, getting 34.5 percent in Buryatia and 32.4 percent in Ust Orda Buryat AO. Because the procommunist vote was split between four candidates, however, Yeltsin received more votes than any other candidate in both these regions did. In the Aga Buryat AO, by contrast, Nikolai Ryzhkov emerged the clear favorite with 47.6 percent of the votes against 17.5 percent for Yeltsin. Two years later, in April 1993, 51.8 percent of Buryatia's voters expressed confidence in Yeltsin, while his support was only 49.8 percent in the Aga Buryat AO and 48.7 percent in the Ust Orda Buryat AO. Strangely enough, the residents of all three territories voted in favor of the new constitution in December of the same year, by 58 percent in Buryatia, 69.9 percent in the Aga Buryat AO and 80.9 percent in the Ust Orda Buryat AO.

In the December 1993 parliamentary elections, 15.6 percent voted for the CPRF list in the Buryat Republic, 9.8 percent in the Aga Buryat AO and 11.9 percent in the Ust Orda Buryat AO. In elections for single-mandate seats in the Duma, Buryatia's voters opted for an Agrarian; those in the Aga Buryat AO for the director of a local state farm; and those in the Ust Orda AO for a member of the pro-government Party of Russian Unity and Concord. In December 1995, the CPRF received 27.9 percent of the votes in Buryatia, 18 percent in the Aga Buryat AO, and 22.8 percent in the Ust Orda Buryat AO.

In the June 1996 presidential election, Zyuganov won 49.5 percent of the vote in Buryatia to Yeltsin's 45.3 percent. The communist leader

204. *IEWS Russian Regional Report*, No. 16, 1998.
205. *IEWS Russian Regional Report*, No. 21, 1998.

did less well in the two Buryat AOs, however: Yeltsin won 49.2 percent in the Aga Buryat AO to Zyuganov's 47.2 percent and 48.7 percent to Zyuganov's 47 percent in the Ust Orda Buryat AO.

In the ensuing period, Leonid Potapov was the only leader of the three nominally Buryat regions who managed to win election to his post. This was less surprising in light of the fact that Potapov had been elected rather than appointed to his office in the first place. In 1990-91, he headed the regional committee of the CPSU, but he resigned from that post in August 1991 and—like so many other canny former communists—shifted sideways to become speaker of the republic Supreme Soviet (soon to be renamed the People's Hural). Potapov was elected president of the Buryat Republic in July 1994, with 72 percent of the votes, having been nominated by the local "Social Justice" election bloc, which included the republic organization of the CPRF among its collective members.[206] Potapov supported Yeltsin's reelection campaign in 1996, but opposed most of the economic policies of the Yeltsin leadership. He denounced the 1992 liberalization of prices and called repeatedly for a return to price controls and state support for agriculture.[207] When his first term in office expired in June 1998, Potapov was reelected with 63.2 percent of the vote in the first round against no fewer than nine other top republic officials.[208] Potapov's campaign was boosted by the fact that he enjoyed the support of the local Communist Party and because he campaigned on a platform of opposition to the free sale of agricultural land. The following month, Potapov organized a republic-wide referendum on imposing a ten-year moratorium on the sale and purchase of agricultural land. In the event, the referendum was invalidated by low turnout. At the same time, however, Potapov's supporters-who, like him, campaigned on an anti-reform platform—won the majority of seats in the People's Hural.[209]

The situation in the two AOs was different. The Ust-Orda Buryat AO held its first direct gubernatorial election in November 1996. Both the Yeltsin-appointed incumbent, who had headed the regional administration for the previous five years, and the CPRF-backed candidate were defeated by a 32-year-old state farm director, Valerii Maleev, who campaigned on a promise to improve living standards.[210] The following February, the post of head of administration came up for election in the Aga

206. See Panorama site <www.panorama.org/bio/potapov1.shtml>

207. *IEWS Russian Regional Report*, No. 21, 1997.

208. *Nezavisimaya Gazeta*, June 23, 1998.

209. *Nezavisimaya Gazeta*, July 7, 1998.

210 *Itar-Tass*, November 18, 1996.

Buryat AO. Bair Zhamsuev, a 38-year-old ethnic Buryat who had risen through the Komsomol and CPSU apparatus, won.[211] Zhamsuev defeated the Yeltsin-appointed incumbent by promising to make good all wage and pension arrears within two years.[212]

Chita Oblast

One of the poorest and most backward regions of Russia, Chita Oblast is the second "red" spot in Eastern Siberia. Average living standards are below the official minimum subsistence level.

The region has been a place of exile and penal servitude since the late seventeenth century, when the first Russian city in the region, Nerchinsk, was founded as a major trading center with China. Under the czars, prisoners toiled in the silver mines east of Nerchinsk. There was little free settlement until the construction of the Trans-Siberian Railroad in the 1890s. The region resumed its role as a center of forced labor in the 1930s. Today mining and primary-ore processing dominate the economy and these include gold, tin, tungsten, molybdenum, lead, zinc, lithium, tantalum and some coal. Forestry is one of Chita's leading industries, although production has slumped by about two-thirds since 1989.

Unlike most of Russia's "red" regions, Chita Oblast is by no means an agricultural center. Agriculture, despite much new plowing in the 1950s, is poorly developed. Instead, livestock raising, especially of sheep, is dominant. Moreover, the population of the oblast is almost entirely Russian. Ethnic Russians constitute 94.4 percent of the population, which is among the highest concentrations in the country. The socioeconomic situation in the region is appalling.[213] People do not receive their wages for years. Teachers and medical personnel regularly declare hunger strikes, though no one seems to pay much attention. In July 1996, pensioners from Chita blocked the Trans-Siberian Railroad in their desperate demand for payment of their retirement benefits.[214]

Voting in Chita Oblast has been uneven, as if the population of the region was on the verge of a nervous breakdown. While 81.6 percent of the region's voters voted in March 1991 in favor of the introduction of an executive presidency, only 36.6 percent voted for Yeltsin in the presidential election three months later. And, while 53.8 percent of Chita voters

---

211. *ORT*, February 24, 1997.

212. *OMRI Russian Regional Report*, No. 8, 1997.

213. For the official statistics (in Russian) see <www.chita.ru/public_html/stat>

214. *Obshchaya Gazeta*, No. 21, 1996, p. 2.

voted no confidence in Yeltsin in April 1993 and 58 percent expressed their disapproval of his economic policies, a majority of 56.8 percent said "yes" to Yeltsin's autocratic constitution in December of the same year. To cap it all off, Vladimir Zhirinovsky's ultranationalist Liberal Democratic Party (LDPR) received nearly three times more votes in the December 1993 election to the State Duma than the CPRF. The LDPR scored 30.5 percent against 11.5 percent for the CPRF. In the 1995 parliamentary elections, the CPRF list scored 21.6 percent and the LDPR 20.6 percent in Chita Oblast, while newspaper editor Viktor Kurochkin, a member of the radical Democratic Russia movement, and the Agrarian Viktor Kolesnikov were elected to the oblast's two single-mandate constituencies.

In the gubernatorial election of October 1996, the Yeltsin-appointed incumbent, Ravil Geniatullin, won with 30.8 percent of the vote. The candidate supported by the PPUoR, Kolesnikov, received only a handful of votes.[215]

The "Whites"

Irkutsk Oblast

As far as federal elections are concerned, Irkutsk Oblast is a "white" region. The oblast is rich in minerals and contains Russia's largest hard rock gold deposits. Its economy is dominated by mining, chiefly coal and iron ore. It also accounts for a large share of Russia's aluminum production. Most of the population is concentrated along the Trans-Siberian Railroad and the Angara River, where there is a developing industrial region based on coal, iron ore, and salt and mica deposits. The oblast contains three huge hydroelectric plants, providing cheap electricity. Agriculture is largely confined to the vicinity of the towns. Reindeer herding and hunting are carried on by the Evenks of the north. The BAM cuts through the center of the oblast.[216]

In the March 1991 referendum on the establishment of an executive presidency in Russia, 70.9 percent of Irkutsk voters voted in favor, while 52.8 percent voted for Yeltsin in the presidential election in June of that year. In the 1993 referendum, 58.6 percent expressed confidence in Yeltsin while, at the end of that year, 74.2 percent expressed approval of his new constitution. In the elections to the State Duma, 9.5 percent of the Irkutsk

215. *Nezavisimaya Gazeta*, October 29, 1998.
216. *OMRI Russian Regional Report*, No. 7, 1997.

electorate voted for the CPRF list in 1993 and 15.7 percent in 1995. As for the oblast's single-mandate constituencies, two of the deputies elected from the region in 1993 joined the pro-government New Regional Policy faction, another the pro-government Russian Unity and Concord, and another the Agrarian faction. In 1995, one Irkutsk representative joined People's Power, another the Agrarians, a third the moderate Russian Regions faction, and a fourth the Our Home is Russia faction. The 1996 presidential election found Yeltsin apparently losing popularity with Irkutsk voters, since the president won only 32.2 percent of the votes in the first round. In the runoff, however, Yeltsin won 52.5 percent against 39.8 percent for Zyuganov.

Social problems in Irkutsk Oblast were acute. Yeltsin appointed Yurii Nozhikov, who had headed the regional executive since 1988, governor of the oblast in September 1991. But their relations were tempestuous. Nozhikov was a thorn in Yeltsin's side, trying hard to improve local living standards and to defend his region's interests vis-a-vis the federal authorities. He twice fought off efforts by Yeltsin to remove him.[217] Among Nozhikov's numerous achievements was the creation of a commission to monitor the observance of human rights in the region. In March 1994, Nozhikov was elected governor for a four-year term.

Nozhikov unexpectedly resigned in April 1997, citing his inability to fulfil his obligations to the electorate. Elections in July 1997 brought Boris Govorin, a Nozhikov ally and mayor of the city of Irkutsk, to office in his stead.

Khakassia

Until 1991, the Republic of Khakassia was an autonomous oblast within Krasnoyarsk Krai. The efforts to upgrade the republic's status and secure its independence, which had cost its leaders dear, seemed to become superfluous when the two Lebed brothers, Aleksei and Aleksandr, were elected prime minister of Khakassia and governor of Krasnoyarsk Krai, respectively.

The Khakass, for whom the republic is named, are the descendants of a number of nomadic Siberian tribes whose lands were incorporated into the Russian Empire in the eighteenth century. In 1910 they made up 98.3 percent of the population of the republic that now bears their name. Today the Khakass constitute a mere 9.8 percent of the population, while 81.7 percent are Russians.

---

217. See the article on Irkutsk Oblast in <www.nns.ru/regiony/irkut96.html>

Herding sheep and goats remains an important economic activity in Khakassia. Mining has been important since copper first attracted Russian settlers in the eighteenth century. Rich iron ore, gold, coal and barite are also mined, and there are several molybdenum deposits. The forests of the republic are exploited for timber. Abakan is the republican capital. Towering over the republic is the economic giant, Sayan Aluminum (SaAZ), whose director, Oleg Deripasko, is reputed to be behind all the important developments in the Khakass republic, including the political process.[218]

Until June 1996, the vote in the region was close to the average in Russia: 67.3 percent of the electorate voted in favor of the introduction of an executive presidency in March 1991; 57.9 percent expressed confidence in Yeltsin in April 1993; and 58.5 percent gave their approval to the new constitution in December 1993. In parliamentary elections in both 1993 and 1995, the vote for the CPRF list was lower in Khakassia than the average for Russia as a whole. As for the republic's single-mandate constituency, the prominent lawyer Mikhail Mityukov represented the republic in the State Duma from 1990 until 1995, when he was promoted to serve as Yeltsin's representative to Russia's Constitutional Court.

As in many other regions, signs of public disappointment with the Yeltsin regime became apparent in Khakassia in 1996. In the 1991 presidential election, Yeltsin received 53 percent of the votes in the republic. Five years later, Yeltsin received only 29.2 percent of the votes in the first round while Zyuganov received 35.5 percent; in the runoff, Yeltsin secured 47.18 percent against 47.15 percent for Zyuganov. The appointment in December 1996 as Khakassia's prime minister of a former army officer, Colonel Aleksei Lebed, younger brother and comrade-in-arms of the charismatic General Aleksandr Lebed, served notice that the republic elite was dissatisfied with developments in Russia. Unlike most of Russia's twenty-one republics, Khakassia does not have a presidency. The prime minister, who is appointed by the republic parliament, doubles as head of state.

Krasnoyarsk Krai

Situated in central Siberia, Krasnoyarsk Krai cuts across the Russian Federation from top to bottom, north to south. Arguably, it is the region whose attempt to secede would represent the greatest threat to the integrity of the Russian Federation. It leapt into the headlines in spring of 1998, when General Aleksandr Lebed was elected governor.

218. See NTV "Hero without a Necktie" with Aleksei Lebed, NTV television, October 9, 1998; *ORT*, October 16, 1998.

The krai's economic importance is threefold: first, it has vast timber resources, exploited chiefly along the Trans-Siberian Railroad; second, it possesses huge mineral wealth; third, it has important hydroelectric potential. One-fifth of Russia's forests lie in the region, along with a third of the country's coal and lignite resources. Nickel, cobalt, platinum and copper are mined at Norilsk, while gold is mined in the southwestern plateau. The krai commands one-fifth of Russia's water resources. The Krasnoyarsk and Sayan hydroelectric stations are among the largest in the world. Industrial giants include Norilsk Nickel, the Krasnoyarsk Aluminum Factory (KrAZ) and many others. A large share of the region's enterprises belongs to the defense sector. Attracted by these rich pickings, organized crime has put down deep roots in the krai.[219]

As is the case elsewhere in Russia, the fabulous wealth of the region has brought little, if anything at all, to its residents. A case in point is a collective hunger strike that about a hundred policemen in Krasnoyarsk and Norilsk held in December 1987 in demand of back wages.[220]

Elections in Krasnoyarsk Krai are examined closely since it is said that voting patterns in the krai are close to the mean for Russia as a whole and that, as Krasnoyarsk votes today, so will the rest of the country vote tomorrow.[221] In the March 1991 referendum on the introduction of an executive presidency, 70.1 percent of Krasnoyarsk voters approved the introduction of such an institution (compared with 71.3 percent for Russia as a whole). In the June 1991 presidential election, 60 percent voted for Yeltsin in Krasnoyarsk (57.3 percent in Russia as a whole). In the April 1993 referendum, 65.7 percent of Krasnoyark voters expressed confidence in Yeltsin (58.8 percent in Russia as a whole). In the December 1995 referendum on the new constitution, 61.8 percent approved the document in Krasnoyarsk (58.4 percent in Russia as a whole). The CPRF has a relatively strong organization in Krasnoyarsk Krai, numbering some 7,000 members. Yet the votes for the CPRF list in the State Duma elections of 1993 and 1995 were lower in Krasnoyarsk Krai—9.1 percent and 18.8 percent, respectively—than the average of 12.4 percent and 22.3 percent in Russia as a whole. In the 1993 election to the Council of the Federation, Krasnoyarsk voters elected their then governor, Valerii Zubov, and Petr Romanov, director of the Yenisei Chemical Complex and noted ac-

219. See in particular the series of articles published in *Izvestia* on November 11-14, 1997.

220. *Novaya Gazeta*, No. 49, 1997, p. 3.

221. See the table "Russia's Analogue," in *Argumenty i fakty*. No. 21, 1998, p. 4.

tivist of the CPRF. In the 1996 presidential election, Yeltsin won 53.4 percent of the vote in Krasnoyarsk compared to 40 percent for Zyuganov. The CPRF was relatively more successful in the elections for seats in the regional legislature in December 1997, when the party won eight out of 25 seats in the Krasnoyarsk Krai Duma.[222]

The CPRF suffered a double setback when, in April 1998, General Lebed ran for the governorship of the krai. Romanov, who also stood, was eliminated in the first round with only 13 percent of the vote, while Zubov won 35 percent and Lebed 46 percent. Making matters worse was the fact that Romanov was no rank-and-file party member, but a highly decorated Hero of Socialist Labor and co-chair of the Russian National Assembly (Sobor) (RNA). He had long been regarded as one of the party's most promising members.[223] In 1994, for example, Romanov competed for the post of Speaker of the Federation Council but lost to Yeltsin's candidate, Vladimir Shumeiko, by a margin of only two votes. Even worse was the refusal of the regional CPRF organization, including Romanov, to obey the call of the national CPRF leadership to deny the election to Lebed by switching their support to Zubov in the runoff.

In the ensuing weeks, Russian television newscasts featured a long line of CPRF leaders, including Zyuganov, State Duma Speaker Gennadii Seleznev and chairman of the Duma's Committee on Security Viktor Ilyukhin, all of whom flew to Krasnoyarsk to campaign for Zubov. Desperate to prevent Lebed from winning, CPRF leaders even offered to join a regional "Government of National Trust" should Zubov be reelected.[224] Their efforts were in vain. In the runoff in May, Lebed defeated Zubov with 59 percent of the votes against 39 percent.[225] The outcome indicated that the Moscow-based leadership of the CPRF had little influence over members in the regions.

Krasnoyarsk Krai includes two other federal subjects—the Evenki AO and the Taimyr AO. The former is larger than the State of Texas but contains only a handful of villages and one urban settlement, Tura. The population numbers about 20,800 people, of whom 75.4 percent are ethnic Russians and 13.4 percent are Evenki. The Evenki are the most numerous and widely scattered of the many indigenous peoples of northern Siberia. They live by reindeer herding, hunting and fishing.

---

222. *Nezavisimaya Gazeta*, December 9, 1997.

223. For Romanov's role in the CPRF see *Nezavisimaya Gazeta*, April 21, 1998.

224. *Sovetskaya Rossiya*, May 14, 1998.

225. *Nezavisimaya Gazeta*, May 19, 1998.

The Taimyr AO lies on the hilly Taimyr peninsula, the most northerly part of the Eurasian continent. It contains only two urban settlements and has a population of 55,000, 56.8 percent of who are ethnic Russians and 18.6 percent of who are indigenous Dolgan people. Reindeer herding, hunting, fishing and fur farming are the principal economic activities.

The inhabitants of the Evenk AO have generally been more willing to vote for the CPRF than those of the Taimyr AO. In the March 1991 referendum, 66.8 percent of the population of the Evenk AO voted in favor of an executive presidency for Russia, while 73.7 percent voted in favor in Taimyr. In the June 1991 presidential election, only 39.1 percent of voters in the Evenk AO voted for Yeltsin, compared to 58.1 percent in Taimyr. In the 1993 referendum, 70.5 percent of the electorate in the Evenk AO expressed confidence in Yeltsin, compared to 76.8 percent in Taimyr. At the end of that year, 68.9 percent of the voters in the Evenk AO, and 81.8 percent of those in Taimyr, gave their approval to Yeltsin's new constitution. In the parliamentary elections of 1993, 7.5 percent of voters in the Evenk AO voted for the CPRF while in Taimyr the figure was 4.7 percent; two years later the figures were 13.7 and 6.1 percent, respectively. Choosing a representative in their single-mandate constituency, the residents of the Evenk AO voted for an independent in 1993 and for a member of Our Home is Russia in 1995. Residents of the Taimyr AO elected a member of Yabloko in 1993 and a member of Our Home is Russia in 1995. Voters in both regions preferred Yeltsin to Zyuganov in the presidential election of June 1996: Yeltsin got 65.8 percent against 28.3 percent for Zyuganov in the Evenk AO, and 71.6 percent against Zyuganov's 21.6 percent in Taimyr.

The Evenk and Taimyr AOs both staged their first direct gubernatorial elections in December 1996. In the Evenk AO, the speaker of the regional legislature, Aleksandr Bokovikov, was narrowly elected with the backing of the CPRF-PPUoR.[226] The vote was so close that the electoral commission ordered a new election. In March 1997, Bokovikov won that election by a convincing margin of 49 percent compared with 38.7 percent for the Yeltsin-appointed incumbent. Meanwhile, in the Taimyr AO, Gennadii Nedelin was elected head of administration with 64.4 percent of the votes. Nedelin was a former district Komsomol leader that Yeltsin had appointed to head the administration as reward for Nedelin's strong backing of Yeltsin during the August 1991 coup.[227]

226. *Nezavisimaya Gazeta*, December 24, 1996.
227. *IEWS Russian Regional Report*, No. 2, 1998.

Tyva

Voting patterns in Tyva tempt one to describe the republic not as "red" or "white" but as "obedient." This would not be an accurate description of the mood in the republic, however.

Tyva, a remote mountain-encircled region on Russia's border with Mongolia, was part of the Chinese empire from 1757 to 1911 and a tsarist protectorate from 1914 to 1917. Between 1921 and 1944, Tyva was nominally an independent country called Tannu-Tyva. In reality, it was under Soviet suzerainty. In 1944, Stalin annexed it without the world paying the slightest attention.

Ethnic Tyvins constituted 64.3 percent of the population of the republic at the time of the 1989 census, and their majority has probably increased since then because of the Russian exodus. There was an outbreak of serious violence between Tyvins and Russians in May-July 1990, and a large number of ethnic Russians left the republic as a result.[228] As the Russian population dwindled, Tyva oriented itself increasingly toward Mongolia and a strong separatist movement developed. However, the republic remains heavily dependent on Moscow for financial support and cannot afford to leave the Russian Federation. Accordingly, Tyva keeps a low profile in both its voting and its politics.

Tyva is an agricultural region; with cattle breeding being the main occupation. Industries include food processing, leather making, woodworking and the manufacture of building materials, but mining, especially of cobalt and asbestos, is the most developed. However, many workers have not been paid for periods ranging from four to five years. Local hospitals have not been financed for six years. Tuberculosis and syphilis are rampant.[229]

Tyva was one of four Russian regions whose leaders refused to conduct the referendum on the introduction of an executive presidency in Russia in March 1991. At the same time, 91.4 percent of the republic's inhabitants voted for the integrity of the Soviet Union in the USSR referendum held on the same day. In the June 1991 presidential election, Ryzhkov won 62.1 percent of the votes in Tyva, contrasted with 15.3 percent for Yeltsin. The June 1996 presidential election produced the op-

228. See Ann Sheehy, "Russians the Target of Interethnic Violence in Tyva," *Report on the USSR*, No 37, 1990. See also the two-part series in *Izvestiya*, March 11 and 13, 1998.
229. Ibid.

posite result: on that occasion, Yeltsin won 63.1 percent of the vote compared to 32.1 percent for Zyuganov.[230]

In 1993, 56.1 percent of Tyvans expressed their confidence in Yeltsin, while 31.2 percent voted to approve his constitution. In elections to the State Duma, 8.4 percent of Tyva's voters voted for the CPRF in 1993 and 11.4 percent two years later. An independent candidate was elected to the republic's single-mandate constituency in 1993, and a representative of Our Home is Russia in 1995. The Tyvan president, Sherig-ool Oorzhak, was elected in 1992; he was reelected to a second term in 1997 with 70.6 percent of the vote.

230. *IEWS Russian Regional Report*, No. 24, 1997.

12: The Far East

Facing Alaska to the north and Japan to the south, the Russian Far East comprises Amur Oblast, the Chukchi Autonomous Okrug, the Jewish Autonomous Oblast, Kamchatka Oblast (including the Koryak Autonomous Okrug), Khabarovsk Krai, Magadan Oblast, Primorsky Krai, the Republic of Sakha (Yakutia) and Sakhalin Oblast. While many of the regions that make up the zone have been marked by conservative tendencies in regard to elections and referendums, only one of them can be called truly "red." This is Amur Oblast on the Russo-Chinese border.

Amur Oblast

The southern part of this remote oblast is cultivated land while the north and east are almost entirely forested. Ethnic Russians make up over 90 percent of the population, with the largest of sixteen indigenous peoples being the Yakuts and Evenks of the north. The regional capital, Blagoveshchensk, is one of the oldest settlements in the Far East and a traditional center of trade and gold mining.

This is the only agricultural region and the only really "red" spot in the Russian Far East. Throughout much of the 1990s, its voters registered a strong protest vote against the Yeltsin leadership. Its electoral history deserves special mention because of the high degree of abuse of power and electoral falsification reported to have taken place there.

In March 1991, 56.6 percent of the voters in Amur Oblast supported Yeltsin's position and approved the introduction of an executive presidency in Russia. In June 1991, however, only 37.7 percent of them voted for Yeltsin in the country's first presidential election. In the referendum of April 1993, 54.9 percent of Amur voters expressed no confidence in the Russian president, and 58.3 percent said "no" to his economic policies.

Amur Oblast was the only region of Russia in which the returns of the December 1993 referendum on Yeltsin's new constitution were ruled to be fraudulent by a court of law.[231] Nonetheless, the original (fraudulent) figure of 50.2 percent in favor of Yeltsin's constitution remains on the official record. According to the regional electoral commission (the same body that is presumed to have rigged the referendum returns), in elections for seats in the State Duma conducted in the oblast on the same day, only 16.2 percent voted for the CPRF list and a liberal candidate,

231. *Sovetskaya Rossiya*, February 24, 1994; *The Independent*, April 9, 1994.

Andrei Zakharov, was elected in the oblast's single-mandate constituency. In elections for seats in the Council of the Federation held that same day, two members of the CPRF, Leonid Korotkov and Pavel Shtein, were elected.

In the 1995 parliamentary elections, 34.9 percent of the electorate voted for the CPRF list in Amur Oblast, and the communist Korotkov was elected in the single-mandate constituency. In the first round of the 1996 presidential election, Zyuganov won 41.9 percent against 37.7 percent for Yeltsin; in the second round, Zyuganov won by 53.1 percent against 40.7 percent for Yeltsin.

In October 1991, Yeltsin appointed the reform-minded Albert Krivchenko to be governor of the oblast. However, the communist-dominated oblast Soviet, chaired by the career communist party official Anatolii Belonogov, insisted that the governor must be elected by universal suffrage. In April 1993, accordingly, Amur became one of the first regions of Russia to conduct a direct gubernatorial election. Aleksandr Surat was declared the winner. Both he and Belonogov resisted Yeltsin's September 1993 decision to dissolve parliament. Belonogov accused Yeltsin of "genocide against the Russian people"[232] and dismissed the decree as "illegal,"[233] which indeed it was. Yeltsin responded by firing Surat and appointing in his place the head of a small geology laboratory, Vladimir Polevanov, who had lost the gubernatorial election to Surat a few months before.

Following his appointment, Polevanov dissolved the oblast Soviet. Although an Oblast Court ruled his move illegal, Polevanov refused to allow the deputies access to the building. When fresh elections were held in December 1993, the elections for seats in the new regional legislature were conducted. The CPRF won the majority of the mandates. Belonogov was reelected to his old post as speaker. A few months later, leaders of fifteen political parties appealed to Yeltsin to investigate Polevanov's financial activities.[234] A commission dispatched from Moscow declared itself "shocked" at the financial violations by Polevanov's team that it discovered.[235] Polevanov was alleged to have misappropriated local forests, gold mines and coal mines to the tune of $17 billion.[236] Yeltsin's response was to put Polevanov in charge of the Russian State Property Commission.

232. PostFactum News Agency, September 23, 1993.
233. *Rossiiskaya gazeta*, September 25, 1993.
234. *Komsomolskaya Pravda*, November 26, 1994.
235. *Segodnya*, September 12 and October 5, 1995.
236. *Moskovskie novosti*, No. 30, 1996, p. 19.

A fresh gubernatorial election was held in the oblast in September 1996. It was won by Belonogov by so narrow a margin that fresh elections had to be organized.[237] Another election was held in March 1997. Once again, Belonogov won, this time with a respectable 60.5 percent of the vote.[238]

Kamchatka Oblast and Koryak Autonomous Okrug

Kamchatka Oblast is located in the extreme northeast of Russia (it was annexed by Russia in 1697). Although many indigenous peoples still inhabit the region, Russians form the largest population group. The major industry is fishing. Kamchatka is distinguished by the tendency of its inhabitants to elect liberal leaders.

In a gubernatorial election in November 1996, Kamchatka's voters chose the Yeltsin-appointed incumbent, Vladimir Biryukov, who won 61 percent of the vote. The local branch of the liberal Yabloko party, which has traditionally been strong in the oblast, endorsed Biryukov; his chances were also helped by the fact that the CPRF did not nominate a candidate for governor.[239]

Administratively subordinate to Kamchatka is the sparsely populated Koryak Autonomous Okrug (AO). Its economy is dominated by fishing, especially for crab, from small settlements along the coast, while fur trapping and reindeer herding also play an important role. The population is composed of Russians (71.5 percent), Koryak (12.3 percent) and small numbers of Ukrainians, Chukchi and Itelmen. What particularly marks the AO out is the fact that it is the only region in all of Russia to be governed by a woman. Indeed, Governor Valentina Bronevich is not only female but also an Itelmen and, almost equally unusual, a supporter of the liberal opposition party, Yabloko. She was elected in November 1996 with 46.1 percent of the vote.[240]

Both Kamchatka and the Koryak AO regularly vote for liberal candidates. In March 1991, 70.7 percent of Kamchatka's voters voted for the introduction of an executive presidency, while in the Koryak AO the approval rating was 82 percent. In June 1991, 60.2 percent of Kamchatka's voters and 42.6 percent of voters in the Koryak AO supported Yeltsin for the presidency. In April 1993, 70.3 percent of Kamchatka's voters and 67

---

237. *Sovetskaya Rossiya*, September 24 and 28, 1996; *Izvestiya*, October 4, 1996.
238. *Sovetskaya Rossiya*, March 15, 1997.
239. *IEWS Russian Regional Report*, No. 14, 1997.
240. *Itar-Tass*, November 18, 1996.

percent of Koryak AO voters expressed confidence in Yeltsin. In December 1993, 71.0 percent of Kamchatka's voters and 73.9 percent of the voters in the Koryak AO approved Yeltsin's new constitution. In the parliamentary election of December 1993, only 5 percent of Kamchatka's voters and 7.3 percent of the voters in the Koryak AO voted for the CPRF list, while liberal reformers were elected in the single-mandate constituencies of both regions. In the 1995 parliamentary election 11.3 percent of Kamchatka's voters (half the Russian average) and even fewer—10 percent—of the voters in the Koryak AO supported the CPRF list. The liberal economist and Yabloko member, Mikhail Zadornov, was elected in 1995 to Kamchatka's single-mandate constituency in the State Duma.

Khabarovsk Krai

While the CPRF has cooperated with many regional or local leaders appointed from above, the governor of Khabarovsk Krai, Viktor Ishaev, appears to be the only Yeltsin appointee to have enjoyed the support of the CPRF-PPUoR in a popular election.[241] It seems that the local CPRF organization embraced the incumbent in order to distance itself from another contender, Khabarovsk businessman Valentin Tsoi. Tsoi made his name in the early 1990s as an outspoken champion of the Communists of Russia faction in the RSFSR Supreme Soviet. Later he attracted a different kind of fame, when he was branded a "criminal" by the central media.[242]

Khabarovsk lies at the junction of the Amur River and the Trans-Siberian Railroad. Almost the entire region consists of taiga, or dense swampy forest. It is rich in minerals, including coal and iron ore. The population is 90 percent of Russian settler origin, with small numbers of Jews and indigenous peoples—Nanais, Evenks, Ulchi, Nivkhs and Orochi—several of whom are on the verge of extinction. The workforce suffers from the common Russian problem of unpaid wages. In early 1998, twenty miners from the region shut themselves underground, without fresh air, for ten weeks. They were protesting the fact that they had not been paid for fourteen months and their families were on the brink of starvation.[243]

The vote in Khabarovsk Krai reveals the gradual increase of communist influence in the region. In March 1991, 71 percent of Khabarovsk

241. For lists of candidates supported in gubernatorial elections by "the people's opposition," see *Sovetskaya Rossiya*, November 14, December 10 and 24, 1996.
242. See, for example, *Izvestiya*, December 5, 1996.
243. *Nezavisimaya Gazeta*, March 24, 1998.

voters voted for the introduction of an executive presidency. Three months later, 59.8 percent of Khabarovsk's voters voted for Yeltsin as president. In the referendums of 1993, 70.2 percent expressed their confidence in Yeltsin, while 70.5 percent supported the constitution. Yeltsin-appointed Governor Viktor Ishaev was elected to the Federation Council in 1993, along with the rector of Khabarovsk State University, Viktor Bulgakov. In the election for seats in the State Duma conducted in Khabarovsk in 1993, 12.1 percent voted for the CPRF list and both of the region's single-mandate seats were won by democratic parties—Russia's Democratic Choice and Russian Unity and Concord. Two years later, 16.1 percent voted for the CPRF in the region—below the national average—but Tsoi and a member of the CPRF were elected to the single-mandate constituencies. In the 1996 presidential election, Yeltsin won 59 percent against 33.7 percent for Zyuganov.

Yeltsin appointed Ishaev, a former factory director, governor in October 1991. Five years later, in November 1996, Ishaev was one of the first of Russia's governors who threatened to stop paying taxes to the federal purse unless the federal government paid its debts to the region.[244] The following month, Ishaev defeated Tsoi in a gubernatorial election with 76.9 percent against 13 percent of the vote. Ishaev's defiance won him the admiration of local communists. When Prime Minister Evgenii Primakov threatened that governors who did not pay taxes would be sacked, a Khabarovsk Stalinist rushed to Ishaev's defense.[245]

In elections to the regional legislature in March 1998, the CPRF won almost half of the twenty-five mandates. A few months later, the Krai Duma demanded Yeltsin's resignation and a change of economic policy. The deputies called on their fellow Khabarovsk deputies in the two chambers of the Russian parliament to support a constitutional amendment making the government accountable to parliament. The appeal was adopted almost unanimously by the Khabarovsk Duma, with only one deputy abstaining.[246]

MAGADAN OBLAST

The very name Magadan strikes a chill through any student of Russian and Soviet history. The city was founded in 1933 as the port and supply center for the gold fields of the upper Kolyma River valley. From that time

244. See *Sovetskaya Rossiya*, November 12, 1996.

245. See *Sovetskaya Rossiya*, October 15, 1998.

246. See *Izvestiya*, October 2, 1998.

onward until 1954, after Stalin's death, Kolyma was the site of a huge complex of forced-labor camps in which over a million prisoners died. Many of the present residents are descended either from former camp prisoners or guards. Today, Kolyma gold has turned the oblast into a war zone for all kinds of Russian criminal gangs.[247] Yet the majority of the local population suffers from the usual Russian malaise of wage arrears; even the region's tax inspectors went on a hunger strike to demand their unpaid wages.[248] In October 1998, 40 percent of the residents were said to be living below the poverty line.[249]

October 1998 saw mass rallies in Magadan in which communists and democrats joined ranks to demand Yeltsin's resignation. Until then, Magadan had been considered a "white" region whose residents voted for Yeltsin through thick and thin. In March 1991, 73.8 percent of Magadan's voters voted for the introduction of an executive presidency; the following June, 50.4 percent voted for Yeltsin in the presidential election. In October 1991, Yeltsin appointed Viktor Mikhailov as governor. Mikhailov, who supported Yeltsin in everything, was defeated in a popular election in November 1996 by Valentin Tsvetkov.

In April 1993, 74.4 percent of Magadan voters expressed confidence in Yeltsin, and in December 68.6 percent approved his new constitution. In elections to the State Duma, 6.0 percent of Magadan residents voted for the CPRF list in 1993 and 12.6 percent in 1995. Independent candidates won the region's sole single-mandate district in both 1993 and 1995. The present governor, Valentin Tsvetkov, was elected to the State Duma in December 1995 as an independent but later joined the Russia's Regions faction. Zyuganov was elected governor in the summer of 1996 but was defeated in the 1996 presidential election with 63.6 percent of the vote against 27.5 percent.

In the 1996 gubernatorial election, Tsvetkov enjoyed the support of the PPUoR-CPRF. Thereafter, however, Tsvetkov proved to be in no hurry to invite communists to join his administration.[250]

CHUKOTKA

The Chukchi Autonomous Okrug is the most easterly part of Russia. A remote peninsula that lies across the Bering Strait from Alaska, nine time

247. See the interview with Magadan Deputy Governor Vyacheslav Kravets in *Nezavisimaya Gazeta*, September 2, 1998.
248. See *Izvestiya*, June 6, 1997.
249. See *Nezavisimaya Gazeta*, October 8, 1998.
250. See *Moskovskie novosti*, No. 51, 1996, p. 6.

zones away from Moscow, it is within the Arctic Circle and covers an area the size of France. The territory was set up in 1930, supposedly for the Chukchi people, though Russian settlers outnumbered them. The Chukchi are closely related to the Eskimo people. Today, the Chukchi comprise 4.3 percent and Russians 73.8 percent of the population. Until 1990, the Chukchi AO was under the jurisdiction of Magadan Oblast. It became administratively independent in 1993.

The region has rich mineral deposits. During the Soviet period, the Soviet authorities enticed people to work in the inhospitable territory by paying them three times the standard wage and offering generous benefits including early retirement. This motivated workers to travel from the European parts of the Soviet Union to work hard for a few years before returning with their savings. The Chukchi were forced from their native villages into Soviet settlements in the 1950s. Collective farms took over their ancient herds of reindeer and their traditional hunts for whales, walruses and seals. The Chukchi became dependent on state benefits. At the time of the 1989 census, the population (numbering 164,000) consisted mainly of gold miners and coal miners. Of these, 66 percent were ethnic Russians, 17 percent were Ukrainians, and 7.3 percent were Chukchi.

After communism collapsed, Russia was no longer able to subsidize the Far East and Far North. Prices of even essential food products grew to five times more in Chukotka than in Moscow and other less isolated parts of Russia. State-owned enterprises were forced to close. Whole settlements shut down as people moved out. The indigenous Chukchi, who lost their traditions during the Soviet period, were especially poorly prepared for the transition to a market economy.[251] During two winters in succession (1997 and 1998) the local authorities failed to obtain enough heating fuel and, therefore, the Ministry on Emergency Situations had to evacuate the population.[252]

Chukotka's voters have nonetheless been very supportive of Yeltsin. In the referendum of March 1991, 73.2 percent gave their approval to the creation of an executive presidency in Russia, and 57.7 percent voted for Yeltsin in the June 1991 presidential election. Two years later, 74.2 percent expressed confidence in Yeltsin and 75.9 percent approved his constitution. In the parliamentary elections, only 6.6 percent voted for the CPRF in 1993, and 11 percent in 1995. In elections to Chukotka's

251. *IEWS Russian Regional Report*, Vol. 3, No. 3, January 1998, and Vol. 3, No. 35, September 1998.

252. See *Izvestiya*, September 2, 1998, p. 2

single-mandate constituency, the independent Tatyana Nesterenko was elected in both 1993 and 1995. Yeltsin appointed Aleksandr Nazarov head of the okrug administration in November 1991, and he was elected in a popular vote in December 1996.

Jewish Autonomous Oblast

The situation in the Jewish Autonomous Oblast is similar to that in Chukotka. As Chukotka left the jurisdiction of Magadan Oblast, Khabarovsk Krai Oblast, The Jewish Autonomous Oblast left the administrative supervision of Khabarovsk Krai in 1991. It is now the only autonomous oblast in the Russian Federation.

Established in 1934, ostensibly as a national homeland for Jews in the Soviet Union, the Jewish Autonomous Oblast is renowned for the scarcity of Jews in its population. It does not even have a synagogue. Jews comprise only 3.5 percent of the population, whereas Russians make up 87.4 percent and Ukrainians 5.1 percent. In the Soviet period, the leaders of the region were Jews. Today, the heads of both the executive and legislative—Aleksandr Volkov and Stanislav Vavilov—are ethnic Russians. The first secretary of the Oblast committee of the CPRF, Vladimir Fishman, appears to be the only Jew in charge of anything in the Jewish Autonomous Oblast today.

Most of the population live along the region's two main lines of communication, the Trans-Siberian Railroad and the Amur River. The oblast has one of the most favorable climates in the Far East and a good half of the territory is suitable for cultivation. Fishing, especially for salmon, is a major part of the economy. Some 40 percent of the territory is covered with trees and forests, and lumber and cellulose production are highly developed.[253] While the region has never been rich, it was hard hit in the 1990s by the transition to the market. Industrial output in the oblast in the late 1990s was only 16 percent of what it had been at the beginning of the decade; the unemployment rate was 15.9 percent; and the average salary was only 75 percent that of the average for Russia as a whole.

Voters in the Jewish AO have tended to oppose change. While 63.2 percent voted in March 1991 for the introduction of an executive presidency, only 42.9 percent voted for Yeltsin in the June 1991 presidential election. In April 1993, 63.2 percent expressed their confidence in Yeltsin's leadership, and 58.6 percent approved the new constitution in December 1993. Volkov and Vavilov were elected to the Federation Council at that

253. *IEWS Russian Regional Report*, No 16, May 1997.

time. In elections to the State Duma, the vote in the Jewish Autonomous Oblast for the CPRF list was precisely the same as the average for Russia as a whole—12.3 percent in 1993 and 23.4 percent in 1995. Anatolii Biryukov, deputy chairman of the Agrarian Party, was elected to the region's single-mandate constituency in 1993 and the CPRF candidate, Sergei Shtogrin, in 1995. Yet neither the CPRF nor the PPUoR put up a "people's" candidate to fight the regional gubernatorial election in October 1996. Instead, they endorsed Volkov's candidacy, as did the Liberal Democratic Party and Our Home is Russia. Appointed by Yeltsin in December 1991, Volkov was elected to head the oblast administration in 1996 with 70.1 percent of the vote.[254]

PRIMORSKY (MARITIME) KRAI

Primorsky Krai lies along the coast of the Sea of Japan. Russia wrested control of the region from China in the mid-nineteenth century and, in 1860, assumed control of it under the Treaty of Peking. Soviet power was declared in the region in December 1917 but, in the spring of 1918, Japan, Great Britain and the United States landed troops in Vladivostok. For a short time, until the Bolsheviks asserted control, the city was the center of Siberian and Allied opposition to Soviet power.

Today, a seemingly endless chain of inter-enterprise debts exacerbated by sharply increased transport and distribution costs has brought about a situation where virtually all the regional workforce seems on permanent strike. Protests have included workers from all categories—teachers, doctors, nurses, miners, electricians, civil servants and sometimes even the military. As a result of the strikes, electricity, gas and water cuts have became another permanent feature of local life, leading to the deaths of women in childbirth and of patients on operating tables.

Aggravating the region's social and economic problems has been the six-year feud between the regional governor, Evgenii Nazdratenko, and the mayor of Vladivostok, Viktor Cherepkov. Tensions between regional governors and the mayors of capital cities are commonplace in Russia. The reason is that the bulk of regional budgets consists of taxes collected in the capital cities. Mayors bitterly resent the fact that the decision on how to spend the taxes collected on "their" territory is made not by the mayors but by the governor. Even so, the epic struggle between Nazdratenko and Cherepkov has surpassed the limits of what may be viewed as normal even in Russia. A retired Navy officer, Captain Cherepkov was

254. *Itar-Tass*, October 21, 1996; *Interfax*, October 22, 1996.

elected mayor of Vladivostok in June 1993 because of his role in unmasking the deaths by starvation of a number of conscripts at a naval base in the region. Cherepkov proved popular as mayor because he abolished charges for public transport and public telephones in Vladivostok. Within months, the city's coffers were empty. The following spring, Cherepkov was forcibly removed from office by local police acting on behalf of the krai administration. The krai authorities argued that the action was justified because the regional prosecutor's Office had charged Cherepkov with corruption. Newspaper reports subsequently claimed that the charges brought against Cherepkov had been trumped up by Nazdratenko's supporters among the local judiciary for the purpose of getting rid of the popular populist mayor.[255]

Though the charges against Cherepkov were dropped in November 1994, Yeltsin supported Cherepkov's ouster and appointed a Nazdratenko ally as mayor in his stead. In 1996 a Moscow court ruled that Cherepkov had been illegally dismissed and he was reinstated in his post as mayor.[256] But the unedifying quarrel between the krai's two leading politicians angered many voters and seems to have added to the level of popular support in the region for the CPRF.

However, the activities of the Primorsky Krai CPRF have so far been chiefly remarkable more for the frequency of their protests and demonstrations than for their voting patterns. In the referendum of March 1991, 69.4 percent of local participants approved the creation of an executive presidency in Russia. In June 1991, 61.5 percent voted for Yeltsin as president. In the referendums of April and December 1993, 64.3 percent expressed confidence in Yeltsin, and 71.5 percent gave their approval to his constitution. In the parliamentary elections of 1993 and 1995, votes for the CPRF in Primorsky Krai were about a third below the national average—8.7 percent in December 1993 and 18.5 percent two years later. But while in 1993 three reform-minded deputies (one member of Democratic Party of Russia, one of Yabloko and one of Russia's Democratic Choice) were elected to the region's single-mandate constituencies, in 1995 the victors were one independent, one Agrarian and Svetlana Goryacheva of the CPRF.

Yeltsin first appointed Nazdratenko as governor in May 1993. In December 1995, Nazdratenko won a popular election, defeating Cherepkov for the post of governor by 68.6 percent to 17.2 percent.

255. *Novaya ezhednevnaya gazeta*, 17, 18, 19, and 22 February 1994.
256. See, for example, the four-part series in *Izvestiya*, July 23-26, 1996.

In the presidential election of June 1996, Yeltsin won 29.5 percent of the votes in the first round against Zyuganov's 24.6 percent, and 52.3 percent against Zyuganov's 39.4 percent in the second round. It may be added that Nazdratenko is notorious for his heavy control over the media in the region. During the time that Cherepkov was out of office, all the local opposition newspapers felt constrained to move their headquarters away from Vladivostok to neighboring Khabarovsk.

SAKHA (YAKUTIA)

With its diamonds, gold and energy reserves, Sakha covers an area more than four times the size of Texas and only slightly smaller than India. It is Russia's largest republic and occupies one-fifth of the territory of the Russian Federation. It was created as an autonomous republic of the Soviet Union in 1922. It takes its name from the indigenous Yakut, one of the major peoples of Russia's Far East. Today they make up 39.6 percent of the population of the republic; Russians are 45.5 percent, and the rest are mostly Ukrainians and Tatars. In the 1970s and early 1980s, the capital, Yakutsk, witnessed racially motivated fights between Russian and Sakha youth. Yet, contrary to the general tendency, no serious clashes between various nationalities have been reported in Sakha in the 1990s.

Sakha's President Mikhail Nikolaev is said to be one of the closest to Yeltsin among the regional leaders.[257] A career administrator, Nikolaev graduated from the CPSU Central Committee Higher Party School in Moscow. Elected Chairman of the Yakut Supreme Soviet in 1990, Nikolaev was elected president of the republic in December 1991. Sakha was one of the first among Russia's republics to introduce an executive presidency on its territory. Nikolaev combined this move with a campaign to win republic control over all the diamonds mined in the region. Attempts by the taxman to levy taxes on the company yielded little fruit thanks to Nikolaev's personal relations with Yeltsin.[258] In December 1996, Nikolaev stood for reelection. He defeated Artur Alekseev, first secretary of the republic CPRF organization, by 60.2 percent to 25.5 percent.

Sakha's voting pattern reveals a very gradual slide toward "pale pink" during recent years. In March 1991, 59.8 percent of republic voters favored the introduction of an executive presidency and 44.9 percent voted for Yeltsin in the June 1991 presidential election. In the March 1993 referendum, 68.1 percent expressed confidence in Yeltsin and 55.0 percent

257. See, for example, *Obshchaya Gazeta*, No. 47, 1996, p. 6.
258. *Obshchaya Gazeta*, No. 50, 1996, p. 2.

approved his new constitution. In the elections to the State Duma, 10.2 percent voted for the CPRF list in 1993 and 17.6 percent in 1995. An independent candidate was elected to the republic's single-mandate constituency in 1993 and a member of People's Power in 1995.

Sakhalin

Situated at Russia's extreme eastern edge, Sakhalin Oblast consists of Sakhalin Island and the chain of Kuril Islands. Fishing, lumbering and coal mining dominate the economy. Oil and natural gas are found in the north but the development of the region's resources has been hindered by a lack of investment.

Sakhalin Oblast was probably the first region in the USSR to have unleashed popular insurrection against corrupt Communist Party leaders. In June 1988, President Gorbachev endorsed the mass protests of Sakhalin residents against the Communist Party boss, Petr Tretyakov. The demonstrations proved, Gorbachev indicated, that his policy of perestroika had reached the region's 700,000 people. Accused of dishonest distribution of new housing to his friends and relatives, Tretyakov was forced to resign as a result of the mass rallies.[259] In 1990, Sakhalin residents elected a Moscow economist, Valentin Fedorov, as speaker of their Oblast Soviet with a mandate to launch market-oriented reform in the region.

Despite Sakhalin's natural wealth, the level of poverty in the region is one of the highest in Russia, with more than a third of the population of 648,000 people officially registered as living below the poverty line.[260] Today, Sakhalin is the scene of terrible instances of desperation. For example, prisoners from a local camp for serious offenders were found to be sharing their bread rations with the hungry children of unpaid Sakhalin workers.[261]

Sakhalin's electoral record classifies it as a "white" region. In 1991, 59.8 percent of Sakhalin's voters voted for the introduction of an executive presidency, and 54.9 percent voted for Yeltsin in the first presidential election in 1991. In the referendums of April and December 1993, 60.9 percent of Sakhalin voters registered their confidence in Yeltsin, while 64 percent approved the new constitution. In the 1993 parliamentary elections, 8.9 percent of Sakhalin's voters (slightly less than the Russian aver-

---

259. See *Pravda*, June 2, 1988.

260. Floriana Fossato, "Sakhalin: Waiting For Oil But Patience Is Running Out," *RFE/RL Newsline* Vol. 2, No. 203, October 20, 1998

261. See, for example, *Moskovskie novosti*, No. 1-2, 1998, pp. 8-10.

age) voted for the CPRF list while in 1995 the figure was 24.6 percent—slightly above the national average. Yabloko's Boris Tretyak was elected to Sakhalin's single-mandate constituency in 1993, but in 1995 the victor was a member of the procommunist People's Power movement, Ivan Zhdakaev. In the presidential election of June 1996, only 29.9 percent of Sakhalin residents voted for Yeltsin in the first round. In the runoff, however, Yeltsin won in Sakhalin Oblast by 53.4 percent while Zyuganov scored 38.8 percent.

Fedorov resigned in protest against Yeltsin's economic policy in April 1993. Yeltsin replaced him with Evgenii Krasnoyarov, who also resigned two years later. A third governor, Igor Farkhutdinov, was appointed in April 1995. A gubernatorial election was held in October 1996. The CPRF-PPUoR proposed a certain A.N. Cherny as their candidate but the incumbent Farkhutdinov won with 39.5 percent of the votes.

Along with the gubernatorial election, an election for seats in the regional Duma was conducted in October 1996. The CPRF failed to achieve a majority in the body, and Yabloko's Tretyak was elected as speaker. In September 1998, the Oblast Duma was the first regional legislature to join Ryazan in issuing a call for Yeltsin's resignation.[262]

262. See *Nezavisimaya Gazeta*, September 4, 1998.

13: Scenarios for the Future

To conclude, it seems appropriate to pose a few fundamental questions about future prospects for the Russian Communist Party. What is the role of the Communist Party in a post-communist Russia? What are the chances of a communist-dominated coalition coming to power in Russia in the foreseeable future? And, last but not least, what would be the implications of a possible CPRF comeback for Russia and the rest of the world?

Ostensibly, there are a number of options for future political developments in Russia, but most of them appear unlikely. Theoretically, the range of possibilities open to the CPRF and its political allies in the Russian Federation includes the following:

1. The most improbable scenario appears to be that of the powers-that-be eliminating the communist threat by purely democratic means—by defeating the communist coalition in the forthcoming parliamentary and presidential elections. All public opinion polls conducted in Russia to date indicate that the CPRF is the most popular single political party for the forthcoming parliamentary elections, and Zyuganov the most successful leader of the presidential hopefuls.[263] On the other hand, according to a survey conducted in early 1999, only 20 percent of those polled said that they would not vote for the communists under any circumstances, while slightly more, 30 percent, said that they would never vote for Zyuganov in a presidential election.[264]

2. In contrast, the possibility that the CPRF might be thrown into the dustbin of history by extra-constitutional contingency means, such as yet another ban by presidential decree, has been under constant discussion in the Russian media since 1991. In early 1999, this option was invoked in connection with various political scandals, even if the

263. See for example the article by Mikhail Gorshkov, the director of the Russian Independent Institute of Social and National Problems, in *Nezavisimaya Gazeta*, February 25, 1999. See also the findings of the All-Russian Institute of Public Opinion Studies (VTsIOM) on the Internet <www.polit.ru>. Apart from these, the results of surveys on the possible outcome of the Russian presidential election carried out by the Russian Public Opinion Institute have been broadcast every Sunday by the NTV weekly news program *Itogi*.

264. Cited by the anchor of NTV's *Itogi*, April 11, 1999.

CPRF was not directly involved. [For example, when the Russian Prosecutor-General Yurii Skuratov attempted to launch an investigation into alleged large-scale corruption by members of the president's family, journalists suggested that Yeltsin could respond by introducing emergency measures, starting with a ban on the CPRF.][265]

3. For its part, the CPRF expects to defeat the Yeltsin regime by constitutional, democratic means. In a recent interview with independent Russian television, Zyuganov cited a poll claiming that his party would win more than half the seats in the next parliamentary elections scheduled for December 1999.[266] To what extent his optimism is justified remains to be seen.

4. Like its political opponents in the Yeltsin camp, the CPRF does not restrict its methods of gaining power to the ballot box. Although most of their other proclaimed means of achieving this goal cannot be dismissed as unconstitutional, neither can they be described as routine democratic proceedings. The alternative means at the CPRF leaders' disposal vary from unleashing a campaign of civil disobedience and industrial action to the impeachment of President Yeltsin, which was initiated by the CPRF parliamentary faction in early 1998. In May 1998, the CPRF issued a Substantiation (Obosnovanie) of the need to remove Yeltsin from office, and began collecting the signatures of fellow legislators in support of the charges stipulated in the document,[267] as required under Article 93 of the Constitution. According to the Substantiation, Yeltsin committed the following grave crimes while in office:

a. The preparation and signing of the Belovezhskie agreements which engineered the collapse of the Soviet Union;
b. The coup d'état of September-October 1993, when Yeltsin dissolved the Russian Supreme Soviet and the Congress of People's Deputies, although forbidden to do so by the Constitution in force at that time;

265. See the contribution by Elena Dikun in *Obshchaya Gazeta* No. 12, 1999, p. 1; *Moscow News* No. 12, 1999, p, 8; *Argumenty i fakty*, No. 13, 1999, p. 2; *Zavtra* No. 13, 1999, p. 1.

266. *Itogi*, NTV, March 28, 1999.

267. For the text see *Sovetskaya Rossiya*, May 23, 1998.

c. The decree that unleashed the war against the rebellious Chechen Republic in December 1994, which the president issued without the consent of either chamber of the Russian Parliament;
d. Serious damage to Russia's defense and security during Yeltsin's rule; and
e. Genocide against the Russian people. (Purportedly, Yeltsin's economic reforms had created "living conditions leading to the physical extermination" of Russia's population.)

Members of other Duma factions agreed with at least some of the aforementioned charges, such as those relating to the Chechen war and the events of October 1993, because of the serious human casualties inflicted by both events. Indeed, the 276 signatories who put their names to the Substantiation included representatives of all factions except the governing Our Home Is Russia (Russian abbreviation NDR). However, the CPRF was the driving force behind the move. The hard-liner Viktor Ilyukhin initiated the process in his address to fellow legislators in March 1998, and, Vadim Filimonov, a party moderate, chaired the special multiparty commission that investigated the accuracy of the charges in the Substantiation over the ensuing nine months. The commission had finished its work by spring 1999. Initially, the decisive Duma vote on impeachment was scheduled for April 15, but it was postponed to May 13, 1999. According to the Constitution, the Duma needs a majority of two thirds (301 votes) to start the impeachment process. After this, the Russian Supreme Court and the Constitutional Court review the charges. Then the parliamentary upper chamber, the Federation Council, must also vote for the removal of the president, and must do so no later than within three months after the vote in the Duma. With such a complex chain of events, the impeachment had no chance of success, even if the Duma had voted to start the process.

But, in the event, the CPRF failed to win even the first stage. At the parliamentary hearing that opened on May 13, 1999, and which lasted for two more days, none of the above five points gained the required majority of 301 votes among Russian legislators. As expected, Yeltsin's waging war against the Chechen republic proved the most unpopular, yet even on this charge, only 286 deputies cast their votes in favor of impeachment.

The failure of their attempt to impeach Yeltsin was viewed as a major setback for the CPRF. According to the findings of opinion polls, as revealed by the NTV television channel on May 16, 1999, the party lost almost one third of its former supporters as a result of this vote.

5. The most likely pattern for future development is probably a continuation of the process which is already underway in Russia. The CPRF could seriously influence the decision-making process by steadily infiltrating the existing power structures. Such a process was evident in the early 1990s, immediately after the December 1993 parliamentary elections, when the CPRF faction reached a series of compromises with the then Prime Minister Viktor Chernomyrdin, and a number of the party's legislators, such as Valentin Kovalev and Ivan Rybkin, crossed the floor to join the Yeltsin administration. The infiltration process gathered momentum in September 1998, when parliament refused to endorse Yeltsin's attempt to reinstate Chernomyrdin as prime minister and arranged in his stead the appointment of former foreign minister Evgenii Primakov. Although no communist himself, at the parliamentary session that was to vote him into office Primakov promised that his government would work in cooperation with the State Duma, as happens in all European democracies.[268] And Primakov was true to his word. After the vote, Primakov appointed as his first deputy a member of the CPRF Central Committee, 61-year old Yurii Maslyukov, and made him responsible for running the economy. The post of deputy prime minister for agriculture was offered to Gennadii Kulik, a representative of the CPRF's faithful ally in the PPUoR, the Agrarian Party; while the key post of head of the Russian Central Bank went to the man who had held the job in Soviet times, Viktor Gerashchenko, who enjoyed the confidence of the communist and procommunist segment of the State Duma. Primakov also nobly offered jobs in his government to representatives of other parliamentary factions, including Grigorii Yavlinsky, the leader of the liberal Yabloko party, who turned the offer down. The birth of Primakov's Cabinet has been regarded as a major political victory for the CPRF, and support for this government became a crucial factor in the party's strategy in late 1998-

268. The session on September 11, 1998 was broadcast live by Russian state television channel RTV.

early 1999. In any case, the gradual integration of CPRF representatives into governing structures suggests that the party's influence in Russia's power lobbies is steadily growing. As a result of this process, even if the CPRF does not achieve ultimate power in 2000, it may be more successful in the distant future.

The replacement of Primakov as prime minister with Yeltsin's veteran political ally Sergei Stepashin on the eve of the ill-fated impeachment performance—on May 12, 1999—seemed to slow down the general trend of communist infiltration, but it is unlikely to reverse the process. The reason for this lies in the general old communist nomenklatura origin of Russia's current ruling elite, as well as in the unpopularity of the Yeltsin regime with most ordinary Russian citizens, rather than in the personality of the second-in-command.

6. Recently, Moscow Mayor Yurii Luzhkov unexpectedly suggested yet another way for the CPRF to achieve power in Russia, albeit not full power.[269] Luzhkov proposed that his newly created "Fatherland" movement (Otechestvo) form a broad coalition with two rival political parties, the CPRF and the liberal Yabloko. According to Luzhkov, the aim of the proposed bloc would be to protect Russia from the election of extremists from either end of the country's political spectrum, including such hard-line members of the CPRF as the anti-Semites Makashov and Ilyukhin.[270] From the perspective of the CPRF, such a coalition would achieve much the same result as before—sharing power with the party's traditional opponents, albeit by way of the ballot box rather than by bargaining and exerting pressure in the corridors of the executive. At the time of writing, however, Yabloko leader Grigorii Yavlinsky has categorically rejected entering into any coalition with the CPRF, which he branded "an immoral party."[271] In any case, it should be borne in mind that the 1993 Russian constitution invests the Russian president with almost absolute power, thus in effect turning any sort of bloc and coalition for the presidential elections into a rather meaningless affair. There is no mechanism by which the junior partners in such a coalition can

269. *Izvestiya*, January 16, 1999; *Kommersant-Daily*, March 25 and April 2, 1999; *Nezavisimaya Gazeta*, March 30, 1999; Moscow News No. 13, 1999.

270. Russian television news broadcasts (*ORT*, NTV and RTV), April 10, 1999; *Izvestiya*, April 10, 1999.

271. See *Izvestiya*, April 16, 1999; *Nezavisimaya Gazeta*, April 17, 1999.

force the victor to respect his obligations to them following an election victory. Nor could they prevent a president from getting rid of his coalition partners, as Yeltsin did in 1993 with his running mate from the 1991 election, Vice President Aleksandr Rutskoi, and again three years later with his junior partner in the second Russian presidential election, Aleksandr Lebed.

All in all, growth in CPRF influence seems almost inevitable following the 1999-2000 parliamentary and presidential elections. The consequences for Russia and the rest of the world of the party's rise in influence could be very different, however, depending on whether it shares power with fellow communists and Russian nationalists or with more pragmatic and pro-democracy parties, such as Yabloko and Fatherland. To an even greater extent, the future of the CPRF will depend on how the party achieves its goal. To begin with, a great deal depends on whether the future of Russian politics takes a democratic or a contingency form.

Dictatorial Scenarios

It is difficult not to be skeptical about the prospects for a democratic transfer of power in Russia in the near future, given the ambivalent record of elections held under the current regime, as discussed in chapter 5. Moreover, there is no example of anything approaching the voluntary handing over of supreme power from one ruler to a successor in all of Russian history. Since the unification of Russia under the Grand Principality of Moscow in the fourteenth century, only two leaders have abdicated—the last Czar Nicholas II and the last Soviet President Mikhail Gorbachev—in both cases rather involuntarily. In all other cases, the succession has been caused either by the death of a ruler or by a palace coup (or its Soviet equivalent, as with Nikita Khrushchev, who was removed in 1964 at a CPSU Central Committee plenary session). Against such a background, it is no wonder that few people in modern Russia seem to have considered the possibility of a democratic succession—by way of the ballot box. It is not unusual, for example, to hear the anchor of the country's most respected news program say that "Boris Yeltsin is not going to hand over power to the reds even in 2000"[272]—even if a "red" candidate wins the next presidential election. In his State of the Nation address in March 1999, President Yeltsin spelled out his intention to ensure that the forthcoming

272. Boris Koltsov on *Itogi*, NTV, April 18, 1999.

273. Broadcast live by all the aforementioned Russian television channels on March 30, 1999. For the text see also *Kommersant-Daily*, March 31, 1991.

Russian elections are conducted in a "clean and honest" way.[273] On many other occasions Yeltsin has declared his intention to resign after the next presidential election in 2000, which he is precluded from participating in by the constitution. Nonetheless, the policies of the president's men in early 1999 were marked by arbitrariness, somewhat unfair treatment of the opposition and little regard for either the law or the well-being of the nation, all of which seems particularly unwise for people who have just over a year in office remaining and who should therefore be interested in setting a good example for their successors. To put it plainly, neither President Boris Yeltsin nor his men are behaving like people who are going to relinquish power next year.

MISTREATMENT OF THE CPRF

The treatment of the CPRF by the authorities, for instance, left the Yeltsin administration open to criticism. In February 1999, to take one example, the Russian Prosecutor-General's office proposed that the Ministry of Justice should check whether the activities of the CPRF "corresponded with the aims proclaimed in the organization's statutory documents." The prosecutors used the anti-Semitic remarks of the communists Makashov and Ilyukhin to justify their request.[274] In response, Justice Minister Pavel Krashenninikov initiated an investigation into the CPRF for alleged violations of Yeltsin's 1991 decree banning the activities of political parties in state enterprises.[275] At the time, Krashenninikov's action was widely seen as an attempt to find a pretext for yet another ban of the CPRF. His move seemed particularly suspicious given that a few weeks earlier Yeltsin had unexpectedly removed the Ministry of Justice from the jurisdiction of the prime minister and made it answerable only to himself and his chief of staff. Krashenninikov's attempt to suppress the country's largest opposition party was condemned by the leaders of all other factions in the State Duma. "If you do not like their ideology, then engage them in ideological debate, but do not resort to administrative measures," said Vladimir Ryzhkov, the leader of the pro-Yeltsin Our Home Is Russia.[276] Ryzhkov went on to claim that the administration has only investigated the CPRF, never other parties, including his own NDR. Zyuganov echoed Ryzhkov's observation, complaining on a number of occasions that the powers-that-be had

274. See *Kommersant-Daily* and *Nezavisimaya Gazeta*, both of February 13, 1999.

275. See *Kommersant-Daily*, February 16, 1999.

276. NTV, "*Segodnya* v polnoch", February 16, 1999; *Nezavisimaya Gazeta*, February 17, 1999.

investigated the CPRF as many as six times, whereas others—such as the loyal NDR, the illiberal LDPR or the "democratic opposition" Yabloko—have all been spared any kind of inspection.[277]

In response to this criticism, Krashenninikov denied that his interest in the CPRF was motivated by political considerations.[278] Nor did he agree with widespread speculation that the administration was looking for a pretext to prevent the CPRF from taking part in the forthcoming parliamentary elections.[279] On April 15, Krashenninikov signed a report stating that the Justice Ministry had not discovered any violations by the CPRF.[280] Apart from irritating the CPRF leadership, the February 1999 inspection caused the party no serious trouble. Within a few weeks, however, Krashenninikov succeeded in inflicting a painful blow on the CPRF, using a completely different excuse. At a news conference in March 1999, Zyuganov said that the CPRF would unleash a mass campaign of protests, including street rallies and industrial action in many enterprises, should Yeltsin engineer the resignation of the Primakov Cabinet.[281] The CPRF, Zyuganov claimed, controlled strike committees and other "structures" elsewhere in Russia, and was therefore in a position to organize such a mass campaign. A few days later, on March 22, 1999, Krashenninikov responded with an official warning in which he classed Zyuganov's statement as "illegal activities" by the CPRF.[282] This was a serious setback for the CPRF. According to the Russian Law on Political Parties, the authorities are entitled to appeal to a court of law with a request that this or that political party be banned after two official warnings have been issued regarding its allegedly illegal activities. Meanwhile, Zyuganov's pronouncement seemed rather mild by Russian standards, given that all kinds of threats and even fistfights are far from uncommon on Russia's political stage. What seems particularly significant is that Krashenninikov (and Yeltsin, who had doubtless Okayed his actions) undertook such a maneuver against the country's strongest political force on the eve of a major change of guard in the Kremlin without any fear of possible retaliation. They seemed to be suspiciously confident that the CPRF would not be in

277. *Izvestiya*, February 17, 1999.

278. *Nezavisimaya Gazeta*, February 17, 1999.

279. See Krashenninikov's interview in *Izvestiya*, March 18, 1999.

280. *Kommersant-Daily*, April 16, 1999; *Izvestiya*, April 17, 1999.

281. The footage of Zyuganov's statement was broadcast in various Russian television news broadcasts on the day it was made, March 19, 1999, and later.

282. See *Izvestiya* and *Nezavisimaya Gazeta*, both of March 23, 1999.

a position to avenge itself. In the light of this, one cannot help but question whether the authorities are indeed prepared to relinquish power in favor of the victor in the next elections?

Fears and Rumors of Cancelled Elections

Due to the lack of democratic traditions and to the record of the Yeltsin regime, allegations of plots designed to lead to another coup d'état, similar to that of September-October 1993, have been a constant feature of political life in Moscow. More often than not, the alleged putsch scenarios include the dissolution of the State Duma and a ban on the CPRF. On one occasion, Yeltsin's entourage did indeed come very close to such a deed. Following the vote in the communist-dominated Duma to denounce the Belovezhskie agreements on March 15, 1996, Yeltsin reportedly considered a ban on the CPRF, to be followed by the dissolution of the Duma. The latter move would have violated the constitution, which stipulates that the State Duma may be dissolved only in two cases: Either if the house rejects the president's candidate for the post of prime minister three times, or if the Duma passes a vote of no confidence in the Government of the Russian Federation twice within a three month period. Yet even in the latter case the president is not entitled to dissolve the Duma within one year of its election, and the Duma in question was elected in December 1995—just three months previously. According to widespread reports, Yeltsin had to abandon his plans on this occasion because of opposition on the part of officials such as the then minister of internal affairs, Anatolii Kulikov. Some reports suggested that Yeltsin had also turned to the Clinton administration for support, but the USA had refused to back him on this occasion.[283] Against this background, it is no wonder that rumors of such malicious plans have become a constant theme in today's Russia.

On occasion, the communist-dominated opposition has been the source of such rumors. In March 1999, for example, the Presidium of the People's Patriotic Union of Russia held a meeting of 89 of its members in the State Duma. Following the session, the body issued a statement in which the PPUoR leadership cited unidentified "reliable sources" in connection with alleged plans by the authorities to cancel the forthcoming parliamentary and presidential elections. According to the PPUoR rumor mill, the malicious blueprints had been drawn up with "the support of the USA." The alleged plan included the replacement of Primakov with an

283. See *Nezavisimaya Gazeta*, March 19, 1996; and *Novaya Gazeta* No. 11, 1996, pp. 1-2.

unacceptable figure, the dissolution of the Duma, and the organization in Moscow and other large Russian cities of a series of terrorist attacks which would claim many victims. The purpose of these monstrous actions, according to the rumormongers, was the introduction to the Russian Federation of an indefinite state of emergency with a ban on all elections and political activities.[284]

Yeltsin's Counteroffensive

For its part, Yeltsin's side is also on record as spreading rumors of a coup, presumably designed to put pressure on the CPRF and other opposition parties in the State Duma. In early April 1999, virtually all the non-communist media, whether they supported the president or his opponents in the liberal camp, published articles to the effect that the president had extra-constitutional contingency plans.[285] In the reports, certain unidentified highly placed officials were quoted as the source of the rumor. According to them, the Kremlin was preparing to counterattack, should the Duma vote to start the process of impeachment of Yeltsin in the ballot originally scheduled for April 15 that year. Such countermeasures were said to include banning the CPRF on the grounds of evidence collected by Krashenninikov's team. In the next stage, Yeltsin reportedly intended to find an excuse for the ensuing dissolution of parliament.[286] Had Yeltsin indeed made such a move it would have amounted to a coup d'état. Article 109, paragraph 4 of the 1993 Russian Constitution states in no uncertain terms that "The State Duma may not be dissolved from the moment it files a charge against the President of the Russian Federation" until the process of impeachment is decided one way or the other by the parliamentary upper chamber, the Federation Council. One can only speculate whether "top Kremlin officials" or anybody in the Yeltsin camp had actually cherished such plans, or whether it was a red herring designed to put pressure on the Duma to drop its impeachment proceedings against

---

284. See *Kommersant-Daily*, March 27, 1999.

285. See *Kommersant-Daily*, April 6, *Izvestiya*, April 9, *Nezavisimaya Gazeta*, April 9, 1999. The rumor in question was also discussed on various political television programs.

286. *Moskovskie novosti* No. 12, 1999, p. 8; and *Argumenty i fakty* No. 13, 1999, p.2, both named Chernomyrdin as Primakov's would-be replacement. They also reported the alleged involvement of Yeltsin's daughter, Tat'yana Dyachenko, in the relevant decision-making process. *Novaya Gazeta* No. 13, 1999, named Chubais.

Yeltsin. Either way, such leaks could not but undermine their credentials as "democrats." Furthermore, Yeltsin's subsequent denials of such contingency plans did little to improve the unfavorable impression created by his rumormongers. At a meeting with the leaders of Russia's republics, Yeltsin said that he was not going to replace Primakov's Cabinet, at least not for the time being. "Today, Primakov is useful to us; as for later, that remains to be seen," said the Russian president.[287] He had no intention of dissolving the Duma either, Yeltsin went on to say. Nor was he going to ban the CPRF, Yeltsin added, saying that such a move would be counterproductive, because the Russian people tend to pity the underdog. [In fact, the removal of the popular Primakov at the time posed a mortal threat to Russia's stability. Moreover, Yeltsin was not entitled to ban a party; such a matter should be left to a court of law.] Sad to say, in the above debate the president demonstrated little concern for the law, civil rights or the welfare of his subjects.

It may be added that Yeltsin's failure to honor his pledge regarding Primakov's cabinet did not improve his credibility with regard to his intentions concerning the fate of the CPRF either.

Unlikelihood of Yeltsin Dissolving Legislature

Despite the rumors, Yeltsin's ill health and the unpopularity of his policies in 1999 meant that there was little likelihood of a move similar to the bloody crackdown on parliament in 1993. There are a number of reasons to be skeptical about such an eventuality.

First, Yeltsin's decree of September 21, 1993 followed an extensive mass propaganda campaign against parliament in the media, which Yeltsin at the time compared to an artillery cannonade (artpodgotovka) preceding an armed attack in a battle.[288] In contrast, the tone of the Russian electronic media in early 1999 was no more anticommunist than usual in the periods of cease fire between Yeltsin and the communist-dominated opposition. Moreover, in an unprecedented manifestation of good will, the veteran Russian TV star Aleksandr Lyubimov marked the fourth anniversary of Russian Public Television (ORT) on April 3, 1999 with a live talk show between ORT Director Igor Shabdurasulov and Zyuganov.

---

287. See *Kommersant-Daily*, April 10, 1999.

288. Yeltsin's address to a meeting of representatives of state-owned radio and television companies, August 12, 1993. For the text see *Sovetskaya Rossiya*, August 14, 1993.

During the session, Shabdurasulov promised Zyuganov that ORT coverage of opposition activities would be fair and objective.[289]

Secondly, Yeltsin claims that he had ensured the blessing of Western leaders (the G7) in advance of his move against the parliament in 1993.[290] There seems little doubt that the West would be reluctant to support violence against parliament should such relations between the Russian executive and legislative branches of power become a regular feature.[291]

Thirdly, most of Yeltsin's subordinates who played a crucial part in the events of the fall of 1993 have resigned since then.[292] Some of them—most notably the former chief of Yeltsin's bodyguard Aleksandr Korzhakov—have even become Yeltsin's enemies.[293] Those who have replaced these former allies in Yeltsin's court do not seem to be so eager to deal with the parliamentary rebels.

The fourth and perhaps the most important reason to doubt the seriousness of Yeltsin's alleged extra-constitutional contingency plans lies in the deterioration of the Russian president's relations with the military, including the specially trained commando forces in the Federal Security Service (the former KGB) and the Ministry of Internal Affairs. Even back in 1993, the military intervened only very reluctantly in the president's battle with the legislature. Those who obeyed the order to fire at the parliamentary building, including Defense Minister Pavel Grachev, became rather unpopular with other officers as a result.[294] In the period following the events of October 1993, the economic crisis brought the problem of unpaid wages to the homes of the majority of Russian officers. Other

289. Lyubimov's show, *Zdes i seichas* ("Here and Now"), is normally broadcast on weekdays. The extract with Zyuganov was aired on a Saturday night. As a result the noted Russian TV critic Irina Peterovskaya branded *ORT* a nest of timeservers (see *Izvestiya*, April 10, 1999).

290. See Boris Yeltsin, Zapiski Prezidenta, Moscow, Ogonek Publishing House, 1994, p. 176-7.

291. In the course of his visit to Moscow in January 1994 US President Bill Clinton made it clear that the West would respect the parliament elected by the Russian people. Clinton's question-and-answer session with a Russian audience was broadcast live by Ostankino television on January 14, 1994.

292. For details, see *Zapiski Prezidenta* op. cit.

293. For details, see Aleksandr Korzhakov, *Boris Yeltsin: Ot rassveta do zakata*, Moscow, Interbuk Publishing House, 1997.

294. See, for example, the memoirs of a General Staff Colonel in Viktor Baranets, *Poteryannaya Armiya: Zapiski Polkovnika Genshtaba,* Moscow, Sovershenno Sekretno Publishing House, 1998, pp. 165 ff.

factors that made the current regime even more unpopular among the military included the collapse of Soviet military industries for lack of funding, rumors of widespread corruption among the top military command, and the manner in which Yeltsin's government conducted and lost the war against Chechnya in 1994-96.[295]

Military Dissidents Support CPRF

Today, the militant wing of the CPRF has close ties with the most disappointed representatives of the military through the Movement in Support of the Army and Military Industries (Russian abbreviation DPA). The DPA was set up in 1997 by the Chechen war hero General Lev Rokhlin, revered by officers for his victories in the campaign. Rokhlin was elected as a deputy to the Duma in 1996 from the list of Our Home Is Russia. In the Duma, Rokhlin was offered the chair of the Defense Committee. After a while, the General became bitterly disappointed with the Yeltsin regime, particularly because of its failure to feed servicemen. By the time the DPA was created, Rokhlin enjoyed the support of the CPRF and other PPUoR factions in the Duma.Many communists, such as the egregious Makashov, Ilyukhin and the veteran CPRF activist Igor Bratishchev, joined the DPA at its founding congress held on September 20, 1997. Thanks to Rokhlin's standing with the military, the DPA is said to have enjoyed widespread support.

On July 3, 1998, Rokhlin was assassinated while sleeping at his country home.[296] CPRF activist Viktor Ilyukhin, the driving force behind the Duma impeachment efforts, replaced Rokhlin as chairman of the DPA. Today, some anticommunist media speculate that at least some officers could disobey the order if Yeltsin opted for a repetition of the events of October 1993, while some of the military could go so far as to side with the Duma against the president, thus sparking civil war on the streets of the Russian capital.[297]

How to Stay in Power

In such circumstances, it seems highly unlikely that Yeltsin would venture to resort to extra-constitutional methods in his feud with the CPRF. But

295. See, for example, Viktor Baranets, *Yeltsin i ego generaly: Zapiski Polkovnika Genshtaba*, Moscow, Sovershenno Sekretno Publishing House, 1998, as well as his Poteryannaya Armiya... op. cit.

296. For a biography, see Andrei Antipov, *Lev Rokhlin: Zhizn i smert Generala*, Moscow, EKSMO-Press, 1998.

297. See, for example, *Moskovsky komsomolets*, April 15, 1999.

does this mean that Yeltsin will resign at the end of his tenure? Between 1994 and 1996, various Kremlin officials suggested that the 1996 presidential election be "suspended" (which in fact meant "annulled").[298] In the middle of the campaign, in May 1996, Korzhakov volunteered his plan for suspending the election in an interview with a British Sunday newspaper.[299] In 1996 the proposal to cancel the election was rejected. There seems to be no reason, therefore, to believe that it would be accepted in the year 2000.

In addition to the options outlined above, a more sophisticated method for Yeltsin to stay in power in the third millennium has been discussed in the media. The Russian Constitution stipulates that no one may serve more than two terms as Russian president. According to Aleksei Mitrofanov, Zhirinovsky's deputy in the LDPR faction in the Duma,[300] Yeltsin could create a new state out of the emerging union of Russia, Belarus and probably Yugoslavia, and then engineer his own election as president of the new country. He would thus retain power essentially in the same way as he came to power, by engineering the collapse of the USSR in 1991, albeit in the opposite direction. This does not appear to be a realistic possibility, if only because of the lack of time available to Yeltsin to arrange such a union. However, should this happen, the CPRF would benefit from a union of this kind, as the party's relations with both Belorussian leader Alyaksandr Lukashenka and Yugoslav leader Slobodan Milosevic are better than their relations with Yeltsin.

A Quasi-Democratic Scenario

The most commonly held view of the future of Russia's leadership may be stated as neither dictatorial nor entirely democratic, but something in between. In this quasi-democratic scenario, Yeltsin would resign as Russian president in favor of a handpicked successor capable of continuing Yeltsin's policies and of guaranteeing immunity for the former Russian president and his family. It is assumed that Yeltsin's heir apparent would fight an election that would be organized in a way that could hardly be termed

---

298. Among such officials were the then speaker of the Federation Council, Vladimir Shumeiko (see *Izvestiya* and *Nezavisimaya Gazeta*, October 7, 1994) and the Governor of Voronezh Oblast, Aleksandr Kovalev (*Obshchaya Gazeta* No. 11, 1996, p. 1).

299. See *The Observer*, May 5, 1996.

300. In an interview with Mitrofanov on the NTV news program *Segodnya*, April 11, 1999.

either free or fair. Thus far, former Russian Prime Minister Viktor Chernomyrdin has been named as Yeltsin's virtual official heir more often than any other Russian politician has.[301] However, the choice of Chernomyrdin would require a considerable amount of pressure to be put on the electorate. In a survey conducted on March 27-30, 1999 by Russia's most prestigious sociological institution, the All-Russian Institute of Public Opinion Studies (VTsIOM), the percentage of respondents willing to vote for Chernomyrdin in the next presidential election was zero (0).[302] Other polls have shown Chernomyrdin's approval rating not to exceed three percent of those polled.[303]

The election of a candidate with such a low rating would require intervention on his behalf by local and regional authorities, the cooperation of electoral commissions at all levels, and control of the media.

Needless to say, none of this would be achievable unless a presidential hopeful held a top position which would enable him either to buy the loyalty of these structures or to impose his will on them. There are only three such positions in today's Russia—the posts of president, prime minister and acting president. According to the Russian Constitution, if the president dies or has to resign due to poor health or impeachment, his duties are temporarily assumed by the prime minister—the acting president. The election of the new president of the Russian Federation must take place no later than three months after the president's early exit from office. This means that a former prime minister could serve as acting president for as long as three months. In Russia's quasi-democracy, the post of acting president would no doubt give its holder a huge (and rather unfair) advantage over all other presidential hopefuls. No serious politician in Russia today appears to doubt that any head of government would win the 2000 presidential race if he chose to participate.

CHERNOMYRDIN'S CHANCES

This very consideration is widely believed to have been behind Chernomyrdin's fall from grace on March 23, 1998, when Yeltsin suddenly replaced him with the young and ambitious banker Sergei Kirienko. Some Russian observers attributed the move to the president's desire to be

---

301. See, for example, *Nezavisimaya Gazeta*, February 3, 1998, and April 16, 1999.

302. See Ibid. (Footnote 1).

303. The figure was revealed by the deputy director of the Russian Institute on Europe, Sergei Karaganov in NTV's *Itogi*: *Predislovie* on April 10, 1999.

succeeded by a younger man with a background different from those of such career communist party apparatchiks as both Chernomyrdin and Yeltsin himself.[304] To an even greater extent, the unwillingness of the parliamentary factions to pave the way for the unpopular Chernomyrdin to the highest office in the land was believed to be behind the refusal of the Duma to consent to Chernomyrdin's comeback in September 1998. The economic crisis of August 17, 1998, when Russia announced the devaluation of the ruble and simultaneously suspended the repayment of its foreign and internal debts, changed Yeltsin's mind about the so-called "young reformers." Kirienko was fired and Chernomyrdin reappointed as acting prime minister. But the Duma that had voted for Kirienko only on the third attempt and by a very small margin flatly refused to cooperate with the president on the appointment of Chernomyrdin six months later. With the sole exception of Vladimir Zhirinovsky's LDPR, all factions swore to face the dissolution of the Duma rather than endorse Chernomyrdin's appointment. Addressing the house during the parliamentary debate on the issue in September 1998, the liberal Yavlinsky advanced the candidature of Evgenii Primakov, saying that Primakov had no presidential ambitions and could therefore ensure the democratic nature of future elections.[305]

Lack of cooperation by parliament may be a major obstacle in Chernomyrdin's path to supreme power in Russia. The current Duma is highly unlikely ever to vote in favor of Chernomyrdin's appointment to the office. One can expect, therefore, that the authorities will try very hard to ensure that a more cooperative chamber is elected at the forthcoming parliamentary elections, scheduled for December 19, 1999. Yeltsin is on record as having said in front of Russian TV cameras that he needs "a different Duma."[306] The statement was significant, as Yeltsin made it during his meeting with the new chairman of the Central Electoral Commission, Aleksandr Veshnyakov. But would the Russian president be capable of achieving such a goal in the next elections for seats in the lower chamber of the Russian parliament? Russian reformers appear to be perfectly sure of their ability to manipulate the will of the electorate. "Modern election technology allows us to influence the public in such a way that

304. See, for example, the editorial in *Nezavisimaya Gazeta*, March 24, 1998. Other Russian analysts to have addressed the issue in the media have opined that Yeltsin might have considered a third term in office, regardless of the Constitutional ban.

305. The proceedings in the State Duma were broadcast live by RTR on September 9, 1999.

306. See *Nezavisimaya Gazeta*, April 14, 1999.

they would not even notice it," said a Kremlin official, identified only as a member of Chubais' "Right Cause" election bloc.[307] Yet the reform-minded parties have never been capable of achieving a clear cut majority in any parliamentary election conducted in the Soviet Union or Russia, not even in the days of almost universal public hero-worship for Boris Yeltsin in the late 1980s and early 1990s. It is very difficult to imagine how on earth they could be more successful today, when Yeltsin's approval rating is reported to be as low as 1.4 percent,[308] while Chernomyrdin's party, Our Home Is Russia, is generally expected to fall far below the five percent barrier required for a party to be elected to the State Duma in December 1999.[309] If NDR fails in the parliamentary election, Yeltsin's family will very probably withdraw their support for Chernomyrdin as the next president and look for somebody with a better showing in the polls.

Potential Presidential Candidates

In such an eventuality, the composition of the short list is very well known. In the past few years, a total of five men have been considered favorites in a potential presidential race, with Zyuganov and Primakov being the front-runners. Yeltsin's team would welcome neither of the two, and in addition, the 69-year-old Primakov has kept saying that he will not take part in the presidential election. The rest of the pool consists of Yurii Luzhkov, Grigorii Yavlinsky and Aleksandr Lebed. According to the most recent survey, 13 percent of the electorate were willing to vote for both Luzhkov and Yavlinsky in the presidential election, while Lebed's support stood at 7 percent.[310] Each of them has friends in different sections of Yeltsin's court. Therefore it cannot be ruled out that Yeltsin may also opt to back one of the three. But it would be more like Boris Yeltsin to advance somebody completely unknown to the general public, as he did with his choice of Ivan Silaev as the first Russian prime minister in 1990, with Colonel Rutskoi as his vice-president in 1991, with Kirienko in 1998, and on a number of other occasions. Prior to their appointments, those speculating in the media on the vacant positions had mentioned none of these names. In this respect, Yeltsin's personnel policies are reminiscent of a well-known anecdote about

307. *Nezavisimaya Gazeta*, April 16, 1999.

308. Lyudmila Telen, citing findings of the Institute of Sociology of the Russian Academy of Sciences and Socioexpress Center in *Moskovskie novosti*, No. 9, 1999, p. 7.

309. See the survey of VTsIOM, op. cit., or the article by Mikhail Gorshkov in *Nezavisimaya Gazeta*, February 25, 1999.

310. The *ORT* news program *Vremya*, April 17, 1999.

that master of the Russian power game, Josef Stalin. Asked whom he saw as his successor, the Soviet dictator grinned and replied: "An unknown young man (neizvestnyi molodoi chelovek)." At least on one occasion, this policy proved useful. Asked why some of his political allies voted for the appointment of Kirienko, Zyuganov told the author: "We did not know anything about this man." It is indeed rather difficult to oppose a candidate of whom neither good nor bad is known.

CPRF Seeks to Share Power With Future President

From the standpoint of the CPRF, almost anyone, including Chernomyrdin, would be easier to deal with than the current president. The only exception may be one of the "young reformers" from the Gaidar-Chubais-Kirienko bloc, but such a choice is unlikely because of the opposition they would face among regional leaders, as well as among the military, security and police elite. Even if Yeltsin decides to back an "unknown young man" and succeeds in pushing his choice through the Russian voting machine, the youth in question is hardly likely to survive in power for long.

No other candidate would need to continue Yeltsin's crusade against the CPRF. The reason for this belief lies in the history of Russia in the late 1980s. Yeltsin arrived at the top of Russian politics just as the nation was beginning to feel tired of seventy years of communism and was eager to try a way of life similar to that of "all civilized countries," as they used to say in the late Gorbachev era. Militant anticommunism has served as the raison d'étre of Yeltsin's rule; negative anticommunist campaigning has been Yeltsin's instrument in his efforts to concentrate almost unlimited power in his hands at various stages of his tenure as president.

For the next generation of Russian leaders, the great evil of the communist era would be ancient history, no more useful to them than the crimes of the emperors Nero or Caligula to a modern Italian politician. Furthermore, with the sole exception of Yavlinsky, all the figures in the list of known presidential hopefuls—Primakov, Luzhkov and Lebed—are on record as having cooperated with communists in their current posts. Like Primakov's choice of Maslyukov and Kulik, Luzhkov in his capacity as Moscow mayor and Lebed as governor of Krasnoyarsk Krai have both selected communists as their deputies. In the case of Luzhkov, this was Moscow Deputy Mayor Valerii Shantsev, who was elected from Luzhkov's list on the day of the Russian presidential election, June 12, 1996. A life-long CPRF activist, in February 1993 Shantsev acted as chair of the Moscow CPRF Organizational Committee that presided over the restoration of the Russian communist party in the capital.[311] More recently, Lebed appointed the former first secretary of the Krasnoyarsk Krai Committee of the CPSU Pavel Fedirko as his new deputy. A resident of Moscow, Fedirko was asked to represent the krai in the Russian Federal government. Fedirko's comeback has been viewed as part of a general change in Lebed's personnel policy. Following his election as governor in March 1998, Lebed gave positions of responsibility in the region to outsiders who came to Krasnoyarsk along with the new broom. Such a policy naturally met with opposition in Krasnoyarsk. Since then Lebed has come to terms with the regional champions of the CPRF, and started to replace his newcomers with local former Communist Party officials.[312] In view of such evidence, it seems safe to assume that any of the three would share power with the CPRF if elected president. Moreover, the tendency to share power with communists does certainly not appear to be limited to the policies of Primakov, Lebed and Luzhkov. It seems to be applicable to any possible replacement for Yeltsin except a "young reformer." Chernomyrdin, too, was said to have promised jobs for the PPUoR during his negotiations with the Duma leaders in August-September 1998. The new Russian prime minister Stepashin and his deputies adopted a similar tactic, having said in their interviews with the Russian media that they are ready to do business with the CPRF, "because the communists are humans."

As for Yavlinsky, even during his short terms in office as Russian and Soviet deputy prime minister in 1990 and 1991 respectively, he was not in a position to share power with any political party, including the CPRF. The closest equivalent to a "young reformer" in the shortlist of hopefuls, Yavlinsky bears no personal responsibility for Yeltsin's policies. On the contrary, he has acted as Yeltsin's main democratic opponent in the parliament since December 1993. Today it may be premature to speculate whether Yavlinsky would offer jobs to the CPRF in the highly unlikely event of his election as president. It is worth noting, however, that one slogan of Yavlinsky's party during the 1995 parliamentary election campaign read: "Yabloko fights poverty rather than communists." In other words, with or without jobs the relations of the CPRF with such a leader would at least be peaceful, with no tanks or bans by decree.

311. See Tarasov A.N., Cherkassov G.Yu., Shavshukova T.G., *Levye v Rossii: Ot umerennykh do ekstremistov*, Moscow, Moskovskii Antifashistskii Tsentr & Informatsionno-Ekspertnaya Gruppa Panorama, Institut Eksperimental'noi Sotsiologii, 1997, pp. 120 and 165.
312. See *Izvestiya*, April 17, 1999.

The Presidency Controversy

Another scenario, advocated by most CPRF ideologists, is either democratic or very undemocratic, depending on who proposes it and to what end. This scenario envisages introducing amendments to the current Russian Constitution to annul the election of the Russian president by universal suffrage. Some of those who advocate the abolition of the executive presidency envisage transforming Russia into a parliamentary republic governed by a prime minister—"the acknowledged head of the party commanding a majority in the parliament." Today's one-man-rule in Russia, they argue, has very little in common with either the US or French presidential democracies, and therefore it should be changed in accordance with the model that prevails in most of Western Europe. For obvious reasons, such a proposal is popular with the more moderate wing of the CPRF and with friendly politicians. (Radical communists advocate the restoration of the Soviets rather than parliamentary democracy). However, some authors believe that the proposed amendments would not benefit the CPRF in the long run. In a brilliant essay, a leader of the St. Petersburg Yabloko organization, Boris Vishnevsky, argues that abolishing the executive presidency in Russia would ultimately diminish the power of the CPRF in Russian politics. First, because the government of a parliamentary republic would not be capable of implementing against the will of the electorate "the radical Bolshevik course of reform", as Vishnevsky termed it, which would give a great boost to the protest vote. Secondly, Vishnevsky continues, because the democrats in a parliamentary republic would have to compete for seats in parliament rather than for posts in the executive branch of the government, and such competition would diminish the electoral success of Zyuganov and his ilk.[313] Perhaps even more important, Vishnevsky writes, the abolition of the presidency would have spared Russia many of the tragic errors of the past decade, including the war against Chechnya, corruption scandals related to privatization and arbitrary taxation. According to Vishnevsky, the presidential system may work very well in a country such as the United States, thanks to Americans' traditional respect for the law. But in Russia, with its lack of a democratic tradition, the existing system creates arbitrariness and autocracy.

Quite naturally, the leaders of the CPRF, the strongest faction in the State Duma, are in favor of the changes advocated by their liberal opponent from St. Petersburg. In the fall of 1998, the speaker of the Federa-

313. See *Nezavisimaya Gazeta*, July 22, 1998.

tion Council, Yegor Stroev, told the Spanish newspaper *El Pais* that the next Russian president should be elected by a constitutional assembly rather than by universal suffrage. Echoing the words of his colleague, the speaker of the State Duma Gennadii Seleznev cited the experience of such West European states as Germany and Italy to support his argument that the president should be chosen by both chambers of the parliament along with the legislative assemblies of the Russian regions. Zyuganov, in turn, opined that a president should be elected by a collegium of electors, consisting of representatives of "all the regions, estates and political forces."[314] All these suggestions were designed to give parliament more say in the affairs of government. The problem is that the introduction of such amendments is highly improbable under a non-communist president. And the communists would hardly insist on their proposals if one of their number were elected president under the current Constitution.

Questioning Universal Suffrage

Others have suggested that the president should remain the absolute ruler, but, at the same time, be elected only by the "best people" rather than by universal suffrage. In an interview with a popular Moscow weekly, for example, the governor of Great Novgorod Oblast, Mikhail Prusak, suggested that ordinary people should not vote in any elections.[315] According to Prusak, parliament should be formed in essentially the same way as the CPSU Central Committee—in other words composed of the best representatives of the regions, such as bankers, industrialists and factory directors. Such a body, Prusak said, should be entitled to chose the president, just as the Central Committee elected CPSU General Secretaries. And the president in turn would appoint the governors, rather than allow the population to elect the regional leaders.

In a very unusual move for modern Russia, on April 6, 1999 a majority of Moscow daily newspapers published a long appeal to the president and government, signed by 33 factory directors and scholars, mostly from Siberia.[316] The signatories stated that power in Russia should be strong, that Russia needs a strong "state ideology," and that the Russian elite needs to be protected from radicals of all kinds by state power. Three days later, the deputy director of the Center of Political Conjecture, Valerii

314. See *Nezavisimaya Gazeta*, October 31, 1998.

315. *Argumenty i fakty*, No. 15, 1998, p. 6.

316. See *Izvestiya*, Novye *Izvestiya*, *Nezavisimaya Gazeta* and *Moskovskii komsomolets*, all April 6, 1999.

Fedorov, translated the rather vague demands of the signatories into clearer Russian.[317] According to Fedorov, the signatories were urging that Yeltsin's successor be chosen "by the common coordinated command of the country's entire political elite." Only this form of succession, Fedorov went on, could bring peace to a quasi-feudal country such as Russia. Such "elections without a choice," Fedorov added, "would be less painful for the public conscience than the tragicomedy of the 'free election' of 1996."

The publication of such an appeal in several newspapers was reminiscent of the beginnings of an old Soviet-style propaganda campaign, which would normally need a sponsor from above. Which of Russia's top officials was behind its publication is as yet unclear. Yeltsin has so far rejected all attempts to amend the Constitution, whether from the advocates of parliamentary democracy or from the self-proclaimed "elite." In his State of the Nation address, however, the president suggested that this issue should be postponed until after the elections to the new Duma in December 1999. "It is unacceptable to amend the Constitution behind the backs of those who are about to replace the current Duma. Let them decide whether they want to introduce any amendments. And let them decide what kind of amendments are to be considered." Should the CPRF indeed win the majority of seats in the parliamentary elections, it cannot be ruled out that the powers-that-be would not want to risk the election of a new president by universal suffrage. In this case, the future Russian president might be chosen by some sort of "elite"—by a board of appointees.

Democratic Scenarios

Since the collapse of the Soviet Union and the communist regime in 1991, the adjective "unpredictable" has become a key term in Russian political vocabulary. Observers seem to have formed a consensus that everything is possible in today's Russia. Although Yeltsin's team makes no secret of their intention to prevent a communist comeback in 2000 by any means necessary, such an eventuality is far from impossible. Given Yeltsin's well-known health problems, for instance, there seems to be little doubt that without Yeltsin political developments in Russia would take on a completely different complexion should Primakov become acting president. It may be argued that Yeltsin is by no means the only man in Russia who has a vested interest in the preservation of the status quo. All of Russia's "new rich" (in particular those who gained from illegal privatization, most of the powerful regional elite, a large section of Russia's gigantic bureaucracy,

317. See Novye *Izvestiya*, April 9, 1999.

many intellectuals, journalists and so on) are quite sincere in their determination to prevent the victory of somebody like Gennadii Zyuganov in the next presidential election. These sections of Russian society are certainly more powerful today than their opponents. But their opponents may outnumber them.

The communist-dominated coalition, the PPUoR, differs from most other Russian political parties because of the variety of options available to it if there is a truly free and fair presidential race. Zyuganov is by no means the only candidate who may suit them. If there is very negative campaigning aimed at Zyuganov personally, he may withdraw in favor of a less controversial figure, such as Kemerovo Governor Aman Tuleev, who withdrew in Zyuganov's favor on the eve of the 1996 presidential election. Tuleev has the advantage of being immensely popular in his region, but his father was a Kazakh, and the Russian nationalist communist electorate regards this as a great disadvantage. Another possible presidential hopeful acceptable to the bloc would be Gennadii Seleznev, the speaker of the State Duma and a moderate member of the CPRF Central Committee. Furthermore, some of the party's moderates reportedly prefer a compromise figure with no direct links with the PPUoR, let alone the CPRF itself. In an interview with Radio Free Europe/Radio Liberty, for example, the prominent Moscow journalist Leonid Nikitinsky cited many sources among moderate CPRF and PPUoR activists as saying that they would rather have Primakov than Zyuganov as the next Russian president.[318] His contacts in the PPUoR, Nikitinsky added, approved of Primakov's policies in both his governmental capacities—as foreign minister and prime minister. At the same time, the journalist went on, they value his image as a less controversial figure that is more inclined to compromise.

Primakov's victory in a presidential election would be no less triumphant than was Yeltsin's in 1991, but only on the condition of two big "ifs": (1) If Primakov becomes acting president; and (2) If he agrees to contest the election. At present, both of these options seem extremely unlikely ever to happen.

Factors Controlling Electoral Success

In Zyuganov's case, or that of another CPRF candidate, the possibility of success in such a race would be conditional upon a number of other factors, such as money, equal access to the media, particularly television, and control

318. As broadcast by the RFE/RL Russian Service's Liberty Live program on April 12, 1999.

of the ballot. At the time of writing, the situation with regard to each of these issues was as follows:

(1) Money. The financial factor is said to have played the decisive role in 1996, when the cooperation of Russian financial tycoons alongside unlimited access to the state coffers contributed to the victory of Boris Yeltsin.[319] Yeltsin had started his campaign with a rating that ranged in different surveys from three to eight percent.[320] The crisis of August 17, 1998 resulted in the bankruptcy of some of Russia's financial oligarchs who had contributed to Yeltsin's election campaign in 1996, and seriously affected the wealth of others. To no lesser an extent, the crisis affected the state's finances, as Russia declared itself unable to pay interest to foreign creditors.[321] At the same time, questionable financial affairs in Yeltsin's campaign gave rise to a number of public scandals, some of which have endured for years, such as that involving the removal of a cardboard box containing $500,000 in cash from the Russian government building.[322] Whether it was the poverty or the scandals—or both—which aroused public concern it has been decided that future elections should represent "competition between candidates rather than between [their] purses."[323]

Despite the good intentions of the newly elected Central Election Commission, it is not hard to predict that the monetary issue will be no less important in 2000 than it was in 1996. After all, money is an even greater temptation for the poor than for the rich. On October 30, 1998, the CPRF Central Committee held a special plenary session behind closed doors at which the party's financial problems were discussed. In his address to the plenum, CPRF first deputy chairman Valentin Kuptsov complained about the party's financial difficulties.[324]

Another highly placed communist told *Kommersant-Daily* that the party's coffers would be exhausted by the end of 1998, and that they had to think about the forthcoming election now.[325] According to the newspaper's analyst, the CPRF had enjoyed the sponsorship of at least

---

319. On October 10, 1996, *Sovetskaya Rossiya* published excerpts from a leaked financial document on the use of taxpayers' money in the course of Yeltsin's campaign.

320. See *NG Stsenarii*, August 29, 1996.

321. Russian television news broadcasts of April 20, 1999.

322. See, for example, *Moskovskii komsomolets*, November 23, 1996, and *Novaya Gazeta*, No. 14, 1999, p. 1.

323. Russian television newscasts, April 13, 1999.

324. NTV's *Segodnya* newscast, October 30, 1998.

325. See *Kommersant-Daily*, October 31, 1998.

two of the very same bankers who had contributed to the Yeltsin campaign—Inkombank and MENATEP.326 Following the crisis of August 17, 1998, the former went bankrupt while the latter was placed under the supervision of the State Bank. At about the same time, the CPRF lost contact with its official sponsor, known in Moscow lobbies as "the red millionaire."

The owner of a Moscow casino and chairman of Rosbiznessbank, Vladimir Semago provided financial assistance to the communists when the party was banned by a series of Yeltsin's decrees in 1991, and for a subsequent few years. In 1992, Semago testified on behalf of the CPSU in the Constitutional Court.[327] Semago joined the CPRF when the party was restored in 1993, and was elected as a deputy from the party list in both 1993 and 1995. As early as January 1996, when Semago accused the party leadership of corruption, the banker's relations with the Communist Party started to deteriorate. Following two years of mutual accusations, the "red millionaire" resigned from the CPRF faction in the Duma in September 1998.[328]

Semago was probably the best known but by no means the only representative of the type to which Zyuganov refers in his interviews as "nationally-oriented capital" (the term implies the non-Russian—in other words, Jewish—origin of other countries' businesses). A glance at the lists of CPRF regional officials reveals the names of people running the local branches of some of Russia's richest companies—such as Aslanbi Sovmis, the General Director of the LUKoil-Nefteproduct share company in North Ossetia, or Sergei Korepanov, the director of Gazprom's representation in Yamalo-Nenets Autonomous Okrug. In addition to members of the CPRF, the governors of "red" regions enjoy the support of local bankers such as Timur Tsoriev, who reportedly controls the finances of Kemerovo Oblast

326. NOTE: According to persistent Moscow rumors, most large Russian financial groups have contributed to the funds of all major competitors in various Russian elections. The explanation for this strange behavior lies in their desire to safeguard their businesses, which are not in fact defended by either custom or law, but have to rely on the mercy of the powers-that-be. At least one former tycoon, the Moscow gasoline king Ilya Kolerov, is reported to have been ruined because he refused to contribute to Yeltsin's 1996 campaign.

327. See *KPSS vne Zakona? Konstitutsionnyi sud v Moskve*, Moscow, Baikal'skaya Akademiya, 1992, pp. 139-148.

328. See *Izvestiya*, January 11, 1996; *Nezavisimaya Gazeta*, August 2, 1997, and September 18, 1998.

under Tuleev.[329] On a federal level, CPRF sponsors included such exotic figures as the former president of Imperial Bank, Sergei Rodionov, who financed the publication of *Pravda*.

Today, the party's most prominent benefactor is Viktor Vidmanov, a member of the party's top ruling body, the Presidium of the CPRF Central Committee (the equivalent of the CPSU Politburo). Vidmanov is chairman of the board of one of Russia's largest banks, Agropromstroibank, which specializes in building up agricultural industry, as well as of dozens of the bank's subsidiaries throughout Russia. As a major contributor to Zyuganov's 1996 presidential campaign, Vidmanov joined the PPUoR; he was elected to the party's Presidium on April 20, 1997. In January 1999, Vidmanov was offered one of the greatest honors for a member of the communist party leadership: He addressed a plenary session of the CPRF Central Committee with a long paper, entitled "How to Lead the Country out of Crisis: The Position of the Communists."[330] Unlike Semago, who enjoyed the sympathy of many journalists, Vidmanov has been attacked in the media. Articles in two popular anticommunist newspapers accused Vidmanov's bank of involvement in two of Russian most infamous financial scandals—the bankruptcy of Chara bank that destroyed the fortunes of many of Russia's cultural figures, and the mysterious disappearance of the budget funds which were supposed to finance the rebuilding of the Chechen Republic, devastated in the infamous war.[331] According to his critics, Vidmanov's business is no less dishonest than those of the reform-minded Russian tycoons.

Apart from its connections with questionable bankers, the CPRF has been routinely accused of lobbying for the interests of various companies in exchange for financial benefits. The Russian Academy of Agricultural Studies, the owner of 6,500,000 hectares (16,049,383 acres) of agricultural land and of many food processing factories, has been named as one such benefactor of the CPRF.[332] At the same time, the CPRF reportedly refused a bribe of $60 million offered if it voted in the Duma to endorse Chernomyrdin as prime minister. A party defector Vasilii Kobylkin has revealed that he was twice offered $10,000 to vote for Kirienko and Chernomyrdin. On both occasions, Kobylkin said, he refused to accept

329. See *Obshchaya Gazeta*, No. 8, 1999, pp. 1-7.

330. For the text see *Sovetskaya Rossiya*, January 26, 1999.

331. See *Nezavisimaya Gazeta*, December 5, 1998; and *Argumenty i fakty*, No. 5, 1999, p. 5.

332. See *Argumenty i fakty*, No. 5, 1999, p. 5.

the offer,[333] as did most of his former CPRF colleagues in the Duma. In short, the CPRF does not appear to be the most corrupt faction in the Russian parliament.

All in all, the financial state of the CPRF today may not be as acute as it was in the fall of 1998, but it is widely believed to be one of the poorest political parties in Russia.[334]

(2) The media. Following the presidential election of 1996, a number of respected international organizations which have monitored the media in various countries issued statements accusing Boris Yeltsin of abuse of power in his use of television for his presidential campaign.[335] Under pressure from the administration, Russian television companies violated all existing laws and norms of civilized behavior in order to give the advantage to one candidate. Other competitors, such as Zyuganov and Yavlinsky, were denied access to the media, sometimes even in prepaid slots. All the comments on Yeltsin in the electronic media were positive, while all the pronouncements about other candidates, particularly Zyuganov, were negative. They were merely criticized and ridiculed. Moreover, a special team of advisers, including people such as the former dissident Gleb Pavlovsky, was busy inventing deliberate lies aimed at blackening Yeltsin's rivals.[336] The television companies were then ordered to broadcast their concoctions in news programs. Needless to say, the media made no attempt to inform the electorate that Yeltsin had suffered a heart attack between the two rounds of the election. And to add insult to injury, Igor Malashenko, the director of the largest Russian private television company, NTV, joined Yeltsin's team of campaigners as a propaganda adviser.

Journalists involved in the 1996 campaign have claimed that they were sincere in their desire to support Yeltsin, viewing him as "the lesser evil," the only option left for them against that great evil embodied by Zyuganov. It should be borne in mind that the entire Russian electronic media is entirely dependent on the president and his team. During his tenure, Yeltsin has fired and replaced the heads of the ORT and RTR television channels on more than one occasion. The private companies, in turn, can be deprived of access to the airwaves at the nod of Yeltsin's

333. See *Moskovskie novosti*, No. 47, 1999.

334. See, for example, *Nezavisimaya Gazeta*, February 18, 1999.

335. See *The ICFJ Clearinghouse*, No. 24, 1996.

336. Pavlovsky revealed this in so many words in his brochure *Prezident* v 1996: stsenarii i tekhnologii pobedy (Kak, pochemu i zachem my pobedili na vyborakh 1996 goda. Nash podkhod k pobede Borisa El'tsina), Fond effektivnoi politiki, August 1996. See also *Obshchaya Gazeta*, No. 48, 1997, p. 7.

appointee, the head of the Federal Service on Radio and Television Mikhail Seslavinsky; alternatively, the rates for their use of state-owned transmitters can be raised at will. According to Pavlovsky, in the absence of political parties or a proper administrative mechanism, television is the only instrument with which Yeltsin can govern Russia.[337] And, last but not least, there is no tradition of objective news coverage among the former Soviet propagandists who make up today's journalistic corps. The concept of news reporting based on accuracy and impartiality is completely alien to the highly opinionated Russian journalists. All attempts by the opposition factions in the State Duma to introduce Western-type multiparty committees to ensure more balanced coverage of Russian political events on the airwaves have been routinely vetoed by Yeltsin as a communist plot aimed at reintroducing censorship in Russia.

More likely than not, media coverage of the next Russian elections will essentially be the same as it was in 1996.

(3) Control over the accuracy of the ballot. In March 1999, the opposition achieved a major victory in its fight for fairness in the next elections when the Duma candidate Aleksandr Veshnyakov was elected chairman of the Central Election Commission. Under the old law, in force in 1996, the Commission consisted entirely of the president's appointees. Subsequently a new law was adopted, and the new fifteen-strong body is composed of five members appointed by Yeltsin, five delegated by the State Duma, and another five elected by the Federation Council. During the elections for the Commission chairman, the candidate advanced by Yeltsin and Primakov, Valentin Vlasov, withdrew in favor of Veshnyakov. Upon his election, Veshnyakov vowed to ensure that the next Russian election be "honest."[338] Moreover, Veshnyakov reiterated the promise during his meeting with Yeltsin twenty days later.[339] Does this mean that the results of the next parliamentary and presidential elections will not be rigged?

There is another reason to be cautiously optimistic about the accuracy of the ballot in future elections. Back in 1996, most governors and heads of local administrations were appointed, and therefore dependent on Moscow. They have since been replaced with elected—and therefore independent—figures. At the same time, the legislative bodies of most Russian regions are controlled by the opposition to Yeltsin, albeit not

337. See an interview with Pavlovsky in *Kommersant-Vlast*, December 15, 1998.
338. See *Nezavisimaya Gazeta* and *Kommersant-Daily*, March 25, 1999.
339. See *Izvestiya*, *Nezavisimaya Gazeta* and *Kommersant-Daily*, April 14, 1999.

necessarily procommunist.[340] It is to be hoped that the new composition of the regional power structures provides certain safeguards against election fraud.

What is the CPRF likely to do if it comes to power?

As cited above, some moderate members of the CPRF have confessed privately that they would prefer the top job to go to a neutral person—such as former prime minister Primakov—rather than to their leader, Zyuganov. At first glance, this preference seems very strange. After all, Primakov is the embodiment of many things that today's Russian communists dislike (to put it mildly). Primakov owed his career to two men who are more than unpopular with the PPUoR, namely Mikhail Gorbachev and Aleksandr Yakovlev. He is a friend of such sworn enemies of the CPRF as Yegor Yakovlev, the editor of the liberal weekly *Obshchaya Gazeta*. Primakov's father was a victim of Stalin's purges, while his mother was Jewish. So why would they have such a man in charge of Russia rather than one of their own number? Could it be because moderate communists are afraid of the vengeful mood of their less moderate comrades? If so, Zyuganov himself may well be one of these moderate communists. Zyuganov does not appear to be a vindictive person, but it may be very difficult for him to resist the pressure of a revengeful mob if he were elected president.

The question of what to expect if there is a communist comeback is not an easy one to answer. It would seem to depend on whether they come to power as the junior partner of a non-communist, such as Luzhkov or Primakov, or on their own. In the partnership scenario, the moderates would have the upper hand. After all, nothing awful has happened with the arrival of the communist Maslyukov in his capacity as first deputy prime minister responsible for economics in Primakov's cabinet: No nationalization, no target economy, no rapid inflation. According to Yeltsin, Maslyukov implemented the very same policies as those advocated by the reformer Kirienko.[341] A larger role for the CPRF under a non-communist successor to Yeltsin may lead to a more nationalist foreign policy. Yet their influence may even be democratic, should the communists indeed make the government answerable to the parliament or introduce something similar to the American Fairness Doctrine for the electronic media. All in all,

340. For details see *Nezavisimaya Gazeta*, December 2, 1998.
341. See *Kommersant-Daily*, March 31, 1991.

as a junior partner the CPRF may be no more dangerous than the former communists who have temporarily come to power in Eastern Europe.

Fruits of Communist Victory?

The situation may be completely different if the party triumphs in the election. First of all, communists today make no secret of their opinion that those responsible for legal violations, such as those during the course of privatization, should be brought to trial.[342] It may be argued that many influential people in today's Russia are widely suspected of involvement in affairs that would be viewed as criminal in any country, such as corruption, abuse of power or election fraud. Yet there is a great difference between a fair trial and a revolutionary tribunal, as it would almost certainly become if the communists were to seek revenge. Once started, revolutionary tribunals tend to be very difficult to stop.

Secondly, Russian communists do not seem to differ much from their Russian liberal opponents in their appreciation of democracy while in opposition. Once in power, both sides tend to change their minds rather quickly. While in opposition, for example, they demand equal access to the media for all. Once in power, they tend to deny such access to their opponents. One case in point is a recent vote in the State Duma on Russian television coverage of the war in Yugoslavia. In the midst of the debates on that day's agenda, a member of the CPRF, Tamara Pletneva, complained about Russian television's "transparent insinuations" about "the alleged suffering," as she put it, of Kosovo Albanians at the hands of the Serbs. Such broadcasts should be stopped, Pletneva argued, because they contradicted the view on the matter of both the president and the government. All attempts by Deputy Chairman of the Duma Committee on Information Policies Yurii Nesterov (Yabloko) to explain that the media does not always have to agree with either the president or the prime minister were in vain. As a result, as many as 192 deputies voted in favor of Pletneva's proposal.[343] The resolution failed but only by a small margin.

Conclusion

To sum up, it can be said that Russia's democrats have made rather poor use of the historic chance accorded them. They have proved incapable of

---

342. See comments on the report of a special commission that investigated privatization in the Federation Council in *Sovetskaya Rossiya*, March 20, 1999.
343. See *Kommersant-Daily*, April 15, 1999.

routing communism in Russia. At the same time they have failed to set an example of fairness, respect for the rule of law, of justice and mercy. No wonder their opponents feel bitter and eager to avenge themselves.

Appendices

In early 1999, Zyuganov announced that the CPRF-PPUoR had decided to contest the parliamentary elections scheduled for December of that year "in three columns"—i.e. in three separate lists. Ostensibly, this tactic was designed to secure the votes of those who might otherwise be reluctant to cast their ballots for the communists. On the other hand, the splitting of the bloc into three "columns" no doubt indicates serious tensions within the CPRF and the PPUoR. Against this background, it seems appropriate to provide this book with brief biographical portraits of the key figures who represent the CPRF proper (Zyuganov and Kuptsov), along with the leaders of its moderate wing (Seleznev and Podberezkin) and the hard-liners Ilyukhin and Makashov. In addition, portraits of two CPRF regional leaders are also given—the governor of Bryansk Oblast Yurii Lodkin and the first secretary of Amur Oblast Gennadii Gamza.

The data in the appendices is based on the following sources:

- *Kto est' kto v Kommunisticheskoi partii Rossiiskoi Federatsii*, Moscow, SPIK-Tsentr, 1997;
- Tarasov A.N., Cherkassov G.Yu., Shavshukova T.G., Levye v Rossii: *Ot umerennykh do Ekstremistov, Moscow, Moskovskii Antifashistskii Tsentr & Informatsionno-Ekspertnaya Gruppa Panorama*, Institute Eksperimental'noi Sotsiologii, 1997;
- Various biographical sites on the Russian Internet, in particular those of the Panorama research center <www.panorama.org> and the National News Service <www.nns.ru>;
- The author's interviews with some of the figures in question.

1. The CPRF Mainstream: Zyuganov and Kuptsov

Gennadii (Andreevich) Zyuganov,
Chairman of the CPRF Central Committee

As CPRF leader and chief ideologue, Zyuganov by definition represents the party's mainstream. Widely believed to have enemies within the CPRF, Zyuganov has nonetheless managed to retain his job for the past six years. The CPRF does not seem to blame the loss of the 1996 presidential election on Zyuganov personally, probably with good reason.

Zyuganov's attempts to turn the Communist Party into a center for the united opposition of great power fundamentalists rather than left-wingers has so far been successful from the point of their electoral performances. A future historian would probably also give credit to Zyuganov for his achievement in making the CPRF far more widely respected an organization than was its predecessor, the CP RSFSR.

- Zyuganov was born into a family of rural school teachers on June 26, 1944 in the village of Mymrino in Orel Oblast.
- In 1961-62 Zyuganov worked as a teacher in a village elementary school. At the same time, he studied at the physics and mathematics faculty of Orel Pedagogical Institute, from which he graduated in 1969. Zyuganov's studies at the institute were interrupted by the draft. While in the Army, Zyuganov served in military reconnaissance in Belorussia, Eastern Germany and Chelyabinsk Oblast.
- In 1966 Zyuganov joined the CPSU.
- In 1967-68 Zyuganov assumed posts in structures of the Young Communist League (Komsomol)—as first secretary of a district committee, then a city committee.
- In 1969-70 Zyuganov worked in his own physics and mathematics faculty of Orel Pedagogical Institute.
- From 1972-74 Zyuganov served as the first secretary of the Orel Oblast Komsomol Committee.
- From 1974-83 he successfully occupied the posts of secretary and second secretary of the Orel City Committee of the CPSU, and subsequently as chief of the propaganda and agitation department of the Orel Oblast Committee of the CPSU.
- From 1970-78 Zyuganov was a deputy of both Orel city and regional Soviets.
- In 1981 Zyuganov successfully defended his candidate dissertation, entitled "Foundations of Planning the Development of the Socialist Urban Way of Life (Based on Examples of the Country's Larger Cities)".
- From 1981-83, while working in Party structures, Zyuganov also taught at the philosophy faculty of Orel Pedagogical Institute.
- In 1983, Zyuganov was made an instructor in the CPSU Central Committee propaganda department. In this capacity, Zyuganov monitored developments in Moscow, the Moscow Oblast and North Caucasus. Zyuganov subsequently worked as organizer, section

head, and later deputy department head of the CPSU Central Committee apparatus.

- From 1989-90 Zyuganov served as deputy head of the CPSU CC Ideology Department.
- In June 1990 Zyuganov was elected to the Central Committee and Politburo of the CP RSFSR. At the same time, he was elected Chairman of the CP RSFSR CC Permanent Commission on Humanitarian and Ideological Problems.
- On May 7 1991, the hard-line communist daily *Sovetskaya Rossiya* published an article by Zyuganov, in which he attacked his former boss, Politburo member Aleksandr Yakovlev, widely credited to have been the architect of Gorbachev's policy of glasnost, or press freedom. At the initial stage of his career as an independent politician, Zyuganov owed his prominence to this and other articles, in which he attacked the openness of the Gorbachev era.
- In 1991-92, Zyuganov participated in the activities of various nationalist organizations. In December 1991, Zyuganov joined the leadership of the Russian Nationwide Union. Although he was not a deputy of the Russian CPD, Zyuganov was elected a leader of the parliamentary "Russian Unity" bloc. In January 1992 Zyuganov was elected Chairman of the Constitutional Council of the People's Patriotic Forces of Russia. In June 1992 he was elected co-chairman of the Central Duma of the Russian People's Sobor (Assembly). From October 1992 to spring 1994 Zyuganov was a member of the National Salvation Front's organizing committee, a member of the NSF Political Council, and one of its co-chairmen.
- In December 1992, Zyuganov joined the Initiative Committee to organize the restoration congress of the CP RSFSR.
- At the Second Restoration congress of the CPRF, held on February 13 and 14 1993, Zyuganov was elected chairman of the CPRF Central Executive Committee. Two years later, his job was renamed Chairman of the CPRF Central Committee.
- On December 12, 1993 Zyuganov was elected as a deputy to the State Duma from the CPRF party list that he headed. He then became chairman of the CPRF faction and a member of the State Duma Council.
- In 1995 Zyuganov joined the leadership of the All-Russian social-political association Spiritual Heritage (Dukhovnoe nasledie). On December 17, 1995 Zyuganov was reelected to his seat in the State

Duma, once again as the first name on the CPRF party list. Consequently, he retained his positions as chairman of the CPRF faction and member of the parliamentary ruling Council (both of which had meanwhile grown stronger as the party's representation in the Duma increased sharply).

- In 1996, Zyuganov stood in the presidential election as a representative of a People's Patriotic Bloc, led by the CPRF. He lost to Boris Yeltsin in the second round.
- At the founding congress of the People's Patriotic Union of Russia in August 1996, Zyuganov was elected chairman of the PPUoR and its Coordination Council.
- Zyuganov is married, and has a son and a daughter.

VALENTIN (ALEKSANDROVICH) KUPTSOV,
First Deputy Chairman of the CPRF Central Committee; decorated with the Order of Lenin, two Orders of the Red Labor Banner, the Symbol of Honor order, and a number of medals.

Kuptsov enjoys the respect of non-Communist observers in Russia thanks to his loyalty to the party that rejected him as its leader twice, with no valid reason on either occasion. Even more credit is given for Kuptsov's loyal services to Zyuganov, who was elected CPRF leader instead of him. For this reason, Kuptsov's name has been cited in the media as an example of honorable behavior to selfish and ambitious non-communist politicians.

In the early 1990s, Kuptsov presided over the process of the Russian Communist Party's restoration and coordinated its defense in the Constitutional Court. In an interview with the author, conducted in his Duma office in November 1997, Kuptsov revealed that he was also secretly behind the setting up of the Socialist Party of Working People (SPWP). If left to his own devices, Kuptsov would certainly have preferred to merged with Marxist reformers like today's members of the moderate SPWP, rather than with the "Ordodox Stalinists" as has happened under Zyuganov. However, party loyalties have apparently prevailed in Kuptsov's heart. Therefore, in the course of the aforementioned interview, Kuptsov attempted to assuage his own conscience, saying that at that point the CPRF was preoccupied with "the national-liberation struggle" rather than with the fight for Socialism.

- The son of a peasant family, Kuptsov was born on December 4, 1937 in the village of Mindyukino in the Cherepovets district of Vologda Oblast.
- From 1955 Kuptsov worked on his collective farm; later he became the director of a reading-room in a village in the nearby Uloma district of Vologda Oblast.
- From 1956-58 Kuptsov served in the Army.
- Starting in 1958, Kuptsov worked at the Cherepovets Metallurgy Complex, initially as a rolling-mill operator, then as a rolling-mill master and later as deputy Party secretary. While working, Kuptsov studied in the North-West Correspondence Polytechnic Institute, and graduated as a "metallurgic engineer" in 1966.
- In 1966 Kuptsov joined the CPSU.
- In 1979 Kuptsov was appointed second secretary and then first secretary of the Vologda City Committee of the CPSU. From 1979 to April 1990 Kuptsov was first secretary of the Vologda Oblast Committee of the CPSU. He was elected to the CPSU Central Committee at the Twenty-seventh party Congress, held in 1986.
- In 1988 Kuptsov graduated from the Leningrad Higher Party School.
- In spring 1989 Kuptsov was elected to the USSR Congress of People's Deputies by the residents of Velikii Ustyug in Vologda Oblast; in the CPD he joined the group of communist deputies. One year later, Kuptsov was elected as a deputy of the Vologda Oblast Soviet. In April 1990, Kuptsov was elected chairman of the Vologda Oblast Soviet of People's Deputies.
- From December 1989 to June 1990 Kuptsov was a member of the Russian Bureau of the CPSU Central Committee—a body reinvented by the Gorbachev leadership in their desperate attempt to prevent the emergence of a Russian Communist Party. In April 1990 Kuptsov was appointed head of the CPSU CC department for work with public and political organizations. He was elected CPSU CC secretary in July 1990.
- In June 1990 Kuptsov stood for the first secretaryship of the newly formed RSFSR Communist Party but lost the race to the egregious Ivan Polozkov. In the following period Gorbachev arranged for Polozkov's resignation. On August 6 1991, General Secretary Gorbachev's initial choice—namely Kuptsov—was elected first secretary of the CP RSFSR.

- Within three days of the attempted coup on August 19-21 1991, the CP RSFSR leadership, headed by Kuptsov, did not dare to spell out their attitude to the putsch.
- Together with the CPSU CC deputy general secretary Volodimir Ivashko, Kuptsov acted as a representative of the Communist Party at the Russian Constitutional Court hearing that reviewed the legality of the ban of the CPSU and CP RSFSR by three Yeltsin decrees.
- In November 1992, Kuptsov was elected Chairman of an Organizational Initiative Committee and charged with convening a unifying congress of Russian communists. Kuptsov presided over the opening session of the Russian CP restoration congress, held on February 13 and 14, 1993. He also gave a report to the congress. Initially expected to become party leader, Kuptsov was forced to withdraw in favor of Zyuganov after the intervention of a hardliner. On February 14, 1993, Kuptsov was elected as a CPRF deputy first secretary along with other communist activists. On March 20, 1993 Kuptsov was elected first deputy chairman of the CPRF Central Executive Committee. He retained this post in reelections to the CPRF ruling bodies in 1995 and 1997.
- From 1993-95 Kuptsov was in charge of the CPRF faction apparatus in the State Duma.
- In December 1995, Kuptsov was elected to a seat in the Duma from the CPRF list. As a member of the CPRF faction, Kuptsov joined the Duma Committee on Tourism and Sport.
- In the course of the Russian presidential election of 1996, Kuptsov managed Zyuganov's campaign.
- In August 1996 Kuptsov was elected to the PPUoR Coordination Committee, in which he represents the CPRF.
- Kuptsov is married with two daughters.

2. THE CPRF MODERATES: SELEZNEV AND PODBEREZKIN

GENNADII (NIKOLAEVICH) SELEZNEV

Chairman (Speaker) of the Sate Duma; Member of the CPRF Central Committee Presidium; Member of the Central Council of the All-Russian social-political association Spiritual Heritage (Dukhovnoe nasledie); Candidate of Historical Sciences, Senior Lecturer at the Moscow Institute of Youth; Chief editor of the weekly *Pravda* Rossii (Russia's Truth);

Professional journalist, former chief editor of several prominent newspapers; Decorated with the Order of People's Friendship and the Order For Services to the Homeland (Second Degree).

It was announced on April 22, 1999 that a group of moderate left-wing politicians would form a separate bloc entitled "Patriots of Russia", chaired by the Duma speaker Gennadii Seleznev, to contest the forthcoming parliamentary elections. The bloc is expected to embrace members of Spiritual Heritage and other similar organizations. This move appears to be an important step in the gradual separation of the speaker from the CPRF mainstream, not to mention the party's hard-liners. The fact that Seleznev has serious differences with the leadership has been evident for some time. Seleznev, for instance, has been less disinclined to cooperate with the powers-that-be than the rest of the party. In this respect he even went as far as to advocate postponement of Yeltsin's impeachment by the Duma until the hostilities in Yugoslavia were over. Contrary to the will of the majority in the communist-dominated Duma, Seleznev has always advocated that the house condemn the anti-Semitic statements of fellow CPRF Central Committee member Albert Makashov. And last but not least, Seleznev's announcement in the fall of 1998 that he would consider running as a candidate in the 2000 presidential election also indicates that there are serious tensions between him and Zyuganov.

Perhaps Seleznev's moderate behavior derives from his position as Duma speaker. This job requires its incumbent to cooperate with president and government, and, equally, Yeltsin and his premiers have had to cooperate with the parliamentary chairmen. For the purpose of comparison, it should be borne in mind that Seleznev's predecessor, Ivan Rybkin, who presided over the State Duma from 1993-95, had been one of the most prominent founders of the CPRF. In his tenure as speaker, Rybkin had gradually come closer to the executive branch of power in Russia and ended up joining the Yeltsin administration.

- Seleznev was born on November 6, 1947 in the town of Serov, Sverdlovsk Oblast. In 1964 he graduated from a trade school as a blue-collar worker.
- In 1965-66 Seleznev worked as a lathe operator in a factory in Leningrad (now St. Petersburg). For the following two years, he served in the Soviet Army.

- From 1968-74 Seleznev served successively as secretary of the Young Communist League (Komsomol) organization in a Leningrad trade school; as an instructor; as chairman of a department in the Leningrad Vyborg district Komsomol Committee; and as deputy head of the Leningrad Oblast Komsomol Committee. Simultaneously, he studied at the journalism faculty of Leningrad State University, from which he graduated in 1974.
- In 1970 Seleznev joined the CPSU.
- From 1974-1980 Seleznev was initially deputy chief editor and then chief editor of the Leningrad Komsomol newspaper *Smena*. In 1980 Seleznev was appointed first deputy head of the Komsomol Central Committee's Propaganda and Agitation Department. In the same year, he was appointed chief editor of the leading Komsomol daily, *Komsomolskaya pravda*, a post he held from 1980-88.
- From 1988 to February 1991 Seleznev was chief editor of *Uchitelskaya gazeta* (*Teachers' Newspaper*).
- At the Twenty-eighth Congress of the CPSU in June 1990, Seleznev was elected to the CPSU Central Committee.
- From February-August 1991 Seleznev served as the first deputy chief editor of the daily CPSU mouthpiece, *Pravda*. After the August 1991 coup against Gorbachev, Seleznev quit the CPSU. Nonetheless, he was elected chief editor of *Pravda* by the journalists working on the newspaper. In this capacity, Seleznev replaced Gorbachev's former adviser, Ivan Frolov, who had been intensely disliked by the newspaper's employees. Seleznev was also elected vice-president of the share company Pravda International.
- Seleznev joined the CPRF in 1993.
- During Yeltsin's dispute with the Russian parliament in 1992-93, *Pravda* sided with the president's opponents. Following the bloody events of October 4, 1993, Yeltsin banned both the CPRF and communist newspapers, but the ban was short-lived. On October 13, 1993, in violation of the Russian Press Law, the then Press Minister Vladimir Shumeiko removed Seleznev from his post as *Pravda's* chief editor. Despite his dismissal, Seleznev retained his positions as a vice president of Pravda International and a member of *Pravda's* editorial board.
- In December 1993 Seleznev was elected as a deputy to the State Duma from the CPRF party list. As a member of the CPRF faction, he was elected deputy chairman of the Duma Committee for Information Policy and Communications. On January 25, 1995,

Seleznev was elected as a deputy chairman of the State Duma. In this capacity, Seleznev replaced a former fellow member of the CPRF parliamentary faction, Valentin Kovalev, who had crossed the floor and was rewarded with the post of Russian Minister of Justice. In his capacity as a deputy speaker of the Duma throughout 1995, Seleznev monitored parliament's relations with the media.

- In January 1995 Seleznev became a member of the CPRF Central Committee. At the plenary session that followed, he was elected to the CPRF CC Presidium and as a party secretary. (Seleznev had to quit this latter party post, however, when he was elected speaker.) In March 1995 Seleznev was given the unpaid job of chief editor of the CPRF weekly newspaper *Pravda Rossii* (*Russia's Truth*).
- Also in 1995, Seleznev was elected to Spiritual Heritage's Central Council.
- On December 17, 1995 Seleznev was reelected as a deputy of the State Duma, again from the party list. On January 16, 1996 the CPRF nominated him for the post of speaker, and he was elected the following day. Seleznev is a member of the CPRF faction, but his stance on matters of importance for Russia has often differed from that of his faction.
- On Seleznev's fiftieth birthday—November 6, 1997—Yeltsin visited the State Duma in person and presented Seleznev with one of the highest honors in the new Russia, the order For Services to the Homeland (Second Degree).
- In September 1998, commenting on the rumors circulating at the time about the alleged presidential ambitions of Moscow Mayor Yurii Luzhkov, Seleznev suggested that he himself might stand as a candidate in the next presidential election. Such a statement could not but spark speculation in the media about Seleznev's relations with Zyuganov. Both leaders said at the time that only the corresponding sessions of the CPRF and PPUoR could decide who would be the alliance's nominee in the election.
- Later, in the fall of 1998, Seleznev revealed that he did not intend to seek election to the next Duma from the CPRF party list, but would rather contest a single-mandate constituency in Leningrad oblast. In April the following year, the Russian media reported that the PPUoR moderates would contest the forthcoming parliamentary election as a separate bloc, headed by Seleznev, rather then jointly with the rest of the CPRF.
- Seleznev is married with one daughter.

ALEKSEI (IVANOVICH) PODBEREZKIN,
Chairman of the All-Russian social-political association Spiritual Heritage (Dukhovnoe nasledie); President of the RAU-corporation; Full member of the Russian Academy of Natural Sciences; Author of approximately 200 publications—including a monograph—on economics, military and foreign policies.

Widely reputed to be an ideologue of the new Russian Communist Party, Dr. Podberezkin is not a member of the CPRF. However, in December 1995 Podberezkin was elected as a State Duma deputy from the CPRF party list, along with a number of the party's other influential allies, such as the film director Stanislav Govorukhin. More often than not, the party's intellectual friends have never been adherents of communist ideology. Unlike most of Yeltsin's political allies, prior to the anticommunist Russian revolution of August 1991 they were not members of the CPSU either. The relations of these intellectuals with the CPRF have been far from cloudless. On the eve of the 1999 parliamentary election, both Podberezkin and Govorukhin were rumored to be on the verge of estrangement from their old friend Zyuganov and the rest of the CPRF.

Podberezkin enjoys the reputation of a "gray cardinal" whose ideas played a key role in the formation of Zyuganov's policies. Podberezkin's determination to "marry" the Russian left-wing political world-view with his own ideology of a national great-power state, at the expense of the purity of Marxist orthodoxy, was sharply criticized by the party faithful. He is also believed to have been the driving force behind the decisions of the CPRF leadership at various times in its brief history to cooperate with the Yeltsin administration rather than continue posing as an "irreconcilable opposition." (Two examples of the willingness of the CPRF to accept the outcomes of rather controversial votes are the referendum on the new Constitution in 1993 and the presidential election of 1996.) More recently, Podberezkin has reportedly advocated the idea that the PPUoR should support Primakov rather than Zyuganov in the next presidential election; this seems to place the PPUoR on the verge of collapse.

- Podberezkin was born on February 7, 1953 to a family of Moscow factory workers. From the age of 15 he worked as a locksmith and later as a factory electrician. At 18 he was conscripted into the

Soviet Army, and after his military service returned to his blue-collar job. While working in a factory he studied at night-school, and enrolled as an external student in the most prestigious Soviet educational institution of the time—the Moscow State Institute of International Relations (MGIMO), which as a rule was attended by the offspring of the top Soviet elite.

- In 1979 Podberezkin received an external degree from MGIMO. He was then assigned to work in the Institute as a specialist on US military policies.
- From 1981-85 Podberezkin led a group of scholars acting as advisers to the Committee of USSR youth organizations. From 1985-1990 he served as a senior analyst in two other highly esteemed Soviet think-tanks—t he Institute of International Economics and International Relations, and the Diplomatic Academy of the USSR Ministry of Foreign Affairs.
- In 1990 Podberezkin successfully defended his doctoral dissertation on "The Significance of the System of Battle Commandment in US Military Doctrine."
- Podberezkin is the president of the opposition think-tank RAU-corporation, which was set up in 1990 under the auspices of the Russian-American University. In 1992-93 he was a member of the editorial board of the newspaper Obozrevatel ("Observer"). Also in 1992, Podberezkin founded a journal with the same title, of which he is chief editor. In the early 1990s he served as an adviser to the then Russian vice-president Aleksandr Rutskoi. At the same time, Podberezkin was a member of the leadership of a Russian nationalist opposition organization—the presidium of the Central Duma of the Russian People's Sobor (Assembly).
- In December 1993 Podberezkin stood for a seat in the State Duma in the town of Lubertsy on the outskirts of Moscow. He was not elected. In the next Russian parliamentary election two years later, Podberezkin lost the run-off in a Moscow single-mandate constituency, but was elected as a member of the State Duma from the CPRF list. As a Duma deputy, Podberezkin served as deputy chairman of the parliamentary Committee on International Affairs.
- At the founding congress of the People's Patriotic Union of Russia, held in August 1996, Podberezkin was elected PPUoR co-chairman. In the PPUoR Coordination Council, Podberezkin represents Spiritual Heritage.

- Podberezkin is a remarried widower. He has two daughters from his first marriage, and a daughter with his second wife.
- Podberezkin is a Russian Orthodox Christian.

3. The CPRF Hardliners: Makashov and Ilyukhin

On February 4, 1998 Colonel Nikolai Batalov, the head of the Volgograd branch of the Movement in Support of the Army and Military Industries (DPA), suggested that the DPA should create its own separate list for the next elections to the State Duma. Batalov was disappointed with the CPRF's performance in the current parliament, because, in his view, the party was not radical enough in its opposition to the Yeltsin regime. Meanwhile, the movement's chairman Viktor Ilyukhin opined that the DPA list would allow some leeway for those who may be wary of voting for the communists. A few weeks later, Ilyukhin issued a statement in which he voiced the movement's loyalty to the CPRF.

The DPA was founded by General Lev Rokhlin, the former Chairman of the Duma Defense Committee, who had twice turned down the order of Hero of Russia offered to him for his tactical victories in the Chechen war. He considered it dishonorable to be decorated for killing Russian citizens. Rokhlin was assassinated while asleep in his country villa on July 3, 1998. Viktor Ilyukhin was subsequently elected chairman and Albert Makashov first deputy chairman of the DPA.

Albert (Mikhailovich) Makashov,
Former Colonel General; Member of the CPRF Central Committee; First Deputy Chairman of the Movement in Support of the Army and Military Industries (DPA); Chairman of the Subcommittee on Issues of the Military Forces' Preparedness for Action and Mobilization of the Duma Defense Committee.

Probably the most notorious Russian communist, Makashov became an international celebrity by virtue of a series of anti-Semitic remarks in October 1998-February 1999. In the Soviet Union, Makashov entered the limelight as early as March 14, 1990 when he attacked Gorbachev at the third session of the USSR Congress of People's Deputies, saying that Gorbachev could not be elected president unless he attended a three-month course at the General Staff Academy. Since then, Makashov's name has frequently been the subject of scandal and ridicule.

For some time, the liberals viewed Makashov as easy prey in their fight against their communist and nationalist opponents. In February 1999 the CPRF leadership also recognized that Makashov indeed posed a problem for the party. Seleznev and Zyuganov condemned the retired general as an "agent-provocateur"; Kuptsov said that he "created problems for the Party", and even fellow hard-liner Viktor Ilyukhin suggested that Makashov would do better to shut up. According to Zyuganov, however, Makashov has not been formally reprimanded for his anti-Semitic outbursts, but merely "rebuked" by the Party leadership. Zyuganov's personal indebtedness to Makashov, to whom he owes his position more than anyone else, may have contributed to the mildness of the party's treatment of him. However, Zyuganov's sentiment does not appear to have been the decisive factor. More importantly, Makashov is believed to have a considerable following among the masses, who feel deprived by the reforms and consider the Jewish "new rich" to be responsible for their troubles. According to *Izvestiya* (March 6, 1996), Makashov also enjoys the support of the reactionary Russian Orthodox Church clergy, who inspired the former general to identify himself as "an Orthodox Stalinist."

- Makashov was born on June 12, 1938 in the village of Levaya Rossosh, Voronezh Oblast, to a petty officer and a nurse. He was registered with the foreign first name Albert, taken by his mother from George Sand's novel Consuelo. At the same time, the boy was baptized in a church under the Russian name Dmitrii.
- Makashov's education was entirely military. In his teens he studied at the Voronezh Aleksandr Suvorov school for military cadets. In 1960 Makashov graduated from the Tashkent Higher Combined Command School. He finished his military schooling at the Mikhail Frunze Military Academy and the Academy of the General Staff. He graduated from both with a gold medal for excellence.
- Makashov served as commander of a reconnaissance platoon, commander of a division reconnaissance company, head of a tank regiment reconnaissance, and as commander of a battalion, regiment and army. He served in the Transcaucasian, Kiev and Ural Military Districts, as well as in the Western Group of Troops in Germany (Soviet occupation forces in the former German Democratic Republic). He received the rank of Major General in 1979. Following the earthquake in Armenia in December 1988, Makashov was

appointed commander of the affected part of Armenia and later the military commandant of the Armenian capital, Yerevan. From January to September 1989 Makashov served as Commander of the Ural Military district. Following its merger with the Volga Military District in January 1989, Makashov was placed in charge of the Volga-Ural Military District.

- In 1989 Makashov was elected to a seat in the USSR CPD from a constituency in Sverdlovsk Oblast. In the Congress he joined the illiberal factions Soyuz (Union) and Otechestvo (Fatherland) as well as the communist group of deputies. In his capacity as a USSR deputy, Makashov acquired nationwide notoriety for his pronouncements attacking Gorbachev's policies. Like many Soviet military men, Makashov was particularly annoyed by the collapse of the Soviet-dominated bodies in Eastern Europe.
- Makashov's address to the founding congress of the CP RSFSR in 1990 was greeted with rapturous applause when he denounced Gorbachev's military cuts and complained: "Patriotism takes centuries to foster, but it is destroyed in two years by the yellow press." Following this session, Makashov was elected to the CP RSFSR Central Committee.
- Along with other like-minded servicemen, Makashov organized the Otchizna ("Native Land") movement in 1990.
- In 1991 Makashov was a candidate in the Russian presidential election. He came in fifth with 3.74 percent of the vote.
- After the August 1991 coup, Makashov was ordered to resign. After this, he was an active organizer of the Russian Communist Workers Party (RCWP) together with other extremists such as Anpilov and Tyulkin. Makashov was a member of the RCWP Central Committee from November 1991 to August 7, 1993. In early 1992 he was elected to the RCWP Organizational Bureau.
- Following the collapse of the Soviet Union in December 1991, a group of reactionary USSR deputies called an extraordinary session of the USSR CPD aimed at resisting the move. Needless to say, Makashov was among the organizers. At the Extraordinary Congress of USSR People's Deputies, held in the village of Voronovo in March 1992, Makashov was elected a member of the Permanent Presidium of the USSR CPD.
- On June 12 and 13, 1992 Makashov attended the founding congress of the Russian National Sobor and was elected a member of its ruling body, the RNS Duma.

- On October 17 and 18, 1992, Makashov attended the Russian Congress of the Soviets of Workers, Peasants, Specialists and White-collar Employees in Nizhnii Novgorod. Makashov became a member of the so-called "opposition Soviet government," formed at the Congress. Later that month, Makashov became a member of the Organizational Committee of the National Salvation Front. At the NSF founding congress on October 24, 1992 Makashov was elected as one of its nine co-chairmen. On the following day, he was elected to the Coordination Council of the Working Russia movement.
- In February 1993 Makashov attended the restoration congress of the CPRF. At the Congress, he insisted that Zyuganov be elected party leader rather than Kuptsov, whom Makashov dismissed as a "Gorbachevite." Standing at the rostrum, Makashov told the congress that he would not move until Kuptsov withdrew in favor of Zyuganov; Kuptsov eventually withdrew. Makashov quit the RCWP for the CPRF on March 7, 1993 and was elected a member of the CPRF Central Executive Committee.
- Following Yeltsin's dissolution of the Russian parliament by decree on September 21, 1993 Makashov offered his services to the rebel parliament. On October 3, 1993 Makashov led the mob attack on the Ostankino TV Center, during which many people, among them a number of Western journalists, were shot dead by soldiers of the Vityaz special police regiment. Following the tank attack on the parliament the following day, Makashov was arrested and imprisoned. He was released in an amnesty on February 26, 1994.
- In December 1995 Makashov was elected as a deputy of the State Duma in a single-mandate constituency in Samara Oblast. In the Duma, he joined the CPRF faction and the Duma Defense Committee. In 1997 Makashov joined the Movement in Support of the Army and Military Industries (DPA), organized by the Committee chairman, General Lev Rokhlin. Shortly after Rokhlin's assassination on July 3, 1998, Ilyukhin was elected the new DPA chair, while Makashov and two others were elected Ilyukhin's first deputies.
- In an address to a workers rally held in Moscow on October 3 and 4, 1998 Makashov said that Russia was ruled by "ten Yids" who should all be killed. Makashov reiterated his suggestion at a similar event in Samara on October 7, 1998. On February 22, while addressing a DPA meeting of Cossacks in Novocherkassk, Rostov

Oblast, Makashov declared that the DPA was to be renamed the DPZh, or Movement Against Yids. Makashov's anti-Semitic outburst served as an excuse for the Russian Minister of Justice to start investigating the party's activities. In March 1999 Zyuganov revealed that Makashov had been criticized by his comrades and had promised to watch his language.

- Makashov is married with one son, two daughters, and five grandchildren. Makashov's son is an officer, and both daughters are married to military men.

VIKTOR (IVANOVICH) ILYUKHIN,
Lieutenant General of Justice, Chairman of the State Duma Committee on Security Matters; Author of six books, several scholarly works and many articles; Author or presenter of many important bills on legal and security matters, including bills On the Fight Against Organized Crime, On the Fight Against Corruption, On Operation and Detective Activities, On Foreign Intelligence, On the Federal Security Service of the Russian Federation, On the Fight Against Terrorism, On the Criminal Implementation Code, etc.; Correspondent member of the International Slavonic Academy of Sciences, Full member of the International Academy of Information Processes and Technologies; Chairman of the Movement in Support of the Army and Military Industries (DPA).

The chairman of the Duma Security Committee, Viktor Ilyukhin is widely believed to be the most dangerous enemy of President Yeltsin and Yeltsin's family and associates. The former senior official of the USSR Prosecutor-General's office is believed to continue to enjoy close ties with his former colleagues, as well as with officers in the military, police and security services. Owing his fame to an attempt to prosecute USSR President Gorbachev for "high treason" in 1991, Ilyukhin has volunteered similar initiatives on a regular basis ever since. In 1998, for example, Ilyukhin initiated the process of impeachment against President Yeltsin.

Regarding his ideology, Ilyukhin appears to be a law and order zealot rather than a fanatical communist or ultranationalist. At the same time, he is no champion of human rights (to put it mildly). Despite his membership of the CPRF Central Committee, Ilyukhin has serious disagreements with the party leadership on important policies. It would be of little surprise should we learn one day that the top CPRF leaders were themselves afraid of Ilyukhin.

- Ilyukhin was born on March 1, 1949 in the village of Sosnovka in the Kuznetsk district of Perm Oblast. His working life began with a job as a laborer in a Kuznetsk timber mill.
- In 1971 Ilyukhin graduated from the Saratov Law Institute. While studying at the Institute, Ilyukhin also worked as a detective in the Penza police.
- In 1971-72 Ilyukhin served in the Navy, spending this year at the submarine base of the Pacific Ocean Fleet.
- From 1972-86 Ilyukhin worked as an investigator in a district and then an oblast Prosecutor's office. From 1984-86 he was a deputy Prosecutor of Penza Oblast.
- In 1986 Ilyukhin was invited to continue his work in the capital. From 1986-89 Ilyukhin was the head of the Main Investigation Administration of the USSR Prosecutor-General's Office.
- From 1989-91 Ilyukhin headed the Administration of the USSR Prosecutor-General's Office on Monitoring the Implementation of Laws on State Security; he was a member of the Board of the USSR Prosecutor-General's Office with the rank of State Councilor of Justice. In this capacity, Ilyukhin was in charge of special groups that investigated the bloody nationalist conflicts in Nagorno-Karabakh, Armenia, Azerbaijan, Fergana (Uzbekistan), the Dniester Republic (Moldova) and Georgia.
- In the spring of 1989 Ilyukhin was appointed to investigate alleged violations by a group of detectives headed by the once famous investigators, Telman Gdlyan and Nikolai Ivanov. (Gdlyan and Ivanov investigated a controversial case of corruption in Uzbekistan, and their fall from the Kremlin's favor in the course of the investigation turned them into national celebrities.)
- On November 4, 1991, Ilyukhin filed a formal charge of "High Treason" under Article 64 of the RSFSR Criminal Code against outgoing USSR President Mikhail Gorbachev. Ilyukhin claimed that Gorbachev had violated the terms of his presidential oath and the Soviet Constitution when he recognized the independence of the three Baltic states. Within a few days, on November 6, 1991, Ilyukhin was fired, and his criminal case against Gorbachev was closed. Subsequently Ilyukhin acted as head of the "public" commission investigating Gorbachev's alleged "unconstitutional activities." As a result, Gorbachev was condemned by a mob trial in a Moscow square. The verdict sentenced the former President to "nationwide damnation and eternal disgrace."

- From 1991-93 Ilyukhin worked as an observer at *Pravda* and as an expert of the Russian Federation Supreme Soviet.
- In January 1993 Ilyukhin was nominated for the post of Moscow Mayor, but no election was held at that time.
- In 1993 Ilyukhin joined the CPRF. Later, he was elected to its Central Committee.
- From July 1993 to April 1994 Ilyukhin was co-chairman of the National Salvation Front.
- In December 1993 Ilyukhin was elected to a seat in the State Duma in a Penza Constituency. In 1994-95 he chaired the Duma Committee on Security Matters. Under Ilyukhin's chairmanship, the Committee became a real force in Russian politics. Despite the absence of other communists among its members, Ilyukhin managed to control the body. He also managed to widen its sphere of competence, incorporating problems of informational security, technological security and so on.
- In the Duma, Ilyukhin has acted as a fount of ideas aimed at the removal of Yeltsin. As early as April 3, 1995, Ilyukhin informed the chamber that the president's advisers were considering suspending the forthcoming parliamentary and presidential elections. Yeltsin's representatives denied this. However, it later became clear that they had indeed considered such a move, but Yeltsin had rejected the idea. On April 8, 1995 Ilyukhin presented to the house a bill on the creation of a State Medical Commission. This commission was to examine top Russian officials to judge whether they were unable to remain in their posts on the grounds of ill health. Only 118 deputies voted for the proposal, and the bill did not become law.
- In December 1995 Ilyukhin was reelected as a Duma deputy in the same single-mandate constituency. On January 30, 1996 he was reelected as chairman of the same Duma committee.
- In November 1996 Ilyukhin made his first attempt to initiate a process of impeachment against Yeltsin. On this occasion, however, he failed to collect the required number of signatures.
- In his address to the Duma on March 4, 1998, Ilyukhin proposed that Prime Minister Viktor Chernomyrdin and his first deputy Anatolii Chubais be prosecuted for corruption.
- In April 1998 the chairmen of two Duma committees, Ilyukhin and Lev Rokhlin, initiated a process of impeachment against President Yeltsin. This time they were more successful than two years previously. By the end of May the CPRF faction had collected the re-

quired number of signatures and published the Substantiation, explaining their reasons for the move.

- On July 8, 1998 Ilyukhin replaced the late Lev Rokhlin as chairman of the DPA.
- On July 21, 1998 Ilyukhin issued a statement in which he attempted to unleash a campaign of civil disobedience. The statement included a call to stop paying taxes, and the military were advised to stay in their barracks if ordered to interfere on Yeltsin's behalf. Ilyukhin also suggested that the people were entitled to overthrow the regime by revolutionary means.
- On December 15, 1998 Ilyukhin addressed the Duma Commission on Yeltsin's impeachment with a presentation aimed at proving that Yeltsin was guilty of genocide against the Russian people. The genocide would not have been possible had Russia been ruled by its native people "rather than the representatives of one single nationality—Jews." The statement caused a scandal in the media, and Ilyukhin retracted it.
- On February 17, 1999 Ilyukhin read a statement urging that the parties involved in the reform be banned. Ilyukhin's presentation included a list of prominent Russian liberal politicians who, in Ilyukhin's view, should be forbidden from taking part in politics for the next ten years. The statement was clearly designed as a response to the investigation into CPRF activities by the Ministry of Justice. In a rare manifestation of disagreement within his party, Zyuganov issued a disclaimer, saying that he did not agree with such a proposal.
- In March of the same year, Ilyukhin denounced Yeltsin and his daughter, Tat'yana Dyachenko, for having illegally diverted $4.8 billion from IMF loans to Russia into their private offshore bank accounts.
- Ilyukhin is married with two children. His wife is also a lawyer.

4. CPRF Regional Leaders: Lodkin and Gamza

Yurii (Evgen'evich) Lodkin

Governor of Bryansk Oblast, journalist and writer, author of numerous articles and of three collections of belles-lettres based on Russian folklore. A winner of the Komsomol literary award for his 1972 book *Khrustal'naya raduga* (*Crystal Rainbow*).

The story of Yurii Lodkin's triumphant comeback in the gubernatorial election held in Bryansk Oblast on December 8, 1996 may serve as a convincing answer to why the population of some regions that voted for Yeltsin in 1991 subsequently joined the "red belt." The story of the Bryansk governors is similar to those described above in the sections on Kemerovo, Amur and Chelyabinsk Oblasts, where popularly-elected governors were illegally fired by decree and replaced with unpopular and corrupt officials. In the case of Lodkin, the degree of lawlessness and abuse reached an extreme unprecedented in other similar cases. In all such territories, including Bryansk, the dismissed governors were triumphantly reelected a few years later. Since his comeback, Lodkin has acted as a leader of the opposition to Yeltsin in the Council of the Federation, despite the Order of Friendship which the Russian president personally presented to Lodkin, presumably in an attempt to let bygones be bygones.

Despite his unhappy personal experience, Lodkin believes that governors should be appointed by the president rather than elected by popular vote. In an interview with the author, conducted in his office in the Council of the Federation on November 11, 1998, Lodkin expressed the opinion that such appointments would not give rise to the arbitrariness evident in the Bryansk saga if presidents appointed the governors with the consent of the local elected legislative bodies. In other countries, such as the USA, governors may be elected by the populace because the individual states rely on their own economies, Lodkin argued, but in Russia most of the territories are dependent on subsidies from the center and therefore should be governed from the center as well. Meanwhile, the Bryansk authorities have abolished direct popular elections for the heads of local executive bodies in the region, and the new mayor of Bryansk was elected by the Bryansk city legislature. It may be added that the CPRF enjoys an overwhelming majority in all the elected bodies in the region. Thus Lodkin has been spared trouble both from the former and the current mayor of the regional administrative center, and from the chairman of the oblast legislative assembly.

- Lodkin was born on March 26, 1938 in the town Dyat'kovo in Bryansk Oblast. Due to his father's participation in the communist partisan war against the Nazi occupation, the family was detained when Yurii was a mere four years old, and Lodkin spent the following eighteen months in a German concentration camp in Lithuania.

- From 1954-58 Lodkin studied glass-making at a local technical college. After graduating in 1958, he worked as the head of a shift in a glass factory. From 1959-61 Lodkin served in the Soviet Army, and afterwards he worked in a military factory.
- A member of the CPSU, from 1963-68 Lodkin held Komsomol and Party jobs, first as a member of the Young Communist League and later of the CPSU City committee in Dyat'kovo.
- From 1967-72 Lodkin studied journalism at a Higher Party School. His career as a journalist included working on a district newspaper and then in the office of the prominent regional daily Bryansky rabochii, where he served as head of the department of industry, transportation, communications and trade.
- From 1984-87 Lodkin worked in the Bryansk Oblast Committee of the CPSU. The ensuing three years were the height of Lodkin's success as a journalist, when he served as the special regional correspondent of the Soviet state news agency, TASS.
- In 1990 Lodkin was elected to a seat in the RSFSR Congress of People's Deputies. In the Congress, he joined the Communists of Russia faction. During the first Russian presidential election in 1991, Lodkin campaigned for Gorbachev's liberal candidate, Vadim Bakatin.
- On December 14, 1991 Yeltsin appointed a reform-minded fellow RSFSR deputy from Bryansk, Vladimir Barabanov, acting head of the regional administration. On January 22, 1992 yet another Presidential decree removed the adjective "acting" from Barabanov's job title. However, Barabanov's policies displeased the regional Soviet, and in accordance with the law in force at the time, elections for governor of Bryansk were called. On April 25, 1993 Lodkin won the gubernatorial election in Bryansk with a small margin in the second round.
- On September 21, 1993 Yeltsin issued his decree No. 1400, by which he dissolved the RSFSR CPD and the Supreme Soviet and suspended the activities of the Constitutional Court. Lodkin was among those regional leaders who criticized the decree as unconstitutional, as it in fact was. In response, on September 25 that year Yeltsin decreed Lodkin's dismissal from office on the grounds of the governor's failure to accept "step by step constitutional reform." Moreover, the President dispatched to Bryansk a regiment

of OMON special police troopers with an order to remove Lodkin from his office by force,

- As a deputy, Lodkin was present at the sessions of the RSFSR CPD in October 1993 when Yeltsin sent tanks to fire at the parliament building. Following the storming of the parliament, Lodkin was detained and spent a few hours in prison.
- On December 12, 1993 Lodkin was elected as a member of the Council of the Federation in a Bryansk regional constituency.
- Upon Lodkin's removal, on the recommendation of Bryansk reformers Yeltsin appointed Viktor Karpov as head of the territorial administration. Karpov subsequently became involved with local criminal structures, at which the leaders of all political parties in the region protested. On August 16, 1995 Yeltsin replaced Karpov with Barabanov. Shortly afterwards, Karpov was arrested and tried for corruption. On December 10, 1995 the Moscow daily *Izvestiya* published an article alleging that Barabanov was wooing the communists in the region. As evidence, the newspaper cited Lodkin as saying that he was no opponent of Barabanov's. As a result, on May 29, 1996 Yeltsin dismissed Barabanov and on June 19 appointed yet another governor, Aleksandr Semernev.
- On December 17, 1995 Lodkin was elected as a deputy of the State Duma in a regional single-mandate constituency. In the Duma he joined the CPRF faction and became a member of the Committee for veterans' affairs.
- In August 1996 Lodkin was elected a member of the PPUoR Coordination Committee, in which he represented Bryansk Oblast.
- On December 8, 1996 Lodkin was elected Bryansk governor for the second time. On this occasion his victory was resounding: Lodkin won over 80 percent of the vote in the first round.
- In 1998 Yeltsin decorated Lodkin with an Order of Friendship on the occasion of his 60th birthday.
- Lodkin joined the CPRF in 1993, and has remained a committed member ever since. However, at the Second Congress of the PPUoR, held in November 1998, Lodkin criticized his comrades in the Communist faction in the Duma for their failure to assist those residents of the Bryansk region who suffered as a result of the 1986 accident at the nearby Chernobyl nuclear power station. Non-communist colleagues, Lodkin complained in his address to the Congress, had been far more responsive to the sufferings of the Bryansk residents.

- Lodkin is married, has a married daughter and two grandchildren.
- During his tenure as Bryansk Governor, a large number of articles in the Moscow media have accused the regional authorities of unfair treatment of the democratic opposition to Lodkin and the CPRF. His most prominent opponent in the region is Igor Sherman, the editor of the only Bryansk opposition newspaper Bryanskoe vremya. According to a report published in *Obshchaya gazeta* No. 16, 1999, the local authorities cut off the electricity supply to the newspaper's offices. In an interview with Radio Liberty, Sherman also accused Lodkin's men of anti-Semitism. Other Yeltsin supporters in the media have routinely blamed Lodkin for the poor living standards of Bryansk residents.
- Lodkin's term in office expires in December 2000. It remains to be seen whether he will be reelected as Bryansk governor.

GENNADII (EFIMOVICH) GAMZA,

Member of the Presidium of the CPRF Central Committee; First Secretary of the Amur Oblast Committee of the CPRF; Chairman of the Far Eastern Bureau of the CPRF Central Committee.

Amur Oblast is the only "red" region in the Russian Far East. The leader of the regional communists, Gennadii Gamza, is little known outside the closed circle of CPRF leaders. Yet within this circle, he is regarded as one of the most esteemed party officials. Gamza appears to be behind some party policies, including the idea to get the leaders of CPRF regional committees elected as deputies of the State Duma from the CPRF party list. According to Gamza, the status of federal legislators opens the doors of every official in the corresponding region to party leaders. Why Gamza has encountered such a problem in a region where the CPRF is the ruling party remains a mystery.

The celebration of the 81st anniversary of the October 1917 Bolshevik Revolution in the city of Blagoveshchensk in November 1998 was probably the most interesting event in our fact finding trip through the Russian regions. On the eve of the holiday, November 6, 1998, Mr. Gamza honored the author with an interview, in which he described the history of the regional CPRF organization. The process of the party's restoration in this remote area appeared to be relatively independent of the events in far away Moscow. Yet in both cases the processes were almost identical. In both places, for example, prior to the restoration they set up the Socialist Party of Working People which was more similar to the former communist parties of Eastern Europe than to the largely unreformed CPRF. At the same time, the CPRF in Amur Oblast differs from that in the center. The CPRF in the region is an old-fashioned party that has managed to preserve many CPSU traditions, including those contradicting Yeltsin's decrees, such as the ban on primary party cells in state-owned enterprises and educational institutions. Moreover, in Amur Oblast government officials are answerable to CPRF bodies, as they were in the good old days of the Communist regime. At the same time, communist meetings in Blagoveshchensk on November 6 and 7, 1998 differed from similar events in Moscow by the absence of neo-Nazi literature and the presence of non-Russian minorities among the crowds of the party faithful. All in all, the scenes of CPRF life in Amur Oblast leave room for speculation on the path that developments in the CPRF might have taken if a more orthodox communist such as Kuptsov had gained the upper hand at the CPRF founding congress in early 1993 rather than Zyuganov.

- Gamza was born on March 11, 1944. A building engineer by training, Gamza studied at the Khabarovsk Polytechnic Institute and Khabarovsk Higher Party School.
- Prior to his studies, Gamza served in the Red Army and worked in a river fleet. He also worked as a joiner, foreman, and later as a senior engineer in a factory. Gamza was a member of the CPSU, and occupied positions of responsibility in various Komsomol and Party bodies. Prior to his election to a seat in the State Duma in December 1995, Gamza served as director of the regional Avrora building and renovation administration.
- In February 1993 Gamza was elected as a deputy of the Amur Oblast Soviet.
- In 1993 he was elected to the CPRF Central Executive Committee, and in 1995 to the CPRF Central Committee. Simultaneously, he was made First Secretary of the Amur Oblast Committee of the CPRF, Chairman of the bloc of Amur Oblast left forces, and Chairman of the Far Eastern Bureau of the CPRF Central Committee.
- In 1994 Gamza was elected as a deputy of the regional legislature, the Amur Oblast Assembly.
- In 1995 he was elected to the State Duma from the CPRF party list. Gamza is a member of the CPRF faction and the parliamentary Committee on International Affaors.

Index

A

B

F

G

L

O

P

R